"Yet another success story in the world of academic publishing. *Linguistics for Translators* is a major undertaking. To reconcile the two perspectives (sentence and text linguistics) and come up with a product relevant to both translator and linguist is a mammoth task, executed seamlessly and most effectively."

Basil Hatim, *American University of Sharjah, UAE*

"*Linguistics for Translators* is a valuable addition to a field where theory and practice are closely intertwined. The authors review a wide range of linguistic concepts that are of relevance for the translator and illustrate them with clear, up-to-date examples in many languages. Frequent questions and tasks test and enhance the reader's understanding."

Jeremy Munday, *Professor Emeritus in Translation Studies, University of Leeds, UK*

"Almanna and House adopt a perspective in their *Linguistics for Translators* which shows convincingly that systematic knowledge of language is a fascinating and necessary resource for understanding translation. They maintain contact with questions arising in translation studies through their valuable linguistic orientation with a strong pedagogical focus. A timely and most welcome contribution to the field."

Erich Steiner, *Professor Emeritus in Translation Studies Englisch, Saarland University, Dept. of Language Science and Technology*

"*Linguistics for Translators* by Almanna and House provides a groundbreaking contribution to translation studies. It reinstates linguistics to the forefront of the field, by demonstrating its crucial importance for understanding what goes on in translation. This book is a must-read for academics, teachers, practitioners and students."

Dániel Z. Kádár, *Ordinary Member of Academia Europaea, Chair Professor, Dalian University of Foreign Languages, China, and Hungarian Research Centre for Linguistics*

Linguistics for Translators

This engaging and accessible textbook, by two leading experts, is a carefully crafted introduction to linguistics for translators, students, and researchers of translation.

Starting with basic concepts and gradually moving readers to the central questions in different branches of linguistics, examples are drawn from English and many other languages, including German, Arabic, Kurdish, Swahili, French, and Chinese. The key areas of linguistics are covered, from morphology and syntax to semantics, pragmatics, discourse analysis, stylistics, sociolinguistics, and cognitive linguistics. Striking a balance between theoretical developments and empirical investigation, readers gain both a comprehensive overview of linguistics and how it informs their work in translation and learn how to argue for analysis and annotate their own answers and translations academically. Each chapter provides the reader with an overview outlining the main points and technical words used in the chapter as well as illustrative examples, recommended readings, and resources and activities to test knowledge.

This is the ideal textbook for undergraduate and postgraduate students of translation in Translation Studies, Linguistics, and Modern Languages.

Ali Almanna is Associate Professor of Translation Studies at Hamad Bin Khalifa University, Qatar. He is the series editor of Routledge Studies in Arabic Translation. His recent publications include *Translation as a Set of Frames* (2021), *The Arabic-English Translator as Photographer* (2019), and *The Routledge Course in Translation Annotation* (2016).

Juliane House is Professor Emeritus, Hamburg University, Germany; Professor at the Hungarian Research Centre of Linguistics, Budapest; Past President of the International Association of Translation and Intercultural Studies; and Director of the PhD in Language and Communication, Hellenic American University. Her translation-relevant publications include *Translation: The Basics* (2018), *Translation as Communication across Languages and Cultures* (2016), and *Translation Quality Assessment* (2015).

Linguistics for Translators

Ali Almanna and Juliane House

Routledge
Taylor & Francis Group

LONDON AND NEW YORK

First published 2024
by Routledge
4 Park Square, Milton Park, Abingdon, Oxon OX14 4RN

and by Routledge
605 Third Avenue, New York, NY 10158

Routledge is an imprint of the Taylor & Francis Group, an informa business

British Library Cataloguing-in-Publication Data
A catalogue record for this book is available from the British Library

ISBN: 978-1-032-13182-5 (hbk)
ISBN: 978-1-032-13181-8 (pbk)
ISBN: 978-1-003-22802-8 (ebk)

DOI: 10.4324/9781003228028

Typeset in Times New Roman
by Newgen Publishing UK

Contents

Acknowledgements

Our deep indebtedness and sincere appreciation naturally go to Basil Hatim (American University of Sharjah, UAE), Jeremy Munday (Leeds University, UK), Erich Steiner (Saarland University, Germany), and Dániel Z. Kádár (Dalian University of Foreign Languages, China), who have gone through the manuscript and provided us with their opinion.

We owe a debt of gratitude to many people for their meticulous feedback on the manuscript. In particular, we would like to thank: Rafik Jamoussi (Sohar University, Oman), Qing Cao (University of Durham, UK), Chonglong Gu (the Hong Kong Polytechnic University, China), Majid Abdullatif Al-Basri (University of Petra, Jordan), Alaa Ashour (University of Basrah, Iraq), Abdolmehdi Riazi (Hamad Bin Khalifa University, Qatar), Shabnam Saadat (the Independent Persian, UK), Mª Carmen África Vidal Claramonte (University of Salamanca, Spain), Narongdej Phanthaphoommee (Mahidol University, Thailand), Juan José Martínez Sierra (Universitat de València, Spain), Mohamed Erebih (Hamad Bin Khalifa University, Qatar), Rawan Mahmood Sabti (translator), Zahraa A. Shakir (translator), Djamel Goui (Université Kasdi Merbah Ouargla, Algeria), Noreddine Hanini (University of Sultan Moulay Slimane, Morocco), Raja Lahiani (United Arab Emirates University, UAE), Fatma Benelhadj (University of Sfax, Tunisia), Malika Kettani (Euroned University of Fes, Morocco), Kadhim Al-Ali (University of Basrah, Iraq), and Fatima Litim (Ecole Normale Supérieure de Sétif (Teacher Education College), Algeria).

Introduction

This book arrives at a time when investigations of translation as a socio-psychological phenomenon are gaining prominence in translation studies, while purely linguistic aspects are relegated to the margins as outdated and old-fashioned interests. Our aim with *Linguistics for Translators* is to emphasize that the linguistic dimension of translation cannot be overlooked, and that linguistics remains, more than ever, a contemporary and exciting field for translators, translation researchers, and translation students to explore.

The significance of this book lies not only in its linguistic orientation, but also in its strong pedagogical focus. Each chapter of the book links linguistic explanation with the process and practice of translation into a variety of languages, providing a range of exercises and suggestions for discussion and further research. Through this approach, the reader is constantly alerted to the crucial role of linguistic knowledge and competence in producing appropriate translations, evaluating translations, and teaching courses on translation. The book is produced by experts in both linguistics and translation studies, with complementary expertise in different branches of linguistics and mastery of various languages.

This book is intended for students and researchers of translation and linguistics, as well as practising translators and interested lay readers. It can be used as a standalone course in departments of translation studies or linguistics or as supplemental material for existing courses. The volume has been carefully designed to be reader friendly. Its 12 chapters offer the reader the opportunity to study theoretical and practical aspects of linguistics and translation through well-thought-out exercises and discussion topics. Each chapter begins with a highly accessible overview of formal and functional linguistic concepts. This is followed by practical sections connecting these concepts with translation, providing examples in various languages.

In Chapter 1, we first provide an overview of linguistics by defining its scope, main branches, areas of study, and interdisciplinary fields. We also introduce the notion of linguistic universals. In the second part of the chapter, we apply these concepts to translation and provide hands-on activities and discussion topics. This introductory chapter sets the scene for the rest of the volume.

DOI: 10.4324/9781003228028-1

Chapter 2 focuses on the areas of phonetics and phonology. We begin by distinguishing between these two areas, and then provide an overview of the main parts of phonetics, the various stages of sound production, and the importance of phonological features in translation.

Chapters 3 and 4 focus on morphology and morphological processes, respectively. Chapter 3 covers the structure of the word, the classification of morphemes and words, and the units that make up words, all illustrated through ample examples from various languages. This theoretical presentation is then related to the types of shifts that may be necessary in translation. Chapter 4 continues the discussion by explaining higher-level linguistic analyses of morphological processes such as inflection, derivation, compounding, and affixation. Through practice activities and discussion questions, we emphasize the importance of understanding these processes for the practice of translation.

In Chapter 5, we delve into syntax, which focuses on the structure of phrases, clauses, and sentences. We explain the various categories at the word level, such as nouns, verbs, and adjectives, as well as categories at the phrase level, such as the noun phrase or verb phrase. We also explore transformation processes and constituent tests and explain their importance for translation.

In Chapter 6, we focus on the area of semantics, discussing important concepts such as denotation and connotation, reference and sense, semantic roles, and principles, as well as frame semantics. We emphasize the importance of understanding these concepts in relation to translation and provide examples to illustrate their significance.

In Chapter 7, readers are introduced to discourse analysis, a branch of usage-based linguistics that covers both social and linguistic approaches. We explain social approaches such as conversation analysis and critical discourse analysis, and linguistic approaches such as functional linguistics, sociolinguistics, and cognitive discourse analysis. We also discuss other approaches like multimodal discourse analysis and intercultural communication and their relevance to translation.

Moving on to Chapter 8, we dive into pragmatics, a discipline particularly important for translation. We define pragmatics and provide a brief history of the discipline. Then we discuss key concepts, such as deixis, reference, inference, conversational implicature, and speech acts. All of these concepts are presented with a focus on their relevance to translation.

In Chapter 9, the topic is functional linguistics, another topic of immediate relevance to translation. The chapter covers various notions such as register, appraisal, cohesion, and coherence that are significant for translators to understand. We explain the importance of these concepts for the translator's work. Additionally, the chapter includes the second author's model for translation quality assessment, which employs a register-based approach to evaluate translation output.

Chapter 10 is about sociolinguistics. Here we explain basic sociolinguistic concepts such as code-switching, convergence, and divergence, and we discuss their immediate relevance to translation.

Chapter 11 of the book complements the sociolinguistic focus addressed in the previous chapter and focuses on language variation, covering regional, social, and stylistic variation, as well as the concepts of diglossia and polyglossia, pidgins and creoles, dialects, accents, and styles. The chapter explores how these variations can pose challenges when translating into different languages, as translators must consider the target audience and the nuances of the target language in order to convey the appropriate meaning and tone.

In Chapter 12, the final chapter of this book, we provide readers with an introduction to cognitive linguistics. We distinguish between cognitive grammar and cognitive semantics and explore the basic principles of cognitive linguistics and various cognitive systems. We demonstrate how familiarity with these concepts is beneficial for producing accurate translations and evaluating translation quality.

In summary, this book covers a broad range of linguistic topics relevant to translation. By exploring these topics and trying out the various practice activities and topic discussions, readers are gradually helped into having a deeper understanding of the translation process and the importance of linguistic knowledge in facilitating it.

Aspects of difference

When it comes to teaching linguistics to translation students at the university level, there are two main schools of thought. One camp argues that linguistics should be taught independently of translation, allowing students to become familiar with linguistic concepts and issues and make connections to translation on their own. To this end, they may use courses not specifically designed for translation students, such as *The Study of Language* (Yule 1985/1996), *A Concise Introduction to Linguistics* (Rowe and Levine 2022), and *Linguistics for Non-Linguists: A Primer with Exercises* (Parker and Riley 1994/2010), among others.

On the other hand, some believe it is important to restrict focus to the linguistic concepts and issues that are of immediate relevance to translation. This approach tailors the curriculum to the needs of translation students and is determined by those overseeing the programme. Titles such as *In Other Words: A Coursebook on Translation* (Baker 1992) and *Translation and Language: Linguistic Theories Explained* (Fawcett 1997) are common examples of this approach. These titles are adopted as textbooks in many translation programmes though they do not provide a comprehensive enough coverage of the area they purport to address.

In *Linguistics for Translators*, we have taken a different approach by connecting the dots between linguistics and translation. Each chapter introduces the basic linguistic concepts and then proceeds to show their relevance to translation students, researchers, and practising translators. In doing so, we give due consideration to both opinions mentioned above. Moreover, *Linguistics for Translators* discusses these linguistic concepts and issues in the context of various languages. In addition to English, it includes French, German, Arabic, Spanish, Italian, Persian, Chinese, Tok Pisin, and Maltese, among others.

The aim of *Linguistics for Translators* is to provide a comprehensive introduction to linguistics that is accessible to students of linguistics and translation at the university level while still retaining a considerable level of detail. The book is intended for a diverse audience, including students of translation and linguistics, practising translators, and readers from neighbouring disciplines who are interested in the subject. At the beginning of each chapter, readers are provided with a route into the primary literature, and the book includes connecting-the-dots sections that establish a connection between linguistics and translation. This approach introduces the reader to various translation theories, approaches, and models throughout the book.

References

Baker, M. (1992). *In Other Words: A Coursebook on Translation*. London/ New York: Routledge.

Fawcett, P. (1997). *Translation and Language: Linguistic Theories Explained*. Manchester: St. Jerome Publishing.

Parker, F. and Riley, K. (1994/2010). *Linguistics for Non- Linguists: A Primer with Exercises*. Boston, MA: Allyn & Bacon.

Rowe, B. M. and Levine, D. P. (2022). *A Concise Introduction to Linguistics* (6th edn). London/New York: Routledge.

Yule, G. (1985/1996). *The Study of Language*. Cambridge: Cambridge University Press.

Setting the scene

1

This chapter provides the reader with a general overview of the discipline of linguistics. It introduces linguistics along with its main branches. Further, it touches on translation universals. It tries to answer the following questions:

- What is 'language'?
- What is the difference between a 'linguist' and a 'native speaker' of the language?
- What is 'linguistics'? And what are its main branches?
- What is 'formal linguistics'? And what are its main areas?
- What is 'interdisciplinary linguistics'?
- What are the 'linguistic universals'?
- What are the main types of 'linguistic universals'?
- What are the main types of 'translation universals', if any?

Language and communication

In order to express your opinions or feelings, tell somebody about something, ask somebody about something, thank somebody for doing something, promise somebody to do something, and so on, you need to communicate with people in one way or another. In this regard, Baker and Hengeveld (2012: 5) state:

How would you define 'language'?

> Using a natural language, humans can in principle communicate with each other about anything in their world, from talking about the weather to writing or reading a scientific article about global warming. Depending on the subject a different jargon may be used – when talking about football, people in a café use words that are quite different from those used in a parliamentary debate about health insurance costs. These different jargons are, however, part of the language as a whole. Also, to a very large extent, they employ the same grammar.

One may observe here that we are talking about linguistic communication. This is because we can communicate without using any language as we can smile to express pleasure or approval, we can laugh to express happiness

What is the difference between 'linguistic communication' and 'non-linguistic communication'?

DOI: 10.4324/9781003228028-2

or disrespect, and so on. These are examples of non-linguistic communication. Building on this, communication can be linguistic communication when a language is used. Otherwise, it is non-linguistic communication. Language, accordingly, can be defined as a system of communication based upon the use of words in a structured and conventional way.

Linguistics

How would you define 'linguistics'?

Linguistics can be defined as the scientific study of language. It is concerned with "the nature of language and linguistic communication" (Akmajian et al. 2010: 5). Knowledge of linguistics, however, is different from knowledge of a language. A speaker of a language can use language without being able to analyse it. Like a person who is able to drive a car without understanding how the engine of the car works, a language user can use language without any conscious knowledge of its internal structure. Conversely, a linguist can know and understand the internal structure of a language without actually being able to speak it. Linguists do work on specific languages, but their primary goal is to understand the nature of language in general.

What is the difference between a 'linguist' and a 'native speaker'?

Scope of linguistics

What are the main branches of linguistics?

Linguistics covers a wide range of areas, such as 'phonetics', 'phonology', 'morphology', 'semantics', 'pragmatics', 'discourse analysis', 'stylistics', 'sociolinguistics', and 'psycholinguistics', to mention only the most well-known areas. These areas can be divided into different branches of linguistics, such as 'formal linguistics', 'usage-based linguistics', and 'interdisciplinary linguistics', as partially shown in the following diagram:

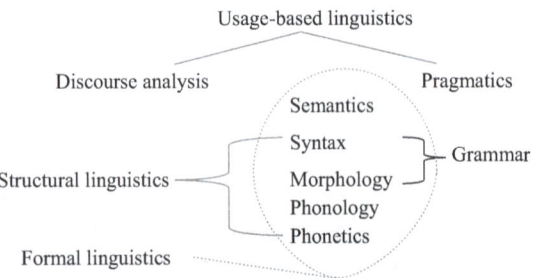

As we can see, inside the circle, there are five areas: 'phonetics', 'phonology', 'morphology', 'syntax', and 'semantics'. These five areas are the main areas of 'formal linguistics'; they "are the 'bread and butter' of linguistics" (Aitchison 1999/2003: 9). When 'semantics' is excluded, then we have what is called 'structural linguistics'. However, when only 'morphology' and 'syntax' are studied, then we talk about what is called

What is the difference between 'formal linguistics' and 'usage-based linguistics'?

'grammar'. As for 'pragmatics' and 'discourse analysis', they are outside the scope of 'formal linguistics'. This is because pragmatics focuses on the study of what is not explicitly said and the role of context in interpreting the speaker/writer's intended meaning while discourse analysis examines how smaller linguistic forms relate in larger linguistic units, such as conversational exchanges or written texts.

Formal linguistics

Formal linguistics, as hinted at above, focuses on studying the structures and processes of language, paying particular attention to how language is organized and how it works. The goal of formal linguists is to identify the common elements among the available structures under consideration in an attempt to discover the most efficient way to describe language in general. Formal linguistics includes five main areas of study.

> What are the main areas of 'formal linguistics'?

Phonetics

Phonetics is a branch of formal linguistics that studies how sounds are produced by the vocal apparatus (the lungs, vocal cords, tongue, teeth, etc.), thus providing a framework for sound classification. Phonetics, more accurately 'auditory phonetics', studies how sounds produced by people are heard, perceived, and then interpreted. In another area of phonetics called 'acoustic phonetics', the focus of attention is shifted towards the frequency, duration, or intensity of the sound.

Phonology

Phonology is another branch of formal linguistics that studies how sounds function in a code (be it a language or dialect) or across these codes. To explain, in English, the sound /p/ has two phones or sounds depending on its position in a word. In words like *'put'*, *'place'*, and *'park'*, it is pronounced with a stronger burst of air than a /p/ in words like *'spin'*, *'apple'*, and *'grape'*.

> What is the difference between 'phonetics' and 'phonology'?

Morphology

Morphology is a branch of formal linguistics that deals with the structure of words. Morphologists "study minimal units of meaning, called 'morphemes', and investigate the possible combinations of these units in a language to form words" (Almanna 2016: 5). The word *'carelessness'*, for instance, is made up of three smaller units called 'morphemes'. They are the root *'care'* and two suffixes *'–less'* and *'–ness'*. The root *'care'* is transformed into an adjective by the effect of the suffix *'–less'*, which is, in turn, transferred into a noun by virtue of the suffix *'–ness'*. For more details on morphology, see Chapters 3 and 4 of this book.

> What are the main dimensions of grammar?

Syntax

Syntax is a branch of formal linguistics that deals with how smaller units, such as words, are put together to form larger units, such as phrases or clauses. The sentence *'Our manager travelled to London yesterday'* is made up of six words. The first two words, *'our'* and *'manager'*, are put together to form a larger unit called a 'noun phrase', whereas the other four words are pieced together to form a larger unit called a 'verb phrase'. To round it off, the above simple sentence is made up of two main phrases. The first phrase, syntactically called a 'noun phrase', is made up of two words: *'our'* (determiner) and *'manager'* (noun). The second phrase, called a 'verb phrase', however, is made up of three phrases: *'travelled'* (finite verb), *'to London'* (preposition phrase), and *'yesterday'* (adverbial phrase).

Semantics

Semantics is another branch of formal linguistics that is concerned with the meaning of morphemes, words, phrases, and clauses. In semantics, the relationship between the referring expressions, such as words or phrases, and what they stand for is given adequate consideration. In other words, the focus in semantics is on "what the words conventionally mean, rather than on what a speaker might want the words to mean on a particular occasion" (Yule 1985/1996: 114).

Interdisciplinary linguistics

Why is 'sociolinguistics', for instance, an inter-disciplinary subject? Discuss.

Interdisciplinary linguistics, like any other interdisciplinary subject, involves at least two different, but somehow related, disciplines, for example 'society' and 'language'. The common branches of interdisciplinary linguistics include:

- 'sociolinguistics' (studying the relationship between language and society);
- 'psycholinguistics' (studying the relationship between language and mind);
- 'ethnolinguistics' also known as 'anthropological linguistics' or 'cultural linguistics' (studying the relationship between language and culture);
- 'computational linguistics' (studying how to apply computers to the analysis and comprehension of texts);
- 'historical linguistics' (studying language change);
- 'philosophical linguistics' (studying the relationship between language and logical thought);
- 'forensic linguistics' (studying the relationship between language and law).

Linguistic universals

Linguistic universals (also known as 'language universals') are "those categories and rules that all human languages, past and present, have in common" (Parker and Riley 1994/ 2010: 149). Examples of linguistic universals include:

- all languages have the categories 'noun' and 'verb';
- all languages have 'vowels' and 'consonants';
- all languages have 'pronouns';
- most languages belong either to SOV, SVO, or VSO type.

To make this point clear, let us translate this English sentence '*I like your car*' into some other languages:

Language	Example
Arabic	أحبّ سيارتك.
Swahili	Naipenda gari yako.
Malay	Saya suka kereta kamu.
German	Ich finde dein Auto gut. Or: Ich finde Ihr Auto gut.
Filipino	Gusto ko ang koste mu.
Tok Pisin	Mi laikim Ka bilong yu.
Chinese	我喜欢你的车 (Wo xihuan ni de che)
French	J'aime ta voiture. Or: J'aime votre voiture.

In French or German, as can be noticed, 'status' as a social dimension is given serious consideration when we use sentences of this kind. To explain, '*J'aime ta voiture*' or '*Ich finde dein Auto gut*' meaning '*I like your car*' is used when we talk about a car owned by a person who is not superior to us, i.e. a friend or a family member. However, '*J'aime votre voiture*' or '*Ich finde Ihr Auto gut*', which has the same meaning in English, i.e. '*I like your car*', is used just to show respect when we talk about a car owned by a person who is superior to us, such as a boss.

Now, let us use the following table to see whether or not all these languages have nouns, verbs, pronouns (including possessive adjectives), and tenses.

Language	Noun	Verb	Pronoun	Tense
English	car	like	I	yes
Arabic	سيارة	حبّ	ك	yes
Swahili	gari	penda	nai, yako	yes
Malay	kereta	suka	saya, kamu	no
German	auto	finde	ich, dein	yes
Filipino	kotse	gusto	ko, mu	yes

If languages do not have a grammatical category of 'tense', how do its speakers talk about the past or future?

Language	Noun	Verb	Pronoun	Tense
Tok Pisin	ka	laik	mi, yu	no
French	voiture	aime	Je, ta/votre	yes
Chinese	车(che)	喜欢(xihuan)	我 (wo)/ 你 ni。	no

As we mentioned above, all languages have nouns, verbs, and pronouns, but not all of them have tenses. Languages such as Malay, Chinese, and creole languages like Tok Pisin do not have tenses. To take the discussion a step further, let us raise this question: Do all languages belong to the Subject–Verb–Object pattern? The answer is 'No' as some languages, such as Arabic, Swahili, and Filipino, start with the verb أحبّ, *'naipenda'* and *'gusto'*, respectively, as can be seen above. Others, such as English, German, Malay, French, Chinese, and Tok Pisin, on the other hand, start with a subject *'I'*, *'Ich'*, *'Saya'*, *'Je'*, 我 (wo), and *'Mi'*, respectively. In addition, in some of these languages, such as Filipino, the noun does not change its form to indicate whether it is singular or plural, but the determiner *'ang'* and *'mga'* used before the noun will see to this, as in:

Gusto ko _{ang} koste mu (I like your car).

Gusto ko _{mga} koste mu (I like your cars).

Now, let us shift our focus of attention to determiners and their position in noun phrases. Do they always precede nouns? The answer is 'No' as in some languages, such as Filipino, Malay, Swahili, and Arabic, to mention but a few, some determiners come after the noun. To explain, the noun phrase *'your car'* can be discussed in the above-mentioned languages. In English, and some other languages, such as German *'dein Auto'* and French *'ta voiture'*, the possessive adjective, which is a determiner, comes before the noun. However, in languages such as Filipino, Malay, Swahili, and Arabic, the possessive adjective comes after the noun, as shown below:

Language	Noun phrase
Filipino	Kotse _{= car} mu _{= your}
Malay	Kereta _{= car} kamu _{= your}
Swahili	Gari _{= car} yako _{= your}
Arabic	سيارة _{= car} ك _{= your}

Unlike English, some languages and creoles, such as Malay, Swahili, Tok Pisin, Arabic, and French, distinguish between a possessive adjective that refers to singular and a possessive adjective that refers to plural. Therefore, when one says *'your car'* in these languages, *'the car'* could belong to one person or more, as shown below:

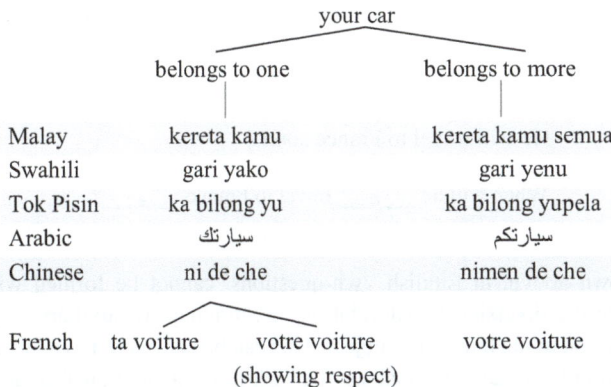

	your car	
	belongs to one	belongs to more
Malay	kereta kamu	kereta kamu semua
Swahili	gari yako	gari yenu
Tok Pisin	ka bilong yu	ka bilong yupela
Arabic	سيارتك	سيارتكم
Chinese	ni de che	nimen de che
French	ta voiture votre voiture	votre voiture
	(showing respect)	

Types of linguistic universals

Linguists distinguish between two kinds of universals: 'absolute universals' and 'implicational universals'. Absolute universals apply to every known language and are quite few in number. For example, all languages have pronouns, verbs, nouns, and the like. Implicational universals, on the other hand, apply to languages with a particular feature that is always accompanied by another feature. For instance, if a language requires a subject–verb inversion for 'yes–no questions', then it also requires a subject–verb inversion for 'wh-questions'. To make this point clear, consider the following sentence in English:

> Why are some universals called 'implicational universals'?

He will travel to France soon.

In this sentence, there is an auxiliary verb *'will'* after the subject of the sentence *'he'*. To form a 'yes–no question' in English, a transformation known as 'inversion' is needed. In the example we are considering, the auxiliary *'will'* is moved from the Infl (short for 'inflection') to the left of the subject, as shown in the following tree:

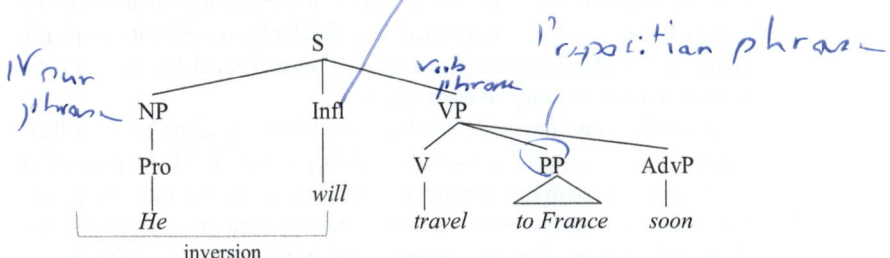

This 'yes–no question' is formed by applying the inversion transformation to the deep structure *'He will travel to France soon'* to produce a surface structure of the following kind: *'Will he travel to France soon?'*.

To form a 'wh-question' in English, in addition to the inversion transformation discussed above, another transformation called 'wh-movement'

> Try to learn the differences between 'deep structures' and 'surface structures'.

is used that can move the 'wh-phrase' from its normal position (indicated by the symbol 'e' that stands for the word 'empty') to a position at the beginning of the sentence, as shown below:

He will travel to France soon.

When will he ___e___ travel to France ___e___?

As shown above, in English, 'wh-questions' cannot be formed without applying the inversion transformation, i.e. moving the auxiliary from its Infl position to the left of the subject. This can be considered as an example of an implicational universal as the 'wh-movement' transformation is accompanied by the 'inversion' transformation.

> What about other languages? Do they need 'inversion' transformation and 'wh-movement' to form 'wh-questions'?

Connecting the dots: Translation universals

From a functional-linguistic perspective, 'universals' can be defined as "those properties that are necessarily common to all human languages" (Comrie 2003: 195). Here a claim is made about the potential of human language where universals are assumed to exist because of how human beings are made, and the physical and cognitive limitations they are subjected to. Thus, for example, certain sounds may not be possible given the nature of the human body, and they are thus universally absent from human language. Another major group of universals relates to the functions of language. The two essential functions of language are (1) to convey information and (2) to establish and maintain social relations between human beings.

The universals posited in the functional approach are used to represent exclusively bottom-up generalizations across languages. Their explanatory potential includes general cognitive, social-interactional, processing, and perceptual, as well as possibly other human faculties. The emphasis is here on empirical cross-linguistic comparison and on the relationship between linguistic forms and language functions. One important functional approach is the systemic-functional one, which places particular emphasis on the relationship between form and function, and which has proved to be most useful for the study of translation.

About the same time as Greenberg and Chomsky came up with their suggestions of linguistic universals, Halliday (1961, 1973) proposed that language as a system of 'meaning making' has a universal meaning potential, which evolved around three motifs that he called 'metafunctions': the ideational metafunction, the interpersonal metafunction, and the textual metafunction (for more details, see Chapter 9 of this book). Ideationally, language reflects our human experience, our interpretation of all that goes on around us, outside and inside, mapping systems of meaning into language such that human beings can capture and construe their individual and collective experiences of the world. Interpersonally, language is a way of initiating and maintaining social relationships, and of construing human

> How many processes are in this complex sentence?
> '"I'll give him a call later", she says'.

language learners and users as personal and collective beings. Textually, language involves the creation of information: it creates discourse, that is, the patterned forms of wording that constitute meaningful semiotic contexts. The textual function has an enabling, facilitative force, which allows the other two functions to operate.

The ideational function contains a general category of process split into material, mental, and relational processes. Processes are happening to, or are being enacted by, human agents in time and space, past or future, real or imaginary, here or there. The interpersonal function is a mode of enacting personal relationships of different kinds, exchanges of speech roles, realizing discourse functions, and implying systems and resources of mood and modality. The textual function is intrinsic to language itself, referring to the resources any language must have for creating discourse and ensuring that each instance of text makes contact with its environment. This 'environment' includes the context of situation (Malinowski 1935), the context of culture, and other instances of text. The resources tapped into here are potentially higher than clauses or clause complexes, setting up relationships which create not only semantic cohesion, but also contributing to the overall grammar of the clause. A typical way of construing the clause as a 'message' is as a combination of two perspectives: that of the speaker and that of the listener, which lead to different types of information flow. All languages display some form of textual organization of the clause. However, how far the tension between the speaker–listener perspectives are weighted one against the other in the languages of the world is far from clear. The textual metafunction also provides for the creation of 'cohesion' of five kinds: reference (or 'phora' [e.g. anaphoric, cataphoric] to distinguish it from reference as defined in the philosophy of language), ellipsis, substitution, conjunction, and lexical cohesion (Halliday and Hasan 1976). In systemic-functional theorizing, it is at this 'deep' metafunctional level of language that we can say 'universality' exists.

Now what might these functional universals mean for translation? Various 'translation universals' as universal tendencies of the translation process, laws of translation, and norms of translation have been suggested in the literature (e.g. Blum-Kulka 1986; Baker 1993; Laviosa-Braithwaite 1998; Toury 2012); see also the contributions to the volume on *Translation Universals: Do They Exist*? (Mauranen and Kujamäki 2004). Toury (2012), in an attempt to formulate probabilistic 'laws' of translation that would hopefully lead to translation universals, has proposed two laws, namely:

(1) The law of growing standardization, referring to the modification of the textual relations of the original text while translating in favour of more "habitual options offered by the target repertoire".

(2) The law of interference, referring to the adaptation of the lexical and syntactic features of the original text in the target language.

As prime candidates for translation universals, the following operations have been suggested: explicitation, simplification, disambiguation,

Is there any difference between 'explicitation' and 'explicitness' in the field of translation studies?

conventionalization, standardization, levelling out, avoidance of repetition, and over- or underrepresentation of source or target language elements, as well as the general manifestation of a so-called 'third code', i.e. translations as opposed to original non-translated texts.

Many researchers who posited translation universals have relied on corpora, the assumption being that through the technical possibilities corpus methodology affords, universals can be found. However, the question we have to ask ourselves is the following: Can there be something like 'translation universals' at all? (House 2008, 2018). Unlike the linguistically based quest for universals of language, the quest for translation universals is, in essence, futile, as there can be no universals at the level of performance, i.e. no proper translation universals, for the following four reasons:

(1) Translation is undeniably an act that operates on language, so universals proposed for language must necessarily also apply to translation. But: these are then NOT universals of translation per se, or *sui generis* universals, but simply universals of language that also apply to translation.

Can you imagine an English-translated text without, for instance, verbs? If not, can we consider this as a translation universal? Discuss.

(2) Obviously, however, translation is not identical to language, let alone to the two linguistic systems involved in translation. Translation can be described as an act of performance, of parole, specific to a certain language pair. This is, of course, reflected in the nature of translation: it is inherently language specific. This language-pair specificity of translation cannot really be offset, such that even corpus-based multi-pair comparisons remain agglomerations of different pairs. Only detailed linguistic analyses of the particular phenomenon suggested to be universal can help us to prove the validity of the claim.

(3) Closely related to the language-pair specificity of translation is the issue of directionality in translation. This means that candidates of universality suggested for one particular translation direction need not necessarily be candidates for universality in the opposite direction. House (2004) has shown on the basis of a corpus of translations of children's books from English into German and vice versa that, for example, procedures of explicitation common in translations from English into German are not traceable in the reverse translation direction at all. In fact, a body of earlier contrastive analyses of many different genres (House 2006) suggested that explicitation holds for translations into German but not the other way round. But even this hypothesis can be disconfirmed if we take the passage of time into account, as was done in the Hamburg research project 'Covert translation' (summary in House 2014). Baumgarten (2007), for instance, has shown that the use of the German sentence-initial coordinative conjunction *'und'*, i.e. *'and'*, has significantly increased over the last 25 years in German academic discourse under the influence of translations from English, which can be taken as indicating an increase of implicitness and vagueness, i.e. a decrease in explicitness regarding this particular functional category.

What about the language-pair that you are familiar with?

(4) Another consideration that militates against the very assumption of translation universals, is genre specificity and the dynamic development of genres over time. In the project 'Covert translation', English original texts, translations from English into German, French and Spanish, and comparable texts in these languages were compared with a focus on how the phenomena 'subjectivity' and 'addressee- orientation' are realized linguistically and how they change over time under the influence of global English. While there is a tendency for explicitation (use of elaboration, extension, and enhancement) in the German translations of popular science texts, this is not the case to the same degree for the different genre of economic texts.

Given the above four arguments, there is no justification at the present time for assuming the existence of translation universals. But the quest needs to go on!

Exercises and discussion

Exercise 1: Mark the following statements as true (T) or false (F).

(1) 'All languages have pronouns' is an example of an absolute universal.	
(2) 'All languages have vowels' is an example of an implicational universal.	
(3) 'All languages have the category noun' is an example of an implicational universal.	
(4) Absolute universals take the form of 'if …, then …'.	
(5) 'If a language has adjectives for shape, then it has adjectives for colours' is an example of an implicational universal.	
(6) All languages have a grammatical category of 'aspect'.	
(7) All languages have a grammatical category of 'duality'.	
(8) All languages belong to the SVO type.	
(9) Formal linguistics covers five main areas. They are *phonetics, phonology, morphology, syntax,* and *pragmatics.*	
(10) Usage-based linguistics covers two main areas: pragmatics and semantics.	
(11) Ethnolinguistics is a branch in linguistics that studies the relationship between language and logical thought.	
(12) Computational linguistics studies how computers simulate languages and their workings.	

Exercise 2: Before translating the following three sentences into a language you know, comment on them by referring to Halliday's three metafunctions: ideational, interpersonal, and textual.

(a) The girl asked this question.
(b) The stupid girl asked this embarrassing question.
(c) It is the girl who asked such a question.

Exercise 3: Select any text from *BBC News* and:

(a) translate it into any language you know;
(b) comment on your translation by referring to such notions as 'explicitation', 'simplification', 'disambiguation', 'conventionalization', 'standardization', 'levelling out', 'avoidance of repetition', 'over-representation of source language elements', and 'underrepresentation of target language elements'.

Discussion and research points

(1) Are procedures of explicitation common in translations between English and your own language or another language which you know and from and/or into which you can translate, or it is influenced by the directionality of translation? Discuss.

(2) It is argued by Frawley (1984) that a so-called 'third code' is different from both the original language and target language as it is a result of the combined impact of the original text and the linguistic and stylistic norms of the target language. Do you agree?

(3) What are the main hypotheses regarding translation universals?

(4) When you translate into your own language, do you have the tendency to make your sentences shorter or longer than the sentences used in the original text regardless of the text type and genre?

(5) Toury's (2012) law of growing standardization refers to the selection of certain linguistic and stylistic options that are more common in the target language at the expense of the patterns used in the original language. With this in mind, carry out a descriptive study to identify some examples in which the translator opted for what is commonly used in the target language, thus modifying the patterns used in the original text while translating.

(6) Carry out a descriptive study of any translated book to answer the following questions:
     (a) What generalizations can you make about the translation process?
     (b) What hypotheses can you propose?
     (c) How would you seek to investigate them?

References

Aitchison, J. (1999/2003). *Linguistics* (6th edn). London: Teach Yourself.

Akmajian, A., Demers, R. A., Farmer, A. K., and Harnish, R. M. (2010). *An Introduction to Language and Communication* (6th edn). Cambridge, MA: The MIT Press.

Almanna, A. (2016). *Semantics for Translation Students: Arabic–English–Arabic*. Oxford: Peter Lang.

Baker, E. A., and Hengeveld, K. (eds.) (2012). *Linguistics*. Oxford: Wiley Blackwell Publishing Ltd.

Baker, M. (1993). "Corpus Linguistics and Translation Studies: Implications and Applications". In Baker, M., Francis, G., and Tognini-Bonelli, E. (eds.), *Text and Technology: In Honour of John Sinclair* (pp. 233–50). Amsterdam: Benjamins.

Baumgarten, N. (2007). "Converging Conventions? Macrosyntactic Conjunctions with English *and* and German *und*". *Text & Talk*, Vol. 27, pp. 139–70.

Blum-Kulka, S. (1986). "Shifts of Coherence and Cohesion in Translation". In House, J. and Blum-Kulka, S. (eds.), *Interlingual and Intercultural Communication* (pp. 17–35). Tübingen: Narr,.

Comrie, B. (2003). "On Explaining Language Universals". In Tomasello, M. (ed.), *The New Psychology of Language*, Vol. 2. Mahwah, NJ: Erlbaum, pp. 195–209.

Frawley, W. (1984). *Translation: Literary, Linguistic and Philosophical Perspectives*. Newark, DE: University of Delaware Press.

Halliday, M. A. K. (1961). "Categories of the Theory of Grammar", *Word*, Vol. 17(3), pp. 241–92.

Halliday, M. A. K. (1973). *Explorations in the Functions of Language*. London: Arnold.

Halliday, M. A. K. and Hasan, R. (1976). *Cohesion in English*. London: Longman.

House, J. (2004). "Linguistic Aspects of the Translation of Children's Books". In Kittel, H., Frank, A. P., Greiner, N., Hermans, T., Koller, W., Lambert, J., and Paul, F. (eds.), *Übersetzung- Translation-Traduction: An International Handbook* (pp. 683–97). Berlin: Mouton de Gruyter.

House, J. (2006). "Communicative Styles in English and German". *European Journal of English Studies*, Vol. 10. pp. 249–67.

House, J. (2008). "Beyond Intervention: Universals in Translation?", *transkom*, Vol. 1, pp. 6–19.

House, J. (2014). "Translation as a Site of Language Contact, Variation and Change". In Ahrens, B., HansenSchirra, S., Krein- Kühle, M., Schreiber, M., and Wienen, U. (eds.), *Translationswissenschaftliches Kolloquium III* (pp. 155–80). Frankfurt/Main: Peter Lang,.

House, J. (2018). *Translation: The Basics*. London: Routledge.

Laviosa- Braithwaite, S. (1998). "Universals of Translation". In Baker, M. (ed.), *The Routledge Encyclopedia of Translation* (pp. 288–91). London: Routledge,.

Malinowski, B. (1935). *Coral Gardens and Their Magic*. London: Allen & Unwin.

Mauranen, A. and Kujamäki, P. (eds.) (2004). *Translation Universals: Do They Exist?* Amsterdam: Benjamins.

Parker, F. and Riley, K. (1994/ 2010). *Linguistics for Non- Linguists: A Primer with Exercises.* Boston, MA: Allyn & Bacon.

Toury, G. (2012). *Descriptive Translation Studies and Beyond* (rev. edn.). Amsterdam: Benjamins.

Yule. G. (1985/ 1996). *The Study of Language*. Cambridge: Cambridge University Press.

Phonetics and phonology

2

This chapter is an introduction to phonetics, phonology, and the main differences between them. It also familiarizes you with the main branches of phonetics, such as 'articulatory phonetics', 'acoustic phonetics', and 'auditory phonetics'. Further, the main stages of sound production, such as 'respiration', 'phonation', 'oro-nasal process', and 'articulation' are explained in this chapter. Added to this, phonological features are discussed in a direct link to translation.

After studying this chapter, you should be able to (1) define phones, phonemes, and allophones; (2) identify vowel and consonant sounds in English; (3) identify the place of articulation and manner of articulation; (4) describe voiced and voiceless consonants; (5) distinguish simple vowels from diphthongs; and (6) assess the phonological features that should be reflected while translating between languages.

Phonetics and phonology (from the word 'phone', meaning 'sound') are the branches of linguistics that study sounds but from different perspectives (for more details, see Ladefoged and Johnson 2010). While phonology focuses on how sounds function in relation to each other in a certain language, phonetics concentrates on how sounds are produced by speakers' vocal apparatus, transmitted by atmospheric air, and perceived by listeners' auditory system. It thus provides "methods for their description, classification, and transcription" (Crystal 1980/2008: 363).

What is the difference between 'phonetics' and 'phonology'?

On this principle, phonetics can be classified into three main branches:

- 'Articulatory phonetics' studies how the vocal organs (lips, tongue, teeth, etc.) are used to produce speech sounds.
- 'Acoustic phonetics' investigates the physical properties of speech sounds in terms of duration, frequency, intensity, and quality.
- 'Auditory phonetics' focuses on how people perceive speech sounds, i.e. how the listener's eardrum is activated by the sound waves on the one hand, and how messages are carried to the brain in the form of nerve impulses on the other.

What about the other languages that you are familiar with?

DOI: 10.4324/9781003228028-3

Why are there more sounds than letters in English?

While the English alphabet is comprised of 26 letters, the sound system of English contains 44 sounds. This is because:

(1) the same sound may be represented by many letters or combination of letters, for example the long vowel /i:/ is presented by the letters 'e', 'ey', and 'ee' in such words as 'he', 'key', and 'see';

Discuss these points in other languages.

(2) the same letter may refer to a variety of sounds, such as the letter 'a' in words like 'cake', 'father', and 'village';

(3) a combination of letters may stand for plenty of sounds, such as the letters 'ch' in words such as 'character' and 'church' or the letters 'th' in words like 'either' and 'through';

(4) a single letter may represent a great deal of sounds, such as the letter 'c' in such two words as 'car' and 'receive';

(5) there may be no letter to represent a sound that occurs in a word, such as the sound /j/ in words like 'cute' and 'use'.

Phone, phoneme, and allophone

A 'phone' (from the Greek word 'phone', meaning 'sound' or more accurately 'voice') is defined as "the smallest perceptible discrete segment of sound in a stream of speech" (Crystal 2008: 361). A 'phoneme', however, is the smallest unit that can bring about a change in meaning; it includes all the phonetic specifications of phones. To explain, let us consider the sound /t/ in the words 'team' and 'stem' as a phoneme. The slight difference in the realization of this phoneme is that the /t/ in 'team' is aspirated [tʰ], i.e. there is a puff of air following the release of /t/, while the /t/ in 'stem' is non-aspirated [t]. Phones that belong to the same phoneme, such as [t] and [tʰ]

How would you define an 'aspirated sound'?

for English /t/, are called 'allophones', as shown in the following diagram:

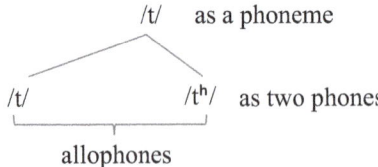

/t/   as a phoneme

/t/   /tʰ/   as two phones

allophones

Sound production

What are the main stages of sound production?

To produce speech, we use our vocal tract, which consists of the passageway between the lips and nostrils on the one hand, and between the lips and the larynx on the other. As such, speech is produced by pushing air from the lungs up through the vocal tract (the first stage) where the vocal folds convert the air into audible sound (the second stage). Then, these audible sounds are distributed to the oral cavity or nasal cavity by the soft palate (the third stage). Finally, these sounds are transformed into intelligible speech sounds with the help of the organs of speech (the fourth stage). Building on this, the stages of sound production are classified into four stages, as shown and explained below.

- Respiration: the air is pushed from the lungs up through the vocal tract.
- Phonation: the vocal folds convert the air into audible sounds.
- Oro-nasal process: these audible sounds are distributed to the oral cavity or nasal cavity by the soft palate (velum).
- Articulation: these sounds are transformed into intelligible speech sounds with the help of the speech organs by manipulating the lips, tongue, teeth, velum, pharynx, and vocal cords.

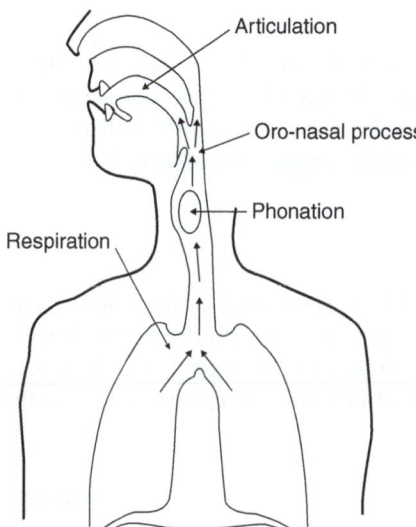

Place of articulation

As stated earlier, in the fourth stage, the audible sounds are transformed into intelligible speech sounds with the help of the speech organs by manipulating the lips, tongue, teeth, velum, pharynx, and vocal cords. In the articulation stage, the vocal tract is constricted at one of the following points, as shown in the following table:

Speech organ	Sound	Place of articulation
at the lips	/b, p, m, w/	bilabial
between the lower lips and upper teeth	/f, v/	labiodental
between the tongue and upper teeth	/θ, ð/	(inter)dental

Be familiar with the main points of articulation.

Speech organ	Sound	Place of articulation
between the tongue and the alveolar ridge	/t, d, s, z, n, l/	alveolar
between the tongue and the palate	/dʒ, tʃ, ʃ, ʒ, j, r/	palatal
between the tongue and the velum	/k, g, ŋ/	velar
at the glottis	/h/	glottal

Manner of articulation

How would you divide consonants according to their manner of articulation?

We have seen that in the fourth stage, i.e. articulation, the vocal tract is constricted at one of the seven points. Now special attention is paid to the way in which the vocal tract is constricted, which can be classified into (1) completely blocked and (2) partially blocked, as explained in what follows.

(1) Completely blocked

Oral stops

What are the 'oral stops' in your own language?

In some sounds such as /p, b, t, d, k, g/, the flow of air through the vocal tract is completely blocked because the two articulators are brought together. These sounds, called (oral) 'stops' (more recently they have been called 'plosives'), can be classified into three groups depending on the articulators used:

Two articulators	Sounds
- the two lips are brought together;	/p, b/
- the tip of the tongue pressed against the alveolar ridge;	/t, d/
- the back of the tongue pressed against the velum.	/k, g/

Nasal stops

How many 'nasal stops' can be identified in your language?

In some other sounds such as /m, n, ŋ/, the flow of air through the mouth is completely blocked but the velum is lowered, thereby forcing the air to go through the nose; hence they are called 'nasal stops' or just 'nasals'.

(2) Partially blocked

Fricatives

What about the other languages or dialects that you are familiar with? Do you have these sounds?

In sounds such as /f, v, s, z, θ, ð, ʃ, ʒ, h/, the flow of air through the vocal tract is impeded, but it is not completely blocked because the two articulators are brought near each other. Here, the air escapes through a narrow passage, thus making a hissing sound. To hear these hissing sounds, try to put your hand very close to your mouth and say these sounds one by one.

Affricates

In sounds like /dʒ, tʃ/, the flow of air through the vocal tract is completely blocked (like the stops /d, t/), but ends with a narrow opening in the vocal tract (like the fricatives /f, v, s, z/). It is worth noting that 'affricates' are quite common around the world, though less common than 'fricatives'.

Do you have these affricates in your own language or dialect?

Approximants

'Approximant' is a term used to cover 'glides' and 'liquids' where there is some or very little obstruction. To begin with 'glides', the flow of air through the vocal tract is constricted, but not enough to block or impede the flow of air, as in: /w, j/. However, in 'liquids', the flow of air through the vocal tract is constricted, but neither enough to block the flow of air nor to cause friction, as in: /l, r/.

Note that unlike the liquids (/ l, r/), which are produced with some obstruction of the airstream, the glides (/w, j/), which are sometimes called 'semivowels', are produced with very little obstruction and are always followed by a vowel.

Voicing

'Voicing' is a term used in phonetics and phonology to characterize speech sounds (usually consonants). Consonants can be described as either 'voiceless' (also called 'unvoiced'; − voice) or 'voiced' (+ voice), as shown in the following table:

Voiced	Voiceless
/b, d, g, v, z, ð, r, l, w, ŋ, y, m, n, ʒ, dʒ/	/p, t, k, f, s, h, θ, ʃ, tʃ/

Note that nasals (/ m, n, ɲ/), glides (/ w, j/), and liquids (/ r, l/) are all voiced. To explain how we can distinguish between voiced and voiceless sounds, try to place your finger(s) on the voice box (i.e. the location of the Adam's apple in the upper throat) and say (1) sssssssssssssss and then (2) zzzzzzzzzzzzzzzz. What do you feel? Is there any vibration? If yes, then the sound is a voiced sound; otherwise, it is a voiceless sound. To put it differently, at the phonation stage, to produce a voiced sound such as /z/, the vocal folds are brought together fairly tightly. However, to produce a voiceless sound like /s/, the air passes through the glottis as the vocal folds are set apart.

In Arabic, as there is no /p/ sound, Arabs sometimes pronounce 'park' and 'bark' in a similar way. Which sound is missing in your language?

Vowels

Unlike consonants, vowels "are produced in a smaller area of the vocal tract – the palatal and velar regions" (Davenport and Hannahs 2010: 39). To produce vowels, people use their tongue, lips, and jaw. As such, in

How many vowels are there in your own language?

describing and classifying the vowels, full consideration is given to these three speech organs. It is worth noting that the most difficult task in describing the vowels is to identify the position of the tongue as it changes its position from one vowel to another without touching any place of articulation (such as teeth, alveolar ridge, palate, velum, or glottis) discussed in the previous section. With this in mind, in producing vowels, there will be no obstruction to the air flow through the mouth. However, the position of the lips and jaw will not cause a big problem as it can be identified by the person without the aid of any instrument.

To begin with, let us try to pronounce these two vowels:

- /iː/ in *'see'*
- /ɒ/ in *'watch'*

Try to pronounce them slowly and then speed up. Now, can you identify the position of (1) your tongue horizontally and vertically, (2) your lips, and (3) your jaw?

Let us begin with the position of the jaw; it is characterized by closeness in /iː/ and openness in /ɒ/. What about the lips? Are they rounded, relaxed/neutral, or spread? They are spread in /iː/ and rounded in /ɒ/, as shown here:

/iː/ as in *'he'*, *'we'*, etc.   /ɒ/ as in *'water'*, *'watch'*, etc.

Now, let us identify the position of the tongue. Horizontally, it is front in /iː/and back in /ɒ/. Vertically, however, it is high in /iː/ and low in /ɒ/.

Building on this, to distinguish one vowel from another, we need to pay extra attention to:

(1) the horizontal position of the tongue (be it 'front', 'centre', or 'back');
(2) the vertical position of the tongue (be it 'high', 'mid', or 'low');
(3) the position of the lips (be it 'rounded' or 'relaxed', also called 'neutral', or 'spread');
(4) the position of the jaw (be it 'close', 'mid', or 'open').

Added to these positions, the length of the vowel (be it 'short' or 'long') can be given serious consideration while describing vowels. The difference between short and long vowels resides in length: long vowels are given symbols written with (ː), as in /iː/ or /aː/, while short vowels are given symbols without (:) like /ɪ/ or /e/ (for more details, see Underhill 1994: 5). Further, English vowels can be classified into two main types: 'monophthongs' (also known as 'pure vowels') and 'diphthongs'. The former phonetically refers to those vowels which remain constant and do not glide, whereas the latter represents those which are composed of a glide from one vowel to another one.

Do you have this complex system of vowels in your own language?

/ɪ/	as in *sit*
/iː/	as in *speak*
/ʊ/	as in *book*
/uː/	as in *tool*
/ʌ/	as in *cup*
/ɑː/	as in *heart*
/ɒ/	as in *box*
/ɔː/	as in *door*
/e/	as in *bed*
/æ/	as in *cat*
/ɜː/	as in *bird*
/ə/	as in *ago*

/eɪ/	as in *may*
/aɪ/	as in *kite*
/ɔɪ/	as in *toy*
/ɪə/	as in *near*
/eə/	as in *dare*
/ʊə/	as in *cure*
/əʊ/	as in *cold*
/aʊ/	as in *mouth*

As one may observe, the vowels in the words *'sit'*, *'speak'*, *'book'*, *'cup'*, and *'bed'* are examples of monophthongs (pure vowels). However, the vowels in the words *'may'*, *'kite'*, *'toy'*, *'near'*, *'dare'*, *'cure'*, *'cold'*, and *'mouth'* are examples of diphthongs.

The question that may arise here is: Why is the letter *'o'* in *'dog'* considered a monophthong while it is a diphthong in *'go'*? This is because the vowel phoneme in *'go'* exhibits some changes where the tongue moves from one position to another, thus showing a change in quality. However, the vowel phoneme in *'dog'* does not show changes in quality as the tongue does not move from one position to another. By quality (more accurately 'sound quality'), it is meant that vowels show considerable differences in three phonetic parameters: tongue shape, tongue position, and lip position.

What about the two words *'boat'* and *'poet'*? Do they have the same vowel?

Building on this discussion, pure vowels can be classified according to the horizontal position of the tongue into (1) front vowels, (2) central vowels, and (3) back vowels. The following table shows vowels from Standard Southern British English:

- front vowels

  - *high front*   /iː/ as in *'seat'*, *'feat'*, etc.

    /ɪ/ as in *'sit'*, *'fit'*, etc.

  - *mid front*   /e/ as in *'left'*, *'bed'*, etc.

	•*low front*	/æ/ as in *'cap'*, *'bad'*, etc.
• *central vowels*		
	•*mid central*	/ə/ as in *'the'*, *'teacher'*, etc.
	•*low central*	/ʌ/ as in *'cup'*, *'bus'*, etc.
• *back vowels*		
	•*high back*	/uː/ as in *'food'*, *'rude'*, etc.
		/u/ as in *'boot'*, *'pull'*, etc.
		/ʊ/ as in *'good'*, *'push'*, etc.
	•*mid back*	/ɔː/ as in *'snore'*, *'law'*, etc.
	•*low back*	/ɒ/ as in *'dog'*, *'want'*, etc.
		/ɑː/ as in *'far'*, *'car'*, etc.

As regards the diphthongs in Southern Standard British English, they are classified into eight vowels, as shown below:

(1) /ɪə/ as in *'beer'*, *'fear'*, *'here'*, *'idea'*, *'beard'*, etc.
(2) /ʊə/, as in *'sure'*, *'moor'*, *'tour'*, *'obscure'*, etc.
(3) /eə/, as in *'there'*, *'where'*, *'chair'*, *'dare'*, *'stare'*, etc.
(4) /eɪ/, as in *'cake'*, *'make'*, *'take'*, *'say'*, *'pain'*, *'they'*, *'vein'*, *'vain'*, *'weight'*, *'wait'*, *'way'*, etc.
(5) /ɔɪ/, as in *'boy'*, *'toy'*, *'enjoy'*, *'voice'*, *'avoid'*, etc.
(6) /aɪ/ as in *'eye'*, *'tie'*, *'die'*, *'high'*, *'buy'*, *'bye'*, *'by'*, *'might'*, *'cry'*, *'shy'*, *'try'*, etc.
(7) /əʊ/, as in *'go'*, *'goal'*, *'snow'*, *'hello'*, *'although'*, *'home'*, etc.
(8) /aʊ/, as in *'house'*, *'loud'*, *'down'*, *'how'*, *'bough'*, etc.

Note that the word *'moor'* has three pronunciations: /mɔː/ UK, /mʊə/ UK, /mʊr/ US.

The best way to memorize them is to divide them into groups, as shown in this diagram (after Roach 2009):

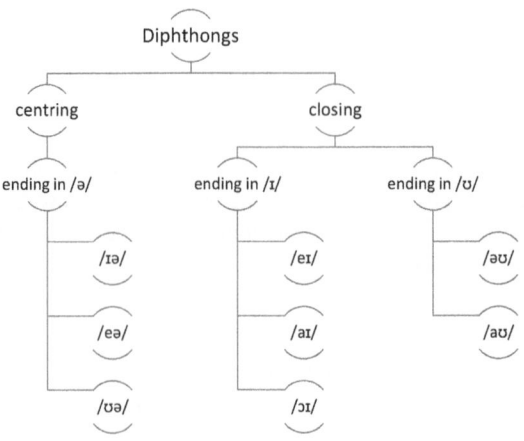

The English-based creole of Papua New Guinea, Tok Pisin, takes most of its words from English, but they are used in different domains and pronounced quite differently. Unlike the lexifier language, i.e. English, Tok Pisin has a limited number of vowels. It only has five vowels (/i/, /o/, /a/, /u/, and /e/). This results in a great number of examples of homophones, which are words pronounced in a similar way. Examples of homophones in Tok Pisin are the word *'was'* resulting from *'watch'* and *'wash'*, and *'sip'* resulting from *'ship'* and *'sheep'*.

What is a 'lexifier language'?

Further, sounds such as /θ/, /ʃ/, /d/, and /f/ are conflated, as shown in this table:

• from /θ/ to /t/ or /s/	
thank	tenk
teeth	tit
something	samting
mouth	maus
• from /ʃ/ to /s/	
show	so
shop	sop
wash	was
ship	sip
• from /d/ to /t/	
blood	blut
• from /f/ to /p/	
finish	pinis
flight	pait
fly	plai
afternoon	apinun
enough	inap

Further, the sound /r/ is not pronounced in many words, such as *'wok'* meaning *'work'*, *'woksop'* meaning *'workshop'*, *'apinun'* meaning *'afternoon'*, *'bepo'* meaning *'before'*, and *'moning'* meaning *'morning'*.

Connecting the dots: Phonological features and translation

Phonologically speaking, each language has its own sounds and some of these sounds are shared by many languages. However, these shared sounds are in an arbitrary relationship with the meanings of the words formed by those sounds, except for a limited number of words. As such, there is no correspondence between any language pair at the phonological level, and content therefore should be given priority at the expense of the sounds. At times, however, when translating between languages, phonological features (here, the very use of the concept of 'phonological features' is no longer tied with the well-known concept of distinctive features proposed by Jakobson and Chomsky) are considered "an important aspect of translation when 'form' comes to the fore in discourse and presents itself as inseparable from content" (Farghal and Almanna 2015: 51). To explain, let us consider the following Chinese conversation between a husband and his wife along with its translation into English (Wong and Shen 1999: 78–9):

ST	Henhao, buyong danxin le. Wo haiyou weiyuan de fufen ne.
	"Moshi de guiyuan?" qizi mei ting qingchu tade hua.
TT	He gave me very good news. We need not look for trouble.
	I have the possibility of being a member of the committee!
	"What's a common tea?" asked the wife, who only vaguely caught the sound.

As can be observed, the Chinese words *'weiyuan'* meaning a member of a committee and *'guiyuan'* meaning longan, which is a type of tropical fruit somehow similar to a lychee, require extra effort from the listener to distinguish between them when being pronounced quickly. Now, the question that rears its ugly head here is: How would you act as a translator in such a situation? Will you ignore the phonological features? Will you change the meaning? Will you opt for using a footnote or endnote? Here, being fully aware that translating them literally would make the whole story behind the use of these two words lost, the translator, as one may see, decided to take care of the phonological features at the expense of the content, thus translating *'guiyuan'*, which is a type of tropical fruit, into a *'common tea'* with the potential to make it rhyme with *'committee'* used in the translation of the Chinese word *'weiyuan'*. This example shows clearly that phonological features are sometimes important and cannot always be ignored on the pretext that there is no correspondence between languages at the phonological level.

To reinforce this point, let us consider the following example where the phonological features emerge as an important aspect that needs to be given serious consideration by translators.

> I think that I used to detest Doctor Fischer more than any other man I have known just as I loved his daughter more than any other woman.
>
> (Greene 1980: 9–10)

Here, the dominant sounds that present themselves as inseparable from the content are /t/, /d/, and /m/. Further, the author introduces two pairs of antonyms, namely *'detest'* versus *'love'* and *'man'* versus *'woman'*, in a very short extract. These antonyms are used in parallel structures, thus acquiring stylistic features that need to be given full consideration. As one

Comment on the translation suggested here by the translator in an attempt to reflect those phonological features.

may notice, there is an example of alliteration used by the author: *'detest'* and *'doctor'*.

Now, giving serious consideration to these phonological features and the antonyms and alliteration employed by the author, one may opt for the following translations:

Arabic	أظنُّ أنني كنتُ أكره الدكتور فشر أكثر من أيّ رجلٍ آخر عرفته في حياتي، تمامًا كما كنتُ أحبُّ ابنته أكثر من أية امرأة أخرى في العالم.
Back translation	I think that I used to hate Doctor Fischer more than any other man I've known in my life just as I used to love his daughter more than any other woman in the world.
German	Ich glaube, daß ich Doktor Fischer mehr als irgend jemanden, den ich je in meinem Leben kannte, immer gehasst habe, genau wie ich seine Tochter mehr als irgendeine Frau in der Welt immer geliebt habe.
Back translation	I think that I have always hated Doctor Fischer more than anyone I have ever known in my life, just as I have always loved his daughter more than any woman in the world.
French	Je pense que je détestais le docteur Fischer plus que tout autre homme que j'ai connu dans ma vie, tout comme j'aimais sa fille plus que toute autre femme au monde.
Back translation	I think I hate Doctor Fischer more than any other man I've known in my life, just as I loved his daughter more than any other woman in the world.

In Arabic, we have more than one option to translate the lexical item *'detest'*. It can be translated into أكره, أمقت, or أبغض roughly meaning *'to hate'*, but the degree of hatred is different. Having paid extra attention to the phonological features and the issues of readability and acceptability that feed into naturalness, the translator opted for أكره, thus making up for the alliteration formed by virtue of the sound /d/ in English.

In German, the lexical item *'detest'* might well have been translated as *'verabscheuen'*, which offers itself as an immediate translational option. However, the translator wisely chose the word *'hassen'* with its strong and hissing double /s/ sound, which is repeated in the conjunction *'dass'* that also features a strong hissing double /s/ sound. This sharp /s/ sound not only better expresses the idea of 'detesting', but it also strengthens it considerably. And the /s/ sound again appears as an initial sound in the adjective *'seine'*, which cumulatively adds to the strong effect of this repeated sound /s/ in German.

In French, the translator has several options to translate the lexical item *'detest'*; these include *'detester'*, *'abominer'*, and *'haïr'*. They have the same denotative meaning with different shades of meaning that show the different levels of hatred. For the sake of readability that feeds into

Alliteration refers to the repetition of usually initial consonant sounds in two or more neighboring words or syllables, as in *'buy'*, *'book'*, *'before'*, etc. Assonance, however, refers to the repetition of the same or similar vowel sounds within words, phrases, or sentences, as in *'seem'* and *'beam'*.

(penso di detestare il dottore Fischer più di ogni altro uomo che ho conosciuto, così come amavo sua figlia più di ogni altra donna. I think I hated D. Fischer more than any other man I known, first as I love his daughter)

naturalness, the translator opted for *'détestais'* to cater for the alliteration used in the original text.

Speakers of Tok Pisin, as explained in this chapter, tend to conflate the sound /tʃ/ in *watch* and /ʃ/ in *wash* with /s/, thus having one word, which is *'was'*, for these two verbs, *'watch'* and *'wash'*. To avoid such confusion, they opt for doubling the word *'was'* without any change, thus having a new word which is *'was was'* to mean *'to wash'*, *'to have a shower'*, or *'to swim'*, as in:

Mi go was was (meaning *'I go swimming'*).

Reduplication is a morphological process where the word or part of it is repeated exactly or with a slight change, as in *'easy-peasy'*.

The second reason for reduplicating the word in Tok Pisin is to show that the action is drawn out over a period, as in *'lukluk'*, literally meaning *'look look'*. In English, when the verb is preceded by the verb *'to keep'*, for instance, as in *'He kept looking at my car'*, it indicates that the act of looking is characterized by multiplexity, i.e. it consists of more than one element/one look. To reflect such a characteristic in Tok Pisin, people opt for reduplication, as in

Em i luklukim ka bilong mi (meaning *'He kept looking at my car'*).

However, to indicate that the matter is characterized by multiplexity, consisting of more than one element, speakers of Tok Pisin tend to attach the suffix *'–pela'* to the pronoun referring to a plural noun, as in:

Asde mi lukim yupela long rod. (*meaning 'Yesterday, I saw you all on the street'*)

Find words in your own language that can express different feelings and meanings depending on the intonation used.

To translate the same sentences from Tok Pisin into English, the phonological feature created by virtue of doubling the words *'was'* and *'luk'* is lost due to the differences between the interfacing languages.

In interpreting, to finish off this section, intonation and stress present themselves as an important aspect that should be given adequate consideration by interpreters to accurately convey the intended meaning. The word *'really'* in English can be discussed here as an example. It can express different feelings depending on its intonation. When it is uttered with rising pitch, it expresses surprise. However, when it is uttered with falling intonation, it expresses disbelief. As such, when paying little or no attention to intonation in interpreting, and the context is of little help, the intended meaning cannot be reflected.

Exercises and discussion

Exercise 1: Mark the following statements true (T) or false (F).

(1) The word *'brother'* begins with a stop.	
(2) The word *'car'* begins with an approximant.	
(3) The word *'sheep'* begins with a glide.	
(4) The word *'sister'* begins with a voiced sound.	
(5) The word *'tree'* begins with a labiodental, affricate, and voiceless sound.	
(6) The letters *'oo'* in words like *'book'* and *'blood'* represent the same sound.	
(7) The word *'see'* ends with a high front vowel.	
(8) Vowels in English are produced in one main area, which is the velum.	
(9) The position of the lips while producing the vowel in the word *'read'* is rounded.	
(10) The words *'some'* and *'sum'* have the same pronunciation.	
(11) In producing vowels, there will be no obstruction to the airflow through the oral cavity.	
(12) The word *'three'* begins with a labiodental, affricate, and voiceless sound.	
(13) The word *'school'* begins with a voiced sound.	
(14) The word *'shop'* begins with a glide.	
(15) The word *'father'* begins with a stop.	
(16) The words *'done'* and *'dune'* have the same pronunciation.	
(17) The word *'she'* ends with a high front vowel.	
(18) The letters *'ou'* in words like *'country'* and *'cousin'* represent the same sound.	

Exercise 2: Fill in the gaps.

(1) The same sound may be represented by two different letters, as in _____ and _____.

(2) English vowels can be classified into two main types: _____ and _____.

(3) To produce vowels, people use their _____, _____, and _____.

(4) There are three branches of phonetics. They are _____, _____, and _____.

(5) The stages of sound production are _____, _____, _____, and _____.

(6) To produce the first sound in *'fan'*, the speaker uses _____ and _____.

(7) To produce the first sound in *'trick'*, the speaker uses _____ and _____.

(8) To produce the last sound in the word *'cook'*, the speaker uses _____ and _____.

(9) The last sound in *'teacher'* is characterized by the following: the lips are_____, and the tongue horizontally is articulated in the _____ of the oral cavity and vertically in the _____ of it.

(10) The vowel in *'cup'* is characterized by the following: the lips are_____, and the tongue horizontally is articulated in the _____ of the oral cavity and vertically in the _____ of it.

(11) To produce the first sound in *'tired'*, the speaker uses _____ and _____.

(12) To produce the first sound in *'photograph'*, the speaker uses _____ and _____.

Exercise 3: Classify the first sound in the following words according to their place of articulation, manner of articulation, and voicing.

Word	Place of articulations	Manner of articulation	Voicing
Time	_____	_____	_____
Ride	_____	_____	_____
Hope	_____	_____	_____
Character	_____	_____	_____

Exercise 4: Choose the words from the box that begin with a 'bilabial', 'labiodental', or 'interdental' sound:

red – war – light– patient – tear – door – this – check – car– horse – father – three

Bilabial	_____
Labiodental	_____
Interdental	_____

Exercise 5: Choose the words from the box that contain 'a high front vowel', 'a high back vowel' or 'a mid-back vowel'.

food – snore – book – fruit – call – seat – cut – flood – home – saw – people – push – rude – sit

a high front vowel	_____
a high back vowel	_____
a mid-back vowel	_____

Exercise 6: The following text is titled *'As you sow, so shall you reap'* quoted from Almanna (2018: 15). Your task is to:

(a)   translate it into any language that you can translate to;
(b)   comment on the phonological features that you have paid extra attention to while translating the text.

One night, three thieves stole a lot of money from a rich man's house. They put the money in a bag and went to the forest. They felt very hungry. So, one of them went to a nearby village to buy food. The other two remained in the forest to take care of the bag of money.

The thief that went for food had an evil idea. He ate his food at a hotel. Then he bought food for his two mates in the forest. He mixed a strong poison with the food. He thought, "Those two will eat this poisoned food and die. Then I will get all the money for myself".

Meanwhile, the two wicked men in the forest decided to kill their mate on his return. They thought that they would divide the money between the two of them. All the three wicked men carried out their cruel plans. The thief who wanted all the money for himself came to the forest with the poisoned food. The two men in the forest hit him and killed him. Then they ate the poisoned food and died. Thus, these evil people met with an evil end.

Discussion and research points
(1)   Go through any translated book to identify the main local strategies opted for by the translator to handle those phonological features presenting themselves as an important aspect that should be given serious consideration while translating.
(2)   Try to find a poem translated into your language to determine how the translator dealt with the phonological features.
(3)   It is argued that translating verse into verse may require a poet translator to deal with the phonological features. What is your opinion?
(4)   At the phonological level, intonation is used by speakers, and then interpreters, to differentiate otherwise identical messages. How would you act if the speaker pays little or no attention to the intonation of a certain word with multiple meanings? Imagine different scenarios.
(5)   In English, words like *'by'*, *'bye'*, and *'buy'*, and *'two'*, *'to'*, and *'too'* are examples of homophones. Translate the following sentence and then comment on the examples of homophones.
He was sent **by** his mother **to** the near**by** supermarket **to buy two** bottles of water.
(6)   Why is Tok Pisin full of examples of homophones?
(7)   Some years ago, the Japanese Prime Minister Mori was given some basic English conversation training before he visited Washington and met President Barack Obama. The instructor told him: "Start your conversation with 'How are you?'. Mr. Obama will say, 'I am fine, and you?' Then, you can say 'Me too'. Afterwards, the translators will do the work for you." When Mori met Obama, he mistakenly

said 'Who are you?' in place of 'How are you?' Mr. Obama was a bit shocked but still managed to react with humour: 'Well, I'm Michelle's husband, ha-ha'. Then Mori replied, 'Me too, ha-ha'. In such a situation, how would you act as an interpreter should you be asked to interpret?

References

Almanna, A. (2018). *The Nuts and Bolts of Arabic-English Translation: An Introduction to Applied Contrastive Linguistics*. Newcastle upon Tyne: Cambridge Scholars Publishing.

Crystal, D. (1980/2008). *A Dictionary of Linguistics and Phonetics.* Malden, MA/Oxford: Blackwell Publishing.

Davenport, M. and Hannahs, S. J. (2010). *Introducing Phonetics and Phonology* (3rd edn). London/New York: Routledge.

Farghal, M. and Almanna, A. (2015). *Contextualizing Translation Theories: Aspects of Arabic–English Interlingual Communication*. Newcastle upon Tyne: Cambridge Scholars Publishing.

Greene, G. (1980). *The Bomb Party*. Harmondsworth: Penguin Books.

Ladefoged, P. and Johnson, K. (2010). *A Course in Phonetics*. Boston, MA: Wadsworth Cengage Learning.

Roach, P. (2009). *English Phonetics and Phonology*. Cambridge: Cambridge University Press.

Underhill, A. (1994). *Sound Foundation: Learning and Teaching Pronunciation*. Oxford: Macmillan.

Wong, D. and Shen, D. (1999). "Factors Influencing the Process of Translating", *Meta*, Vol. 44(1), pp. 78–100.

Morphology

3

In this chapter, the structures of words, the classification of morphemes ('free' or 'bound', 'lexical' or 'grammatical', 'inflectional' or 'derivational'), the classification of words ('simple', 'compound', or 'complex') and the units that make up words are introduced and exemplified. Then an attempt is made to connect the dots by touching on (1) two types of translation: 'rank-bound translation' and 'unbound translation' and (2) types of 'shift' that may occur through translation.

After studying this chapter, you should be able to (1) differentiate morphemes from words; (2) identify the allomorphs of a morpheme; (3) identify homonymous morphemes; (4) differentiate between roots and stems; (5) differentiate between simple and complex words; (6) identify the type of morpheme ('bound' versus 'free', 'lexical' versus 'grammatical' and 'inflectional' versus 'derivational'); and (7) differentiate between 'rank-bound translation' and 'unbound translation'.

Morphology, morphemes, and words

'Morphology' (from the Greek word '*morphē*', meaning 'form' or 'shape') is the study of the structure of words; it is also concerned with word formation. The term morphology was coined in the nineteenth century by the German poet, novelist, playwright, and philosopher Johann Wolfgang von Goethe (1749–1832) in a biological context to refer to "the study of the form and structure of organisms" (Aronoff and Fudeman 2005: 1).

What is the difference between 'morphology' and 'syntax'?

Morphologists study minimal units of meaning, called 'morphemes', and investigate the possible combinations of these units in a language to form words.

'Morpheme' is "the smallest unit of language that has its own meaning, either a word or a part of a word" (www.cambridgedictionary.org). Building on this, a word can be made up of one morpheme, two morphemes, three morphemes, or more. Consider these examples:

What is the difference between a 'word' and a 'morpheme'?

- *'friend'*: one morpheme {friend}
- *'friendly'*: two morphemes {friend} + {–ly}
- *'friendliness'*: three morphemes {friend} + {–ly} + {–ness}

DOI: 10.4324/9781003228028-4

The first formal definition of the term 'word' was proposed by Bloomfield (1933/5: 178; also discussed in Jackson and Amvela 2000: 58). Bloomfield "contrasted the word with other significant units: the morpheme or minimal meaningful unit and syntagme or structure, consisting potentially of more than one word" (1933/5: 178). The term 'word' is defined by Fromkin and her associates as a "meaningful linguistic unit that can be combined to form phrases and sentences" (2000: 25). Words can be simple, compound, complex, or compound complex. When a word is made up of one morpheme, then it is simple. Simple words cannot be broken down into smaller meaningful units, as in:

How would you define 'simple words'?

> cover, arm, gentle, wash ...

When a morpheme is added to these words, as in:

> cover[ing], arm[s], gent[ly], wash[er] ...

then they are not simple anymore as they are made up of two morphemes and can be broken down into smaller meaningful units, as in:

- {cover} + {–ing}
- {arm} + {–s}
- {gentle} + {–ly}
- {wash} + {–er}

How would you define 'complex words'?

How would you define 'compound words'?

Note that the above words are made up of independent morphemes ('cover', 'arm', 'gentle', 'wash') and dependent morphemes ('–ing', '–s', '–ly', '–er'); therefore, they are complex words. By contrast, when words are made up of two independent morphemes, then they are compound words, as in:

> hardcover, armchair, gentleman, white board

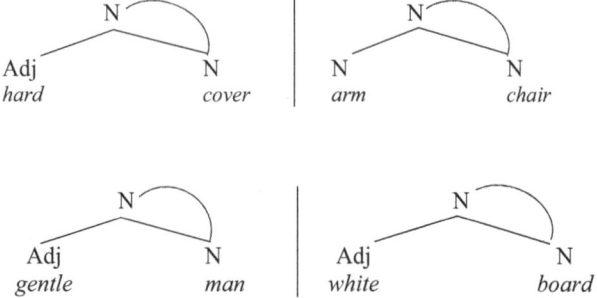

Each compound word contains an independent morpheme. This independent morpheme is also called a 'free morpheme' as it can stand as a word on its own (for more details, see the discussion on 'free morphemes' versus 'bound morphemes' in this chapter).

Each word should belong to a specific part of speech, such as a noun, verb, adjective, adverb, or preposition.

Productivity

It is argued by morphologists that the occurrence of the morpheme in different words can be used as evidence that it is a separate morpheme. In this regard, Parker and Riley (1994/2010: 80; their emphasis) rightly comment: "The more combinations a morpheme can occur in, the more **productive** it is said to be; the more productive a morpheme is, the stronger the evidence that it is a separate morpheme". To put this differently, when a morphological pattern is considered productive, "we mean that this pattern can be extended to new cases, can be used to form new words" (Booij 2012: 70). As such, the suffixes '*–er*' and '*–s*' are productive morphemes as they occur in different combinations with the same meaning and function, as shown in the following examples:

> What kind of evidence could be used to argue that '-er' and '-s' in the word *'teachers'* are morphemes?

–er	–s
*buy*_{er}	*boy*_s
*sell*_{er}	*dog*_s
*read*_{er}	*book*_s
*ask*_{er}	*friend*_s
*interview*_{er}	*day*_s
*found*_{er}	*car*_s
*clean*_{er}	*door*_s
*analys*_{er}	*window*_s
*consum*_{er}	*girl*_s

> Find more examples.

What about irregular words, such as the plural form of *'man'*, i.e. *'men'*? Is it a simple word? How many morphemes are there?

The word *'men'* is not simple because it has two morphemes: the root {man} and the inflectional affix PLU (standing for plural). The word *'men'*, like any plural noun such as *'boys'* or *'girls'*, can be represented morphologically as a root {man} + {PLU}, regardless of the form of the plural morpheme.

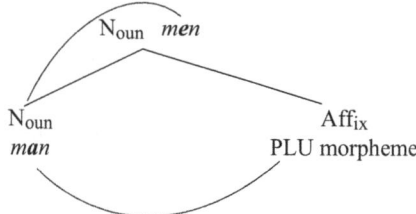

Homonymous morphemes

The function of the suffix *'–er'* in *'bigger'* differs from that of the *'–er'* in *'teacher'*. While the function of the former is to form a comparative degree, the function of the latter is to indicate a person who performs the act of teaching. As these two functions are different and unrelated, these two morphemes are homonymous. To elaborate, the word *'bigger'* can be represented morphologically as a root {big} + {COMP} (standing for the comparative degree), which is why it is called a comparative morpheme. However, the word *'teacher'* can be represented morphologically as a root {teach} + {AG} (standing for the agent of the act), which is why it is called an agentive morpheme. Examples of homonymous morphemes in English (adapted from Almanna 2016: 57) include *'a– '*, *'dis–'*, *'–er '*, and *'–ly'*, as in:

		Meaning	Examples
a–	a.	not or without	*amoral, apolitical, asexual, asymmetric, atheist, atypical, agnostic*, etc.
	b.	in the state of	*ablaze, afloat, asleep*, etc.

Find some examples in other languages.

		Meaning	Examples
dis–	a.	not	*dislike, disbelieve, displeasure, distrust, disagree, disobey, dishonest, disapprove, disappear, disconnect*, etc.
	b.	to know some-thing or to make it known	*discover, disclose*, etc.

		Meaning	Examples
–er	a.	as an agentive morpheme	*writer, reader, designer, farmer, driver, diver, teacher, builder*, etc.
	b.	as a comparative morpheme	*taller, shorter, older, smaller, bigger, richer, nicer*, etc.

Is the word *'manly'*, for example, an adjective or an adverb? Discuss.

		Meaning	Examples
–ly	a.	every	*hourly, daily, weekly, monthly, annually, yearly, etc.*
	b.	having the quality of	*manly, neighbourly, friendly, scholarly,* etc.

Allomorphs and conditioning factors

Now, let's shift our focus of attention to the prefixes *'a–'* and *'dis–'* in words like *'apolitical'* and *'dishonest'*. As one may observe, these two morphemes have the same meaning, i.e. 'not', as modelled here:

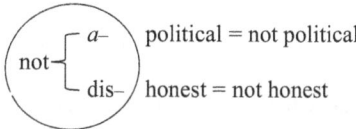

$$\text{not}\left\{\begin{array}{l} a- \\ dis- \end{array}\right. \quad \begin{array}{l}\text{political} = \text{not political} \\ \text{honest} = \text{not honest}\end{array}$$

The question that may spring to mind here is: Are these two morphemes examples of homonymous morphemes? The answer is 'No' as they share the same meaning and function, but are phonologically different. Morphemes do not always come in an identical phonological shape, but they some-times have variant forms. When we have two or more morphemes that have the same meaning or function, but are phonologically different, then these are allomorphs. Consider, for example, the negative prefixes *'un–'*, *'in–'*, *'im–'*, *'ir–'*, *'il–'*, and *'non–'*. These prefixes, in addition to the prefixes *'a–'* and *'dis–'* discussed above, are allomorphs as they have the same meaning and function – they change the word to which they are attached from affirmative to negative, as modelled below:

How would you define the term 'allomorph'?

in–	*correct, visible, tangible, accurate, dependent, expensive, complete ...*
im–	*perfect, possible, polite, moral, mobile, portable, mature, modest ...*
ir–	*rational, regular, resistible, reconcilable ...*
il–	*legal, logical, literate, legible ...*
not– un–	*usual, interesting, healthy, just, fair, important, able, wise, tensed ...*
non–	*essential, sense, conformist, fiction, payment, smoker, finite, tensed, linguistic ...*
a–	*moral, mature, political, sexual, symmetric, typical, theist ...*
dis–	*agree, appear, approve, loyal, honest, similar, believe ...*

Similarly, in Arabic, morphemes like غير, مو, ليس, or لا meaning 'not' are examples of allomorphs as they share the same meaning and function: to change the meaning from affirmative to negative. The only difference is that these morphemes in Arabic are free morphemes while their equivalents as shown above are bound morphemes. Similarly, in Farsi, the morphemes نـ and نا meaning 'not' are examples of allomorphs, as in these examples:

Find examples of allomorphs in your own language.

نـ	بردم I carried/took it > نبردم I did not take it
	خرید He bought it > نخرید He did not buy it
نا	برابر equal > نابرابر unequal
	پیدا visible > ناپیدا invisible

The same phenomenon can be observed in German, as you can see in the following examples where the morpheme *'un–'* meaning 'not' changes the meaning from affirmative to negative:

freundlich (friendly)	>	unfreundlich (unfriendly)
aufmerksam (attentive)	>	unaufmerksam (unattentive)
beliebt (popular)	>	unbeliebt (unpopular)

How would you define 'conditioning factors'?

A question that may arise here is: Which allomorph of a morpheme will the language user use? Is it up to him/her? Actually, the use of a certain allomorph, thus excluding others, is determined by certain factors called conditioning factors (for more details, see McGregor 2009: 68). These factors can be classified in this book into four factors, namely:

- phonological factors;
- lexical morphological factors;
- regional factors;
- formality-related factors.

To begin with, the indefinite articles *'a'* (pronounced /ə/) and *'an'* (pronounced /ən/) are allomorphs as they have the same meaning and function. However, the choice between them is determined by phonological factors, i.e. whether it is followed by a word that starts with a consonant or a vowel, as in:

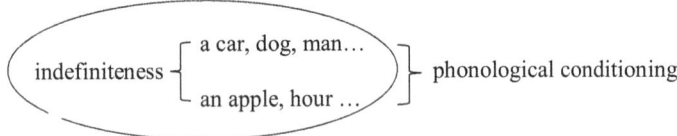

Think of some examples in your own language.

Secondly, the PP (past participle) morphemes *'–ed'*, *'–en'*, and *'–t'* are examples of allomorphs as they have the same meaning and function. However, the choice among them is determined by the morpheme to which the PP morpheme is attached, on the one hand and, on the other hand, by the area in which the morpheme is used, as in:

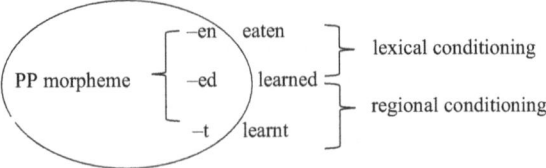

Reflect on your own language to find similar examples.

Thirdly, the comparative and superlative morphemes *'–er'* and *'–est'* are attached to some adjectives to indicate the comparative and superlative degrees, respectively. Building on this, can we add these morphemes *'–er'* and *'–est'* to adjectives such as *'good'* to have * *'gooder'* and * *'goodest'* or *bad* to have * *'bader'* and * *'badest'*? The answer is 'No'.

It is worth noting that some languages do not have verb tenses and aspects to indicate when and how an event or action occurs. Examples of these languages are Indonesian, Malay, Mandarin Chinese, and many creole languages. In these languages, people rely on certain words to indicate periods of time. The verb *'merokok'* in Malay meaning *'to smoke'* is a case in point. The form of the verb is the same in the past, present, and future, as shown in these examples:

Saya merokok (meaning *'I smoke'*).
Saya sudah merokok or Saya telah merokok (meaning *'I smoked yesterday'*).
Saya sedang merokok (meaning *'I am smoking'*).
Saya akan merokok (meaning *'I will smoke'*).

And in Malay the words *'sudha'* or *'telah'* meaning *'already'* can be used to indicate that the event or action occurred in the past. They are synonyms, and the only difference between them is that *'telah'* is more frequently used in writing (formal) rather than in speaking, while *'sudah'* is more frequently used in speaking (less formal). Consequently, *'telah'* and *'sudah'* in sentences of the following kind *'Saya sudah merokok'* or *'Saya telah merokok'* meaning *'I smoked'* are examples of allomorphs, as shown below:

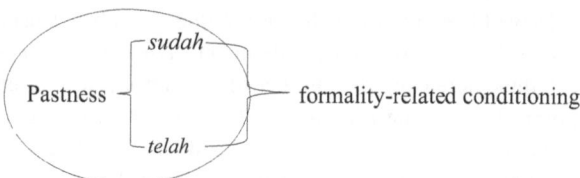

In Persian, for instance, to form a tag question in a sentence of the following kind:

امروز هوا گرمه. مگه نه؟ (meaning *'Today is warm. Isn't it'?*)

What is the difference between 'tense' and 'aspect'. Go to Chapter 5 of this book to learn more about them.

people may opt for مگر نه, مگه نه or مگر اینطور نیست. The choice among these allomorphs is determined by the social context in which they are used. In a formal situation, مگر نه or more formally مگر اینطور نیست is used. However, in an informal situation, مگه نه is opted for.

What do we call this conditioning factor?

Types of morphemes

As stated above, the word *'teacher'* contains two morphemes, the root {teach} and the agentive morpheme *'–er'*.

While the morpheme *'teach'* can stand alone as a word as in *'I teach at one of the universities'*, the morpheme *'–er'* cannot stand alone, but should be attached to another morpheme. Morphemes can be classified into two main types, namely 'free morphemes' and 'bound morphemes'.

How many morphemes are there in a sentence of the following kind? *'I called my sister yesterday.'*

It is worth noting that what is expressed by a morpheme (be it free or bound) in one language is not necessarily expressed by a corresponding morpheme in another. To make what we have in mind here quite clear, consider the following sentences:

Language	Example
English	I like your car.
German	Ich mag dein Auto.
Tok Pisin	Mi laikim ka bilong yu.
Malay	Saya suka kereta kamu.

While in English and German there are four words and five morphemes, in Tok Pisin, there are five words and six morphemes, and in Malay there are four words and four morphemes. Because in Tok Pisin and Malay verbs are simple and there are no endings to be added to the verb to indicate periods of time, there is no morpheme to indicate the tense in the above examples. In English and German, however, there is a morpheme to indicate the tense, which is present. Further, in Tok Pisin, the suffix '−im' is added to any transitive verb to indicate transitivity and flow of energy. However, in English and Malay, there is no need for such a suffix. To indicate possession in Tok Pisin, the preposition 'bilong', derived from the English word 'belong', is always used in this way, i.e. 'ka bilong yu', which literally means 'car belong (to) you', i.e. 'your car', thus increasing the number of the morphemes. To elaborate on this point, the noun phrase 'my brother's house', which consists of four morphemes ('my', 'brother', '−s', and 'house') becomes 'haus bilong brata bilong mi', which consists of five morphemes in Tok Pisin. Had articles been used in Tok Pisin, the number of morphemes would have been increased, but luckily articles are not used.

Further, what is expressed by a free morpheme in one language is not necessarily expressed by a free morpheme in another, as shown in the above example. To reinforce this point, the morpheme 'she' in a sentence of the following kind

She went to school with her dad yesterday.

is a free morpheme as it is used as a word on its own. However, in Arabic, its equivalent ت cannot be used as a word on its own, but should be attached to the verb, as in:

ذهبتْ إلى المدرسة مع أبيها أمس.

How many morphemes are in this sentence? '*I teach at one of the universities.*'

Another difference between English, Arabic, and Farsi is the possessive adjectives *(my*, ي, م, etc.) filling a semantic role of possessor. Unlike in English, in Arabic and Farsi, they cannot be used as words on their own, but they have to be attached to a noun filling a semantic role of possessed, as in:

English	Arabic	Farsi
my book	كتابي	كتابم
his book	كتابُهُ	كتابش
her book	كتابُها	كتابش

Approached from another perspective, morphemes can be classified into 'grammatical morphemes' (prepositions, articles, conjunctions, PLU, PAST) and 'lexical morphemes'. By way of example, let us discuss the following simple sentence:

The teachers asked us to be on time.

Here, while the morphemes '*teach*', '*ask*', '*us*', '*be*' and '*time*' in the above example have meanings in and of themselves, the morphemes '*the*', '*–er*', '*–s*', '*–ed*', '*to*', and '*on*' do not have meanings in and of themselves. As regards the morphemes '*–er*', '*–s*' and '*–ed*', they are bound, grammatical morphemes. These bound, grammatical morphemes can be further classified into 'inflectional morphemes', as in '*–s*' and '*–ed*' and 'derivational morphemes', as in '*–er*', as summarized below.

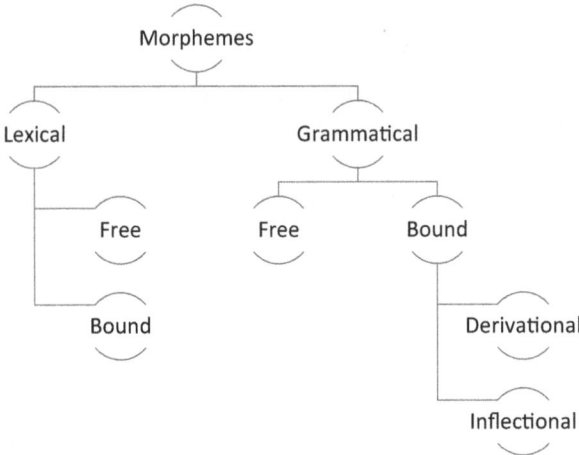

Connecting the dots (1): Shift Theory

A 'shift', according to Catford (1965: 73) in his book *A Linguistic Theory of Translation*, refers to any departure from "formal correspondence" in the process of translating a text from language *A* called the source language to language *B* called the target language. Therefore, when we translate, for example, a noun into an adjective, a verb into an adverb, a word into a phrase, or a grammatical category into a lexical item, to mention but some cases, a type of shift will occur. Shifts are classified by Catford (1965) into two main types:

(a) 'Level shifts' occur when we translate a grammatical category, such as tense, aspect, and voice, into lexis due to the differences between the interfacing languages. For example, to express the past tense in Malay, which does not have a grammatical category for tense and aspect, one can opt for lexical items, such as *'sudah'* or *'telah'* (depending on the formality of the social context). As such, to translate the English sentence *'I smoked yesterday'* into Malay, one may say *'Saya **sudah** merokok'* or *'Saya **telah** merokok'*, as shown below:

*I smok**ed** yesterday.* {*-ed*} PAST morpheme

level shift

*Saya **sudah** merokok.* lexical item
*Saya **telah** merokok.* (*sudah*, *telah*)

Try to find examples of shift that may occur when you translate between other languages.

(b) 'Category shifts', on the other hand, occur when we change through translation the structure (e.g. from passive to active), unit (e.g. from one word to many), class (e.g. from an adjective to a noun) or system (e.g. from a corresponding system to a non-corresponding system). Consider the following examples translated from English into French, German, Malay, and Arabic, respectively:

ST	TT	Type of shift
The teacher sent many emails to his students yesterday.	Plusieurs emails ont été envoyés aux étudiants par leur enseignant hier.	Structure shift
	Back translation: *Several emails were sent ...*	active > passive
He changed the meaning in a dramatic way.	Er änderte die Bedeutung dramatisch.	Unit shift
	Back translation: *He changed the meaning dramatic(ally).*	phrase > word
I will give you a ring later.	Saya akan menelefon kamu nati.	Class shift
	Back translation: *I will ring ...*	noun > verb
Statistics show that about 9 out of 10 tobacco users start before they're 18 years old.	أظهرتِ الإحصائيات أن ما يقرب من 9 أشخاص من أصل 10 يبدأون التدخين قبل سن الثامنة عشر.	Intrasystem shift
	Back translation: *Statistics show**ed** ...*	present > past

How would you translate these verbs *'to email'*, *'to text'*, *'to google'*, *'to hijab'* and *'to bottle'* into your language? Is there any type of shift?

In translating the French simple sentence *'Il n'a pas caché que'* meaning *'He didn't hide that'* into *'He made it clear'*, there is a type of shift. What do we call this?

Here, there are four types of shift. In the first sentence, the translator changed the voice from active (*The teacher sent ...*) to passive (*Plusieurs emails ont été envoyé ... = Many emails were sent ...*), thus enacting a structure shift. In the second sentence, the phrase *'in a dramatic way'* was translated into one word *'dramatisch'* meaning *'dramatic'*, thereby resulting in a combination of both a class shift and a unit shift. In the third sentence, the noun *'ring'* was translated into the verb *'menelfon'* meaning *'to ring'*, thus resulting in a class shift. In the fourth sentence, a simple present *'show'* was translated into a simple past أظهرت meaning *'showed'*, thereby leading to an intrasystem shift.

Morphologically speaking, shifts are classified in this book into several types:

(1) 'Level shift': when a grammatical morpheme lends itself to a lexical morpheme or the other way round.
(2) 'Unit shift': when one morpheme lends itself to more than one morpheme or the other way round.
(3) 'Position shift': when the morpheme changes its position in a larger unit.
(4) 'Status shift': when the morpheme changes its status from free to bound.
(5) 'Word structure shift': when the word changes its structure, thus changing its type from, for instance, compound to simple or simple to complex.

> Think of any type of shift that is not listed here.

As far as translation is concerned, Catford (1965) distinguishes between two types of translations, namely 'rank-bound translation' and 'unbound translation'. In a rank-bound translation, an equivalent is sought in the target language at a morpheme-level category or word-level category, thereby usually resulting in an unacceptable translation where the target text "is either not a normal TL [target language] form at all, or is not relatable to the same situational substance as the SL [source language] text" (Catford 1965/2004: 143). In an unbound translation, however, an equivalent is not tied to a particular rank, but rather is sought at the level of phrase, clause, or sentence. To put this differently, translators and translation students in the first stage of translation ('pre-translation') are encouraged to analyse the source text from different perspectives, including its words along with their morphemes to identify the elements of meaning. However, when they embark on the actual act of translating in the second stage ('translation'), equivalents should not be sought at the level of morpheme or word, but should be sought at a larger level, such as a phrase or clause.

> The translation process at its macro level is classified into three main stages, namely 'pre-translation', 'translation', and 'post-translation'.

Connecting the dots (2): Analytic morphology versus synthetic morphology

What about your own language? Does it have an analytic morphology, synthetic morphology, or something else?

In some languages (e.g. English), words can be easily analysed into smaller parts (i.e. morphemes), while in some other languages (e.g. Arabic) words do not lend themselves to such a morphological mechanism. Consider, for example, the English word *'unbelievable'*. This complex word represented in one orthographic word can be analysed into three smaller units, i.e. morphemes, namely *'un-'*, *'believe'*, and *'-able'*, as shown here:

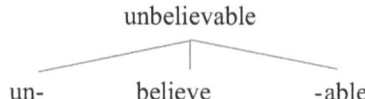

Languages with such a concatenative nature (for more details, see the next chapter) are characterized by having an analytic morphology while others, which do not have such a concatenative nature, are characterized by having a synthetic morphology. When we translate from language *A* to language *B*, the elements of meaning associated with the form of the word are given priority regardless of the form of the word, whether it is represented in one orthographic word or more. To make this point clear, let's go back to the word *'unbelievable'* to discuss the elements of its meaning across languages. This complex word represented in one orthographic word in English lends itself to more than one orthographic word in languages such as Arabic, German, Malay, and Indonesian. However, it lends itself to one orthographic word in languages, such as French, Swahili, Persian, Turkish, and Russian, as shown in this table:

What about your language? How would you translate the word *'unbelievable'*?

Language	Word
English	unbelievable
Arabic	لا يصدّق or لا يمكن تصديقه
German	nicht zu glauben
Indonesian	*luar biasa* or *tidak dapat dipercaya*
Malay	sukar dipercayai or *tidak dapat dipercaya*
Swahili	isiyoaminika
Turkish	inanılmaz
Persian	باورنکردنی
Russian	невероятно
French	incroyable
Thai	ไม่น่าเชื่อ /mai na chuea/

So, we can see that there is no one-to-one correspondence between the elements of meaning of a word and its form across languages. This needs to be taken into consideration by translators. In addition, when we translate from a language with synthetic morphology, such as Arabic, into a language with analytic morphology, such as English, serious consideration should be given to the semantically related words as they may well lend themselves to morphologically unrelated words (for more details, see Farghal and Almanna 2015: 55). Let us consider, in this connection, the following example quoted from Almanna (2016: 38):

ST	استقتل من أجل أن يتزوّجها إلا أنه طلّقها بعد شهرين.
TT	He had made every effort in order to marry her, but divorced her after two months.

Note that the root ق-ت-ل, i.e. *'to kill'*, functions as the input for semantically related words, such as قاتل, i.e. *'to fight'* and استقتل, *'to make every possible effort'*. Those semantically related words driven from the root ق-ت-ل, i.e. *'to kill'*, function as the input for other semantically related words, which often confuses translators. By way of explanation, let us consider the following example quoted from Almanna (2016: 39) along with its two translations:

ST	تمارض أحد أصدقائي البارحة كي لا يخرج معنا.
TT1	One of my friends got sick last night in order not to go out with us.
TT2	One of my friends pretended to be ill last night in order not to go out with us.

Here, it seems that the translator in the first translation confused the two semantically related words مرض *'to feel sick'* and تمارض *'to pretend to be ill'* as they share the same root, i.e. م-ر-ض. Being confused, he mistakenly rendered the word تمارض into *'to get sick'*. Not only did he change the intended meaning, but he also produced an incoherent translation.

Think of semantically related words in your own language and how they might confuse translators.

Exercises and discussion

Exercise 1: Mark the following statements (T) if they are true and (F) if they are false.

(1)	The word *'cut'* in *'I had my hair cut yesterday'* contains two morphemes.	
(2)	The word *'men's'* in *'I found the men's books'* contains two morphemes.	
(3)	The suffix *'–er'* in *'hotter'* is a derivational morpheme.	
(4)	While the word *'come'* in *'They come early every day'* contains two morphemes, the word *'come'* in *'They have just come'* contains three morphemes.	

(5) The word *'carelessness'* is made up of a root and two derivational morphemes.

(6) In *'The men's shirts were found by the cleaner'*, there are 12 morphemes.

(7) The comparative morpheme COMP is attached to adjectives.

(8) The plural morpheme PLU is attached to nouns.

(9) The agentive morpheme AG is attached to verbs.

(10) The suffix *'–er'* in *'shorter'* is a comparative morpheme.

(11) The word *'feet'* is made up of two morphemes.

(12) The word *'sheep'* in *'There are a lot of sheep in the picture'* contains one morpheme only.

Exercise 2: Read the following words and follow the instructions in (1) to (5) below:

achievable – impolite – independent – wireless – imperfection – translator – co-worker – bigger – carelessness – quickly – books – unemployment – beautifully – children – childish – activate

(1) Identify the types of morphemes used in the above words, whether they are 'free' or 'bound'.
(2) Identify the function achieved by each 'bound morpheme'.
(3) Identify the part of speech of each word.
(4) Use the 'bound morphemes' identified by you to create as many words as you can.
(5) Translate them into your own language to identify if any morphological shift occurred through the process of translation.

Exercise 3: Read the following sentences and then (1) identify the number of words and morphemes used in each sentence; (2) divide the morphemes used in each sentence into 'free' and 'bound'; (3) translate the sentences into your own language; and then (4) comment on any shift that might occur.

(1) The teacher asked the students to re-write their homework.
(2) The novel was written by a well-known writer some years ago.
(3) You must switch off the lights before leaving your office.
(4) The mother of the boy and girl are travelling to the UK this summer.
(5) My youngest sister has sent us a great number of emails recently.

Exercise 4: Read the following sentences and (1) identify the number of words and morphemes used in each sentence; (2) divide the morphemes used in each sentence into 'grammatical' and 'lexical'; (3) translate the sentences into your own language; and then (4) comment on any shift that might occur.

(1) The key was found by the girls' father.
(2) She decided to live in the city independently.
(3) My youngest brother is taller than me.
(4) This is one of the most beautiful cities that I have visited recently.
(5) I felt very tired last night, so I did not prepare for the quiz.

Exercise 5: Read the following sentences and (1) identify the number of morphemes used in the following sentences and (2) divide them into 'free' and 'bound'.

(1) I bought it yesterday.
(2) I cooked it yesterday.
(3) My brother bought this gift for me last week.
(4) When will your sister arrive?
(5) Where did your brother travel last month?

Then, reflect on the meaning of the above sentences in your own language and answer the following questions:

(1) How many morphemes are used in each sentence?
(2) Is there any example of a 'free morpheme' that is changed to a 'bound morpheme'?
(3) Is there any example of a 'bound morpheme' that is changed to a 'free morpheme'?
(4) Is there any example of morphological addition or morphological omission?

Exercise 6: Translate the following text adapted from the World Health Organization (WHO) (www.who.int) into your own language. Then comment on the types of morphological shifts that may occur.

The world is in the midst of a COVID-19 pandemic. As WHO and partners work together on the response – tracking the pandemic, advising on critical interventions, distributing vital medical supplies to those in need – they are racing to find a vaccine.

Vaccines save millions of lives each year. Vaccines work by training and preparing the body's natural defences – the immune system – to recognize and fight off the viruses and bacteria they target. If the body is exposed to those disease-causing germs later, the body is immediately ready to destroy them, preventing illness.

Discussion and research points
(1) The following sentence was translated from English into Arabic and German by changing the voice from passive to active, thus resulting in two types of shift, namely 'structure shift' and 'intrasystem shift'. Do you agree with this opinion?

ST	I was asked a difficult question by the teacher.
TT1 (Arabic)	سألني المدرّسُ سؤالًا صعبًا.
Back translation	The teacher asked me a difficult question.
TT2 (German)	Der Lehrer stellte mir eine schwierige Frage.
Back translation	The teacher asked me a difficult question.

(2) In translating the following sentence from French to English, there is a kind of shift where the style is modified to live up to the target language readers' expectation. Can we consider this a stylistic shift? Discuss.

ST	Il a lu le livre de la première à la dernière page.
Back translation	He read the book from the first page to the last page.
TT	He read the book from cover to cover.

(3) Vinay and Darbelnet (1995: 140) have argued that the frequency of using the passive form in English "arises from an attitude towards reality. English chooses a certain objectivity, noting a phenomenon or event either without attributing it to a particular cause or mentioning the cause or the agent only secondarily". If you agree with this, how would you deal with this voice-related issue while translating out of or into English?

References

Almanna, A. (2016). *Semantics for Translation Students: Arabic-English-Arabic*. Oxford: Peter Lang.

Aronoff, M. and Fudeman, K. (2005). *What is Morphology?* Oxford: Blackwell Publishing.

Bloomfield, L. (1933). *Language*. New York: Henry Holt and Company.

Booij, G. (2010). *Construction Morphology*. Oxford: Oxford University Press.

Catford, J. C. (1965). *A Linguistic Theory of Translation*. Oxford: Oxford University Press.

Farghal, M. and Almanna, A. (2015). *Contextualizing Translation Theories: Aspects of Arabic– English Interlingual Communication*. Newcastle upon Tyne: Cambridge Scholars Publishing.

Fromkin, V., Rodman, R. and Hyams, N. (2000). *An Introduction to Language*. Boston, MA: Cengage Learning.

Jackson, H. and Amvela, E. Z. (2000). *Words, Meanings and Vocabulary: An Introduction to English Lexicology*. London/New York: Continuum.

Lieber, R. (2009). *Introducing Morphology*. Cambridge: Cambridge University Press.

McGregor, W. (2009). *Linguistics: An Introduction.* London/ New York: Bloomsbury Publishing.

Parker, F. and Riley, K. (1994/ 2010). *Linguistics for Non- Linguists: A Primer with Exercises.* Boston, MA: Allyn & Bacon.

Vinay, J. P. and Darbelnet, J. (1958/1995). *Stylistique comparée du français et de l'anglais. Méthode de traduction.* Paris: Didier. Trans. and ed. J. C. Sager and M. J. Hamel, *Comparative Stylistics of French and English: A Methodology for Translation.* Amsterdam/ Philadelphia, PA: John Benjamins.

Morphological processes

4

This chapter builds on the previous chapter and introduces students to the higher level of linguistic analysis of morphological processes. In this chapter, the main morphological processes, such as 'inflection', 'derivation', 'compounding', and 'affixation', are discussed and then linked to the actual act of translation.

After studying this chapter, you should be able to (1) identify the main morphological processes; (2) distinguish between declension and conjugation on the one hand, and between derivation and compounding on the other hand; (3) recruit these morphological processes to learn as many words as you can; and (4) utilize these morphological processes to overcome certain difficulties while translating interlingually.

Identify the type and morphological process of these words: *'newspapers'*, *'undisputable'*, and *'asked'*.

Words can be formed by different morphological processes, such as inflection, derivation, compounding, and affixation. It is worth noting that some of these morphological processes are more productive than others, because they are, to a certain degree, exceptional processes. In general, morphological processes can be divided into two main processes (1) inflection and (2) word formation. An inflectional process can be subdivided into (a) declension (an inflectional process applied to nouns and adjectives) and (b) conjugation (an inflectional process applied to verbs). Similarly, word formation can be subdivided into two main processes, namely (a) derivation and (b) compounding, as shown in the following diagram:

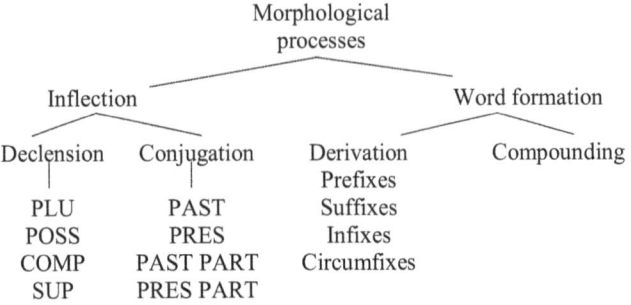

	Morphological processes	
Inflection		Word formation
Declension	Conjugation	Derivation	Compounding
PLU	PAST	Prefixes
POSS	PRES	Suffixes
COMP	PAST PART	Infixes
SUP	PRES PART	Circumfixes

DOI: 10.4324/9781003228028-5

In what follows, these morphological processes will be introduced and exemplified.

Inflection

In English, there are eight inflectional morphemes:

What about other languages that you are familiar with?

(1) PLU (standing for 'plural') attached to nouns, as in *'boys'*, *'girls'*, etc.
(2) COMP (standing for 'comparative degree') attached to adjectives, as in *'bigger'*, *'shorter'*, *'taller'*, etc.
(3) SUP (standing for 'superlative degree') attached to adjectives, as in *'biggest'*, *'shortest'*, *'tallest'*, etc.
(4) PRES (standing for 'present') attached to verbs, as in *'likes'*, *'eats'*, *'teaches'*, etc.
(5) PAST (standing for 'past') attached to verbs, as in *'called'*, *'asked'*, *'played'*, etc.
(6) PAST PART (standing for 'past participle') attached to verbs, as in *'driven'*, *'given'*, etc.
(7) PRES PART (standing for 'present participle') attached to verbs, as in *'writing'*, *'reading'*, *'signing'*, etc.
(8) POSS (standing for 'possessive') attached to nouns, as in *'girl's'*, *'Tom's'*, *'man's'*, etc.

Identify the inflectional morphemes in this sentence: *'She has read his best novels recently'.*

What about the comparative and superlative degrees *'better'* and *'best'*? How shall we treat these? Shall we say they are a root + COMP or SUP? The answer is 'Yes'; the word *'better'*, for example, is made up of two morphemes: the root {good} and the COMP morpheme.

What about *'like'* in *'I like to have a cup of tea'*: Is it made up of one morpheme or two morphemes? It is made up of two morphemes: the root {like} and the PRES morpheme – just change the subject to *'he'* or *'she'* to have a clearer picture.

What about *'bought'* in *'She bought it two days ago'*: Is it made up of one morpheme or two morphemes? The word *'bought'* is made up of two morphemes: the root {buy} and the PAST morpheme.

What about *'put'* in these two sentences: *'I have put it somewhere recently'* and *'I put it somewhere yesterday'*? The word *'put'* in these sentences is made up of two morphemes. While the word *'put'* in the first sentence is made up of the root {put} and the PAST PART morpheme, the word *'put'* in the second sentence is made up of the root {put} and the PAST morpheme.

What about the word *'girl's'* in *'The girl's books are clean and tidy'*: Is it made up of one morpheme or more than one morpheme? Here, there are two morphemes: the root {girl} and the POSS morpheme {–'}.

Word formation

Note that in a sentence of the following kind *'The girls' books are clean and tidy'*, the word *'girls"* is made up of three morphemes: the root {girl}, the PLU morpheme {–s} and the POSS morpheme {–'}.

Apart from the eight inflectional morphemes, all other bound, grammatical morphemes are derivational morphemes in English. Unlike inflectional morphemes, derivational morphemes are not limited in number. They come in the form of affixes ('affixes' referring to 'prefixes' and 'suffixes'). Examples of derivational morphemes in the form of prefixes include *'un–'*, *'dis–'*, *'im–'*, *'re–'*, and *'co–'*, as in:

unkind, **dis**like, **im**polite, **re**-do, **co**-worker

What about your own language?

Examples of derivational morphemes in the form of suffixes include *'–ful'*, *'–er'*, *'–ize'*, *'–ness'*, and *'–less'*, as in:

care**ful**, driv**er**, criti**cize**, sad**ness**, wire**less**

Affixation

Affixation is a morphological process in which a prefix, suffix, or infix (an 'infix' means a letter or a group of letters added within the word stem in some languages, such as Arabic) is added to the root or stem of the word. To illustrate, the root *'friend'* can be discussed here.

Paradigm 1	V	befriends, befriended, befriending, unfriend, unfriends, unfriended, unfriending
Paradigm 2	N	friend, friends, friend's, friends', friendliness, friendlessness
Paradigm 3	Adj	friendly

Can you find an example of 'circumfixation' in your own language?

It is worth noting that a prefix and a suffix are sometimes attached to the root or stem of the word to change, for example, an affirmative word to the negative. In this case, we have what is called circumfix, which is used in some languages such as Malay, Georgian, Chickasaw (a Muskogean language spoken in Oklahoma), and German (for more details, see Fromkin and Rodman 1974/1998: 73). To make this point clear, let us discuss how the past participle of regular verbs, such as *'lieben'* meaning *'to love'* and *'machen'* meaning *'to do'* or *'to make'* in German are formed. With regular verbs such as *'lieben'* and *'machen'*, the past participle is formed by adding the prefix *'ge–'* and the suffix *'–t'* to the root, i.e. *'lieb'* and *'mach'*, respectively, as modelled here:

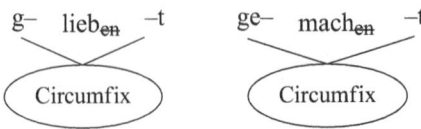

In Farsi, the paradigm of a word can be changed from, for instance, a noun to an adjective by adding the prefix با, as in باسواد, i.e. *'educated'* or باهنر, i.e. *'artist'*. Some suffixes like مند can make changes in the part of speech from a noun to an adjective, as in هوشمند, i.e. *'intellectual'* or سالمند, i.e. *'old'*. If the suffix ی is added to the end of these words their part of speech becomes a noun again with a different meaning, as in:

Noun	Adjective	Noun
سواد education	باسواد educated	باسوادی the state of being educated
هنر art	باهنر artist	باهنری the state of being an artist

The use of the prefix با and the suffix ی in words like باسوادی referring to the state of being educated or باهنری referring to the state of being an artist can be considered as examples of circumfixation. Another interesting example of circumfixation in Farsi is the use of the prefix می indicating progressive aspect and the suffix م showing the present tense conjugation together with some verbs. Let us here consider the following example:

Farsi	من به مدرسه می روم.
English	I am going to school.

In the above example, the root رو meaning *'to go'* is used. To indicate the tense, which is present, the suffix م is attached to the root, and to indicate the progressive aspect, the prefix می is attached to the root, thus resulting in می روم, which is an example of circumfixation.

Compounding

In English, compound words are formed by joining two words together to create a new word with a different meaning. For example, the simple words *'pass'* and *'port'* can stand on their own as words, each with a specific meaning. However, when they are joined together, they form a new word *'passport'* with a different meaning. Another interesting example is the compound word *'brainstorm'*. This word is made up of two simple words, namely *'brain'* and *'storm'*. Sometime the meaning of the compound word is somehow related to the meaning of at least one of its components. Consider the following examples:

- full + moon = full moon
- white + board = whiteboard
- air + port = airport
- police + man = policeman
- dry + cleaning = dry-cleaning

To say *'I do not want'* in Maltese, one can use *'Ma rridx'*, as in *'Ma rridx noqgħod hawn'* meaning *'I do not want to sit here'*. Can we consider the use of *'ma'* meaning *'not'* and the *suffix* *'-x'* attached to the verb as an example of circumfixation? Discuss

Concatenation versus non-concatenation

Focusing on the morphological process itself, whether the word is formed by the effect of linking together a base (be it a root or stem) with another base or linking together two bases as in a chain or not, these morphological processes can be divided into concatenation and non- concatenation, as shown in the following diagram:

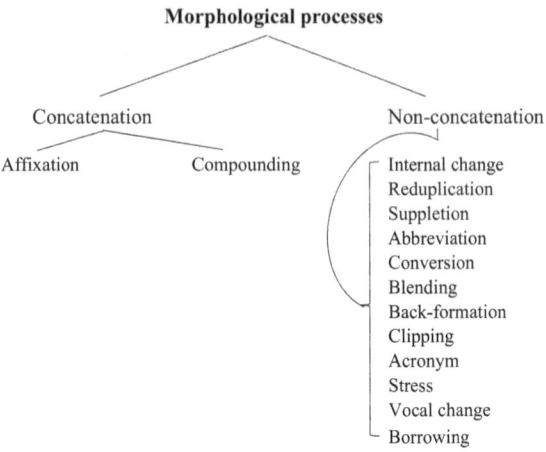

Morphological processes

Concatenation

Concatenation is a morphological process where the root or stem is linked together with affixes as in a chain. Thus, the word *'carelessness'* is formed by linking together the root *'care'* and the suffix *'–less'* to form the word *'careless'*, which is, in turn, linked as a stem with the suffix *'–ness'* to form the word *'carelessness'*. The following diagram representing its internal structure makes this point clear:

Identify the type of the words *'mindfulness'* and *'untouchables'* and then identify the 'root' and the 'stem' used to form them.

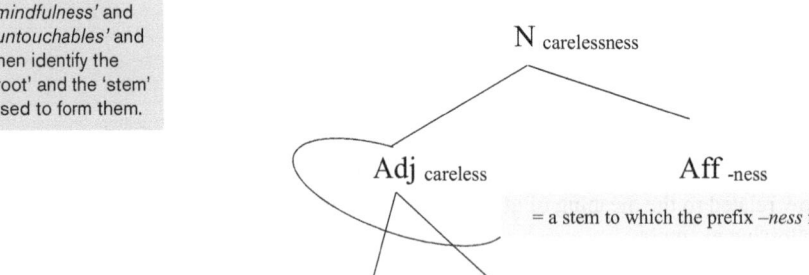

Connecting the dots (1): **Non-concatenative processes of word formation and translation**

Within the same language, words are not formed by virtue of concatenating only; there are also non-concatenative processes where the paradigm of the word can be changed from, for example, a noun to a verb, a verb to a noun, an adjective to an adverb, and so on. By way of exemplifying, words like *'brunch'*, *'hijab'*, and *'flu'* can be examined.

To begin with the word *'brunch'*, it is formed by a non-concatenative process called 'blending' where the first part of the word *'breakfast'* and the last part of the word *'lunch'* are used to form *'brunch'*. The word *'hijab'* is borrowed from Arabic as a noun to refer to the scarf used by women to cover their hair, but more recently it has been used as a verb in a phrase of the following kind *'To hijab or not to hijab?'*. Here we have two non-concatenative processes, namely 'borrowing' and 'category extension'. Regarding the word *'flu'*, it is a shortened form of *'influenza'*. In what follows, these non-concatenative processes are introduced and discussed in a direct link to translation.

> Think of some examples in your own language.

> How would you translate *'To hijab or not to hijab?'* into your own language?

(1) Suppletion

In English, to form the past tense of verbs such as *'play'*, *'walk'*, *'want'*, and *'talk'*, the suffix *'–ed'* is added, thus resulting in *'played'*, *'walked'*, *'wanted'*, and *'talked'*, respectively. To form the comparative degree from such adjectives as *'short'*, *'big'*, and *'small'*, the suffix *'–er'* is added, thus leading to *'shorter'*, *'bigger'*, and *'smaller'*, respectively. To form the plural form of nouns such as *'boy'*, *'book'*, and *'friend'*, the suffix *'–s'* is added to form *'boys'*, *'books'*, and *'friends'*, respectively. Here, as explained earlier, the root is linked with the suffixes *'–ed'*, *'–er'*, and *'–s'* as in a chain, thereby resulting in complex words consisting of two morphemes: a free morpheme (the root) and a bound morpheme (the suffix).

> Why is the word *'boys'* complex? Discuss.

However, there are many exceptional cases. What about the past tense of verbs such as *'to say'* and *'to go'*? Or the comparative degree of *'good'* and *'bad'*? What about the plural form of *'man'*, *'teeth'*, and *'sheep'*? Here, we do not add suffixes, but non-concatenative processes are resorted to.

To begin with, to form the past tense of the verb *'to say'*, two processes are used: vowel change, i.e. changing the vowel /eɪ/ in *'say'* to /e/ in *'said'* and concatenation, i.e. the addition of the suffix *'–ed'*. However, to form the past tense of the verb *'to go'*, the inflected form, i.e. *'went'*, bearing no relationship with the root {go}, is used (for more examples, see Stageberg 1965/1981: 143). To form the comparative degree of *'good'* and *'bad'*, we do not add the suffix *'–er'* to have **'gooder'* or **'bader'*, but the inflected forms, i.e. *'better'* and *'worse'*, bearing no relationship with their roots, i.e. {good} and {bad}, respectively, are used. As such, they are considered suppletive forms. Similarly, the rule that forms the plural forms from singular forms cannot be applied to nouns such as *'man'*, *'tooth'*, and *'sheep'*. The plural form of *'man'* is *'men'* (vowel change) and the plural form of

> Analyse the plural forms of these words: *'ox'*, *'mouse'*, *'thief'*, and *'thesis'*.

> Is there any difference between *'sheep'* (singular) and *'sheep'* (plural) in terms of the number of morphemes?

'tooth' is *'teeth'* (vowel change). However, the plural form of *'sheep'* is *'sheep'* (no change).

As far as translation is concerned, these examples of suppletion are not problematic at all as languages conceptualize experiences differently. So, what is considered as an example of suppletion in one language might not be so in another language. Consider the following example:

I went with my brother to the supermarket yesterday.

Here we have an example of suppletion in the complex word *'went'* consisting of two morphemes: the root {go}, and the past morpheme. As explained above, the inflected word *'went'* bears no relationship with the root, *'go'*, in English, but what about other languages? Let's translate it into some other languages:

German	Ich bin gestern mit meinem Bruder in den Supermarkt **gegangen**.
Azerbaijani	Dünən qardaşımla supermarketə **getdim**.
Maltese	Ilbieraħ **mort** ma' ħija s-supermarket.

In German, Azerbaijani, and Maltese, the verbs *'gegangen'*, *'getdim'*, and *'mort'* meaning *'went'* still have relationships with the verbs *'gehen'*, *'gedirəm'*, and *'mur'*, respectively, meaning *'to go'*.

(2) Category extension and transposition

Category extension (also known as 'conversion' or 'functional shift') is a morphological process by which a word belonging to a particular word-level category, such as a noun, is transferred to another word-level category, such as a verb, without altering the base in terms of spelling or pronunciation. Words such as *'chair'*, *'water'*, *'bottle'*, *'commission'*, *'skype'*, *'text'*, *'google'*, and *'email'* are nouns. However, more recently, they have been used as verbs, thereby extending their category to be used as nouns and verbs. Similarly, words such as *'better'*, *'empty'*, *'dirty'*, and *'wrong'* are adjectives, but more recently they have been transferred to another word-level category, thus being used as verbs.

> What about changing a countable noun to a non-countable noun? Is it an example of the category 'extension'? Discuss.

To clarify this point, let us discuss the lexical item *'email'*. The word *'email'* was first used as a noun in English. However, more recently, it has extended its category to be used as a noun and verb, as in the following diagram:

English	**Maltese and Arabic**
email N.	
↓	Category extension
V.	*'send an email'*

My sister emailed me yesterday.   Oħti bagħtitli email ilbieraħ.

بعثت لي أختي إيميلاً البارحة.

Here the word *'email'* as a verb was translated into Maltese as 'baghtitli email' and into Arabic as بعثت لي إيميلًا meaning *'send an email'*, thus resulting in a combination of two types of shift, namely 'class shift' (from a verb to noun) and 'unit shift' (from a word to a phrase).

In translation studies, many scholars (e.g. Vinay and Darbelnet 1958/ 1995; Catford 1965; Newmark 1988; Chesterman, 1997/2000) have talked about this morphological process, i.e. 'transposition', that can be used by translators as a local strategy.

Vinay and Darbelnet (1958/ 1995) classify the local strategies, or procedures as they label them, into two main types: 'direct translation', which is subdivided into three types – 'borrowing', 'calque', and 'literal translation' – and 'oblique translation', which is subclassified into four types – 'transposition', 'modulation', 'equivalence', and 'adaptation' (Vinay and Darbelnet 1958/1995: 84–91), as shown below:

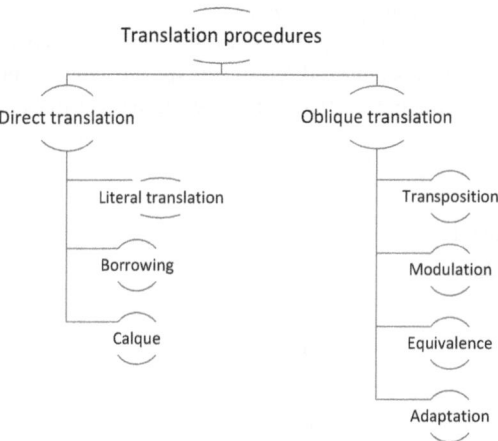

So, in the second type, 'oblique translation', translators may for many different reasons opt for transposition, i.e. changing one part of speech for another without changing the meaning, thus leading to a morphological shift. However, it is worth mentioning that Vinay and Darbelnet advise translators to opt for transposition only if "the translation … obtained fits better into the utterance, or allows a particular nuance of style to be retained" (89). This is because the transposed materials might have a different impact on the target-language reader.

Transposition is labelled 'class shift' by Catford (1965). Class shift, as explained in the previous chapter, occurs when the lexical item in the original text is translated into a lexical item belonging to a different grammatical class in the target language. Transposition, according to Newmark (1988), refers to all types of grammatical changes, such as changing the singular to plural or changing the word class. In this regard, Chesterman (1997/2000) holds that any local strategy adopted by the translator contains a sort of change by default. He classifies those changes into three main types: 'semantic change', 'syntactic change', and 'pragmatic change'. Chesterman labels one of the syntactic changes 'transposition', referring to

Changing a noun from the singular to plural through translation is not a 'class shift' according to Catford (1965). What is it called?

the change that occurs when the word changes its structure (from a noun to a verb, from an adjective to an adverb, from simple to complex, from compound to simple, etc.), thus resulting in a morphological shift labelled in this book a 'word structure shift' (for more details, see Chapter 3 of this book).

(3) Shortening

Shortening can be classified into two main types: clipping and abbreviation.

Clipping

Clipping (also known as 'form clipping', 'form shortening', or 'truncation') is another morphological process where a preexisting form of a word is shortened to form a new word with the same meaning, as in *'flu'* from *'influenza'*, *'lab'* from *'laboratory'*, *'car'* from *'motorcar'*, *'econ'* from *'economics'*, *'gym'* from *'gymnasium'* or *'gymnastics'*, *'info'* from *'information'*, and *'pop'* from *'popular music'*.

As one may notice, in some of these examples the initial part of the word is kept while the rest is removed. This is the most common type of clipping known as 'final clipping' or 'back clipping'. Examples of final clipping in English include:

How would you translate these terms into your language?

• doctor	>	doc
• advertisement	>	ad
• memorandum	>	memo
• vegetable	>	veg
• brother	>	bro
• Professor	>	Prof
• facsimile	>	fax
• demonstration	>	demo
• mathematics	>	math
• examination	>	exam

However, when the final part is kept while the beginning part is removed, this is called 'initial clipping', as in:

• omnibus	>	bus
• motorcar	>	car
• telephone	>	phone
• Internet	>	net
• turnpike	>	pike
• alligator	>	gator
• airplane	>	plane
• raccoon	>	coon
• robot	>	bot
• parachute	>	chute

How would you translate these terms into your language?

There is another type of clipping which is called 'medial clipping' in which the medial part is kept while the initial part and final part are removed, as in:

- influenza   > flu
- refrigerator   > fridge
- detective   > tec

Finally, there is a fourth type of clipping called 'complex clipping' where a compound word is shortened, as in:

- optical art   > op art
- navigation certificate   > navi cert
- microphone   > mike
- popular music   > pop
- organization man   > orgman
- web log   > blog

What are the main types of 'clipping' in your language, if any?

It is worth noting that in some clipped words, the pronunciation might be changed, as in the shortened form *'soc'* from *'society'*.

Abbreviation

An abbreviation is another form of shortening in which some letters of the word are left out. There are three types of abbreviations: 'initialism', 'acronym', and 'contraction'.

Do you have examples of 'abbreviation' in your language?

An initialism is made up of the first letters of a group of words in a phrase, and these letters are pronounced individually with the name of the letters of the alphabet, as in:

- FBI from '**F**ederal **B**ureau of **I**nvestigation'
- VIP from '**v**ery **i**mportant **p**erson'
- BA from '**B**achelor of **A**rts'
- CD from '**c**ompact **d**isc'
- USA from 'The **U**nited **S**tates of **A**merica'
- UK from 'The **U**nited **K**ingdom'
- UN from '**U**nited **N**ations'
- CEO from '**C**hief **E**xecutive **O**fficer'
- MP from '**m**ember of **p**arliament'
- ASAP from '**a**s **s**oon **a**s **p**ossible'

How would you translate these terms into your language?

Note that if the first letters of the words in a phrase are capital letters, then the initialism is written in capital letters, as in *'UN'*, *'USA'*, and the like. Otherwise, it is a style choice as both are acceptable. Consider the word *'compact disc'*; its initialism can be written *'CD'* or *'cd'*. Further, unlike in

American English where full stops are sometimes used for initialism as in *'U.S.A.'* or *'USA'*, in British English, the full stops are not usually used for initialisms, as in *'USA'*.

Like initialisms, acronyms are made up of the first letters of the words in a phrase, as in:

How would you translate these terms into your language? In translating them, will you follow one procedure?

- NASA from '**N**ational **A**eronautical and **S**pace **A**dministration'
- NATO from '**N**orth **A**tlantic **T**reaty **O**rganization'
- PIN from '**p**ersonal **i**dentification **n**umber'
- RAM from '**r**andom **a**ccess **m**emory'
- SIM from '**s**ubscriber **i**dentification **m**odule'
- VAT /vat/ from '**v**alue **a**dded **t**ax' (used here as an acronym)
- OPEC from '**O**rganization of **P**etroleum **E**xporting **C**ountries'

However, unlike initialisms, acronyms are pronounced as one word. With this in mind, full stops are not used here as the acronyms are treated as one word (for more examples, see Jackson and Amvela 2000: 102–3).

Contractions are the third type of abbreviation. There are two types of contraction:

(1) A contraction of one word where some letters from the middle of a word are dropped, as in *'Dr'* from *'Doctor'*, *'govt'* from *'government'*, *'Mr'* from *'Mister'*, etc.
(2) A contraction of more than one word, as in *'he's'* from *'he is'*, *'I'll'* from *'I will'*, *'they're'* from *'they are'*, *'we're'* from *'we are'*, etc.

As regards translation, this depends on the language that you are translating to. For example, a contraction of more than one word, as in *'I'll'* in a sentence of this kind, *'I'll travel to the UK tomorrow'*, is lost through translation when we translate it into Arabic or German as these languages do not have such a mechanism:

What about your own language?

Arabic	سأسافرُ إلى المملكة المتّحدة غدًا.
Back translation	I will travel to the United Kingdom tomorrow.
German	Ich werde morgen nach Großbritannien reisen.
Back translation	I will travel tomorrow to Great Britain.

The same holds true when we translate examples of initialisms, such as *'UK'*, *'UN'*, and *'VIP'*, into languages such as Arabic or German – we cannot use the shortened forms, as shown in the above example. To reinforce this point, let us consider the following translations offered by the official website of the United Nations:

French	Dans le cadre des événements commémoratifs marquant le 75e anniversaire des Nations Unies, l'Assemblée générale a tenu une réunion le lundi 26 octobre 2020 dans la salle de l'Assemblée, au Siège des Nations Unies à New York.
Spanish	Como parte de los actos conmemorativos del 75º aniversario de las Naciones Unidas, la Asamblea General ha celebrado una reunión el lunes 26 de octubre de 2020 en el Salón de la Asamblea, en la Sede de la ONU en Nueva York.
Arabic	عقدت الجمعية العامة ── في إطار الاحتفالات بالذكرى السنوية الخامسة والسبعين لإنشاء الأمم المتحدة ──اجتماعا يوم الاثنين 26 تشرين الأول/ أكتوبر 2020 في قاعة الجمعية بمقر الأمم المتحدة في نيويورك.

The initialism '*UN*' was translated into '*Nations Unies*' in French and الأمم المتحدة, i.e. the United Nations in Arabic. In Spanish, however, it was translated into '*Naciones Unidas*' in the first occurrence and '*NU*' in the second occurrence.

(4) Back-formation and coinage

Back-formation

Back-formation is another morphological process by which what is mistakenly supposed to be an affix added to a preexisting word is subtracted, thus creating a new word. To explain, the verbs '*to edit*', '*to sculpt*', and '*to wordprocess*' are formed by deleting the suffix '*–or*' from '*editor*', '*sculptor*', and '*wordprocessor*', respectively, on the basis of analogy with word pairs such as '*act/actor*', '*translate/translator*', or '*create/creator*'. By the same token, the verbs '*to peddle*', '*to hawk*', '*to stroke*', '*to swindle*', and '*to buttle*' are formed from '*peddler*', '*hawker*', '*stroker*', '*swindler*', and '*butler*', respectively, by deleting the suffix '*–er*', which, along with the suffix '*–or*', is an allomorph of the agentive morpheme, as discussed in the previous chapter.

Other examples of back-formation include the following verbs (for more details on back-formation, see, for example, Stageberg, 1965/1981; Fromkin and Rodman 1974/1998; Parker and Riley 1994/2010; Plag 2002; Lieber 2009):

- '*to televise*' from '*television*'
- '*to resurrect*' from '*resurrection*'
- '*to orient*' or '*orientate*' from '*orientation*'
- '*to escalate*' from '*escalation*' or '*escalator*'
- '*to donate*' from '*donation*'
- '*to enthuse*' from '*enthusiasm*'
- '*to surveil*' from '*surveillance*'
- '*to liaise*' from '*liaison*'
- '*to lase*' from '*laser*'
- '*housekeep*' from '*housekeeper*'

Find more examples in English and your own language.

- *'baby-sit'* from *'babysitter'*
- *'typewrite'* from *'typewriter'*
- *'hedgehop'* from *'hedgehopper'*

Do you agree with this claim? Discuss.

It is worth noting that translators, while translating, usually do not spend a lot of time, effort, and energy on figuring out the morphological process by which the concerned word is formed. Rather, they do their best to find an appropriate equivalent that can be used to reflect the intended meaning, on the one hand, and safeguard acceptability, readability, idiomaticity, authenticity, and well-formedness that feed into naturalness on the other hand. To make this point clear, the following example that contains the word *'televise'* formed by subtracting the suffix *'-sion'* from the word *'television'* can be translated as follows into some other languages:

Don't worry, it will be televised.

German	Keine Sorge, es wird im Fernsehen übertragen.
Indonesian	Jangan khawatir itu akan disiarkan di televisi.
French	Ne vous inquiétez pas, ce sera télévisé.
Spanish	No se preocupe, será televisado.
Thai	ไม่ต้องกลัวไป มันจะถ่ายทอดทางโทรทัศน์เอง
Turkish	Merak etmeyin, Tv'de yayınlanacak.
Arabic	لا تقلق، سيتَم بثه تلفزيونياً.
Farsi	نگران نباش، از تلویزیون پخش خواهد شد.

As can be observed, some languages, such as Thai, Turkish, Arabic, and Farsi, do not have the equivalent of the verb *'to televise'*, thus opting for 'class shift' to use Catford's (1965) term.

Coinage

Coinage is a morphological process by which a word is formed on the basis of an analogy with word pairs existing in the linguistic system. In English, for instance, the prefix *'co–'* can be added to words such as *'translator'*, *'author'*, *'worker'*, etc. to create new words such as *'co-translator'*, *'co-author'*, and *'co-worker'*, respectively. On the basis of an analogy with these word pairs, a word such as *'co-wife'* can be coined to be used, for example, as an equivalent for the Arabic word ضرة or شريكة meaning another wife that a man has along with his first wife at the same time. Preexisting words such as *'ex-wife'* or *'second wife'* denote different meanings, hence the need for coining a word to fill such a cultural gap.

Think of examples of coinage in your language.

(5) Blending

Blending is another morphological process where parts of two words (or more) are pieced together to form a new word. It is worth noting that the parts of the preexisting words used in forming the new words are not themselves morphemes. Words such as *'smog'*, *'brunch'*, *'motel'*, *'Singlish'*, *'culguage'*, *'chunnel'*, *'splog'*, *'fishburger'*, *'chickenburger'*, *'cheeseburger'*, and *'vegeburger'* are some examples. Words like *'smog'*, *'brunch'*, *'motel'*, *'Singlish'*, *'culguage'*, *'chunnel'*, and *'splog'* are formed by utilizing the first part of the words *'smoke'*, *'breakfast'*, *'motor'*, *'Singapore'*, *'culture'*, *'channel'*, and *'spam'*, and the last part of the words *'fog'*, *'lunch'*, *'hotel'*, *'English'*, *'language'*, *'tunnel'*, and *'blog'*, respectively, as shown below:

- smoke + fog = *smog*
- breakfast + lunch = *brunch*
- motor + hotel = *motel*
- Singapore + English = *Singlish*
- culture + language = *culguage*
- channel + tunnel = *chunnel*
- spam + blog = *splog*
- sheep + people = *sheeple*

However, the words *'fishburger'*, *'chickenburger'*, and *'cheeseburger'* are formed by combining the first word without any subtraction and the second part of the word *'hamburger'* (for more details on blending, see Jackson and Amvela 2000: 101).

With respect to translating such examples of blending, the context in which it is used, text type, purpose of translation, readership, and the like should be given serious consideration. To explain, let us consider the following example taken from a conversation between two friends criticizing both the political situation and those who obey authorities like livestock:

I don't think that such sheeple [judgement: negative and explicit] will wake up one day to politically change things [appreciation: negative and explicit]*

Here, we have an example of evaluative language where the speaker expresses his/her attitude towards (1) certain people, thus describing them as 'sheeple' (judgement: negative and explicit) and (2) the political situation in the country (appreciation: negative and explicit). This should be reflected in our translations. Different local strategies, such as paraphrasing, literal translation, functional translation, and transcreation, to mention but a few, can be used to reflect this, and it depends on the translation brief, taking into consideration such aspects as the readership, text type, genre, and purpose of translation, context. Opting for a functional translation, for instance, requires the translator to pay extra attention to issues such as acceptability, readability, idiomaticity, authenticity, intelligibility, and well-formedness. The translation, as a result, does not strike the target-language reader as unusual, as shown below:

Margin notes:

How would you translate these terms into your own language?

Analyze the word 'frenemy'

What about the word *'vegeburger'*? Is there any subtraction? Discuss.

A translation brief can be defined as a set of instructions or pieces of information (e.g. readership, purpose of translation, the medium over which the text will be transmitted, and the time and place of text reception) that would help translators in adopting a certain global strategy and excluding others.

Arabic	لا أظنُّ أن إمَّعاتٍ كهولاءٍ سيستفيقون ذات يوم ليغيّروا الأوضاع سياسيًّا.
Back translation	I don't think that yes-people like those will wake up one day to change situations politically.
German	Ich glaube nicht, dass solche Schafe eines Tages aufwachen werden, um Dinge politisch zu ändern.
Back translation	I don't think that such sheep will wake up one day to change things politically.

In order to reflect the language user's negative attitude towards the people and situations described, on the one hand, and safeguard aspects such as acceptability, readability, and idiomaticity that feed into naturalness on the other hand, the translators opted for إمَّعات, i.e. *'yes-people'* in Arabic, and *'solche Schafe'*, i.e. *'such sheep'* in German.

Opting for الخرفان, i.e. *'sheep'*, in Arabic, for example as a translation for the blended word '*sheeple*', reflects the speaker's attitude towards the people (judgement: negative and explicit) and the political situation (appreciation: negative and explicit).

(6) Borrowing

Find more examples of borrowing out of your language or into it.

Borrowing is a process by which a lexical item is transferred from one language to another because of, for instance, a gap in the linguistic system of the language to which the word or phrase is transferred. Religious words such as *'Imam'*, *'Jihad'*, and *'hijj'* are transferred from Arabic to English. On the contrary, sports words such as '*goal*', '*corner*', '*penalty*', '*offside*', and '*linesman*' or technology-related words such as '*computer*' and '*mobile*' are transferred from English to Arabic. In Papua New Guinea, Tok Pisin, one of its official languages, is used as a lingua franca among the population. Most of the words in this creole are taken from other languages, such as English, German, Malay, and Portuguese. Below are some examples:

Tok Pisin	Language	Meaning
Ka	English	*car*
maski	German	*macht nichts* meaning 'it doesn't matter'.
Susu	Malay	*Susu* meaning 'milk'.
pikinini	Portuguese	*Pequenino* meaning 'child', 'little', etc.

In translation studies, Malone (1988: 15) provides a list of five local strategies that can be employed by the translator when dealing with the text at hand. These are 'matching' ('equation' versus 'substitution'), 'zigzagging' ('divergence' versus 'convergence'), 'recrescence' ('amplification' versus 'reduction'), 'repackaging' ('diffusion' versus 'condensation'), and 'reordering', as shown below:

matching	equation
	substitution
zigzagging	convergence
	divergence
recrescence	amplification
	reduction
repackaging	diffusion
	condensation
reordering	

In this section and in the next one, the first two local strategies, 'matching' and 'zigzagging', are given full consideration. Matching, according to Malone (1988), can be classified into two main types, namely 'equation' and 'substitution'. Matching (along with carry-over matching, i.e. 'borrowing', and 'calque'), according to Malone (1988), is somehow similar to Vinay and Darbelnet's (1958/1995) 'direct translation' that covers three main procedures: 'literal translation', 'borrowing', and 'calque'. On this subject, Almanna (2016: 65) holds that matching, particularly 'equation', is one of the common strategies in "dealing with culturally specific words and neologies". Equation, according to Almanna, can be in the form of 'borrowing', 'calque', 'lexical creation', 'coinage', and the like (for more information, see Almanna 2016: 64). Consider the Arabic word فلافل, i.e. a mixture of ground vegetables, such as chickpeas or fava beans, formed into balls or patties and then fried, in the following examples where the word has travelled all over the world by virtue of borrowing:

> An inexperienced Italian translator may confuse the Italian word *'camera'* meaning *'room'* with the English word *'camera'*. Can we consider this as an example of equation? Discuss.

What would you like to eat? Would you like to have falafel?

German	Was möchten Sie essen? Möchten Sie Falafel haben?
Spanish	¿Qué te gustaría comer? ¿te gustaría comer falafel?
French	Que voudriez-vous manger? Aimeriez vous avoir du falafel?
Indonesian	apa yang ingin kamu makan Anda mau makan falafel?
Maltese	Xi trid tiekol? Tixtieq tieħu falafel?
Farsi	دوست داری چی بخوری؟ آیا دوست دارید فلافل داشته باشید؟

It is worth noting that a 'calque' is a type of borrowing whereby an expression form is borrowed from another language, and then the components of the borrowed expression are translated literally, as in the following example that has several calques in different languages:

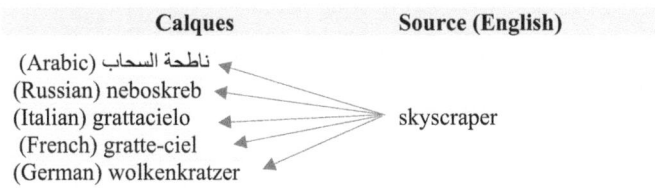

| | Calques | Source (English) |

(Arabic) ناطحة السحاب
(Russian) neboskreb
(Italian) grattacielo   skyscraper
(French) gratte-ciel
(German) wolkenkratzer

Here are some more examples:

Language pair	Calques	Source
English–Arabic	The straw that broke the camel's back.	القشة التي قصمت ظهر البعير.
German–English	Die Schau stehlen.	Steal the show.
English–German	beer garden	Biergarten
English–French	Adam's apple	pomme d'Adam
French–English	Le mariage est une association à cinquante-cinquante.	Matrimony is a fifty-fifty association.
Italian–English	la Casa Bianca	the White House

Vinay and Darbelnet (1958/1995) hold that, like borrowing, many calques become "an integral part of the language" with time and with some "semantic change" might also turn into false friends (85), as in the Maltese word *'ħażin'* meaning *'bad'* borrowed from the Arabic word حزين meaning *'sad'*. Now, to translate, for instance, *'Huwa ħażin'* from Maltese into Arabic, an inexperienced translator may opt for إنه حزين meaning *'He is sad'*, thus resulting in an unacceptable semantic shift.

Substitution, on the other hand, refers to a type of rendering that "may bear little or no morpho-syntactic or semantic relations to the source text" (Taylor 1998: 52). For example, the *of*-structure in English is substituted by the *idafa*-construction in Arabic, a complex prepositional phrase in Tok Pison, and the similar structure *'das Auto meines Bruders'* in German, as shown below:

English	The car of my brother …
Tok Pisin	Ka bilong brata bilong mi …
German	das Auto meines Bruders …
Arabic	سيّارةُ أخي ...

Connecting the dots (2): Translating causativity

> To be able to identify the semantic roles or verb-specific semantic roles in any clause, you need to be able to identify the noun phrases employed. For example, identify the noun phrases used in the following sentence: *'"I'll bring it back tomorrow',* *she says'.*

Causativity (from the verb 'to cause') is an operation where the number of 'arguments' (syntactically known as 'noun phrases') is increased, thus indicating that the doer of the action/activity causes somebody or something else, to do, or to become, something else. To illustrate, the verb *'to laugh'* in the following example can be discussed.

> She laughed a lot yesterday. What made her laugh was his funny haircut.

In the first sentence *'She laughed a lot yesterday'*, only one argument, i.e. a noun phrase, can be identified, which is in the form of a pronoun *'she'* filling a semantic role of Actor/Behaver and a verb-specific semantic role of Laugher (for more details on semantic roles, see Chapter 6 of this book). In the second occurrence, however, through the effect of the analytic causative *'to make'*, an argument-increasing operation occurs where the source of laughing is mentioned, i.e. *'his funny haircut'*. In *'What made her laugh was his funny haircut'*, the interaction between the source of laughing and the person who laughed is unidirectional where the flow of energy goes in one direction (for more details on causativity and flow of energy, see Chapter 12 of this book).

In general, there are three main types of causatives: 'analytic causatives', 'lexical causatives', and 'morphological causatives', as summarized in the following English examples:

(1) 'Analytic causatives' are formed by virtue of verbs, such as *'to make'*, *'to have'*, *'to get'*, and *'to force'*, as in *'The dean got her to type the letter'*.
(2) 'Lexical causatives' are formed by certain verbs, such as *'to kill'* (causing somebody to die), *'to send'* (causing somebody to go), and *'to feed'* (causing somebody to eat), as in *'He was sent by his father to the nearest pharmacy'*.
(3) 'Morphological causatives' are formed by adding certain suffixes, such as *'-en'* and *'-ify'*, as in *'This evidence weakens the case for the prosecution'*.

Now, let's go back to the sentence *'She laughed a lot yesterday. What made her laugh was his funny haircut'* to translate it into some languages, such as German, French, Malay, Indonesian, Swahili, and Arabic, to see how causativity is expressed in these languages:

German	Sie hat gestern viel gelacht. Was sie zum Lachen brachte, war sein lustiger Haarschnitt.
French	Elle a beaucoup ri hier. Ce que la faisait rire, c'était sa drôle coupe de cheveux.
Malay	Dia ketawa banyak semalam. Rambutnya yang lucu membuatnya ketawa.
Maltese	Ilbieraħ daħqet ħafna. Dak li għamilha daħka kien il-haircut umoristiċi tiegħu.
Arabic	ضحكتْ كثيرًا أمس. ما أضحكها هو قصة شعره المضحكة.

How would you translate this into your own language? What type of causative would you normally use in your language to express this 'analytic causative' expressed in English by the verb *'to make'*?

As we can see, causativity is reflected in all these languages, but each language has its own way to express it. Some of them, like German, French, and Malay, would rather use analytic causativity, i.e. *'zum Lachen brachte'*, *'ce que la faisait rire'*, and *'membuatnya ketawa'*, respectively, to stand for *'to make her laugh'*, while others, like Arabic, opt for a lexical causative, which is typically expressed by a lexical item that has implicit causativity.

In Maltese, a structural calque taken from colloquial Arabic *'ghamilha'*, i.e. عملها meaning جعلها *'made her'* is used, thus resulting in an analytic causative.

How would you translate these two sentences into your language? Can you think of an example of divergence?

To clarify this point, let us discuss the verb *'break'*. In English, this verb can be used as a transitive verb, as in *'She broke your phone'* and as an intransitive verb, as in *'The dish fell to the floor and broke'*. To translate this lexical item into Arabic, for instance, the translator needs to go through a process of selecting the most appropriate equivalent from a potential range of alternatives. This process is labelled by Malone (1988) as 'divergence', as opposed to 'convergence'. Divergence occurs when the denotative meaning of the lexical item in the source language is wider and less specific than its counterpart in the target language. Convergence, as opposed to divergence, occurs when the denotative meaning of the lexical item in the target language is wider and less specific. Dickins and his associates (2002) use different terms, namely 'particularization' and 'generalization', to respectively refer to the same ideas. So, when we try to translate the verb *'to break'* into Arabic, we have an example of divergence or particularizing, as shown below:

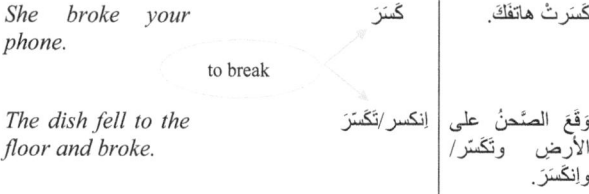

| *She broke your phone.* | كَسَرَ | كَسَرتْ هاتفَكَ. |
| *The dish fell to the floor and broke.* | إنكسر/تَكَسَّرَ | وَقَعَ الصَّحنُ على الأرضِ وتَكَسَّرَ/ وإنكَسَرَ. |

to break

Exercises and discussion

Exercise 1: Mark the following statements (T) if they are true and (F) if they are false.

(1) The suffix *'–ly'* in *'brotherly'* is an adverbializer.	
(2) The word *'better'* contains two morphemes.	
(3) The suffix *'–er'* in *'farmer'*, the suffix *'–ee'* in *advisee*, and the suffix *'–or'* in *'actor'* are examples of allomorphs.	
(4) The suffix *'–ize'* or *'–ise'* is a class-maintaining suffix.	
(5) The word *'flu'* is an example of initial clipping.	
(6) The suffix *'–en'* can be added to nouns.	
(7) The suffix *'–er'* is more productive than the suffix *'–ress'*.	
(8) The word *'smog'* is made up of two words, namely *'smoke'* and *'fog'*.	
(9) The root of the word *'carelessness'* is *'careless'*.	
(10) The word *'sat'* in *'He sat for the exam yesterday'* has two morphemes.	

Exercise 2: Match the following words on the left with those words on the right to form as many compound words as you can, and then translate them into your language:

A	B
• back	• lash
• heart	• brow
• eye	• print
• toe	• nail
• nail	• cap
• finger	• drum
• ear	• line
• skull	• ball
• waist	• lobe
• knee	• beat
• foot	• bone
• jaw	• lid

Exercise 3: Make the opposites of the following adjectives by putting the correct prefix in front of them. Choose from 'a–', 'un–', 'in–', 'im–', 'ir–', 'il–', 'dis–', or 'non–'. Then translate them into your language.

___ healthy	___ regular	___ typical	___ usual
___ polite	___ believable	___ pleasant	___ political
___ correct	___ legal	___ accurate	___ expensive
___ visible	___ fair	___ essential	___ perfect
___ possible	___ successful	___ just	___ literate

Exercise 4: Identify the type of causative (analytic, lexical, or morphological) in the following sentences before translating them into your language. Then comment on any type of shift in causativity.

(1) My father made me wash his car yesterday.
(2) His wife had him sign the contract.
(3) The thief was killed by the police while leaving the house.
(4) Her mother sent her to the nearby supermarket.
(5) Before going to bed, I sent my little girl to bed.
(6) The thought of dying has recently terrified her.

Exercise 5: The following short text is taken together with its translation into English from *My Languages: Maltese Reading*. Your task is to:

(1) identify any examples of 'direct translation' in the sense that Vinay and Darbelnet (1958/1995) use the term;
(2) translate the English translation into your own language;
(3) comment on the local strategies you used by referring to Malone's (1988) first two strategies, namely 'matching' and 'zigzagging'.

Maltese	Kulħadd għandu l-jedd għall-edukazzjoni. L-edukazzjoni għanda tkun b'xejn, għallinqas fil-gradi elementari u fondamentali tagħha. L-edukazzjoni elementari għanda tkun obbligatorja.
English	Everyone has the right to education. Education shall be free, at least in the elementary and fundamental stages. Elementary education shall be compulsory.

Discussion and research points

(1) Go through any translated book from English into your own language to identify the main local strategies opted for by the translator to translate the English prefixes and suffixes.

(2) Go through any translated text from English into your own language to identify any type of morphological shift, including shifts in causativity.

(3) Comment on the translation of *'Valentine Day'* into your language by referring to the morphological processes discussed in this chapter.

(4) Reflect on the language pair that you are familiar with to find examples in which you, as a translator, diverge or converge words.

(5) In translating a phrase of the following kind *'il-karozza ta' ħuti'* from Maltese into English, the translator has two options, namely *'my brother's car'* and *'the car of my brother'*. Can this be considered an example of divergence? Discuss.

(6) An inexperienced French translator may translate '*Passe une bonne journée'* meaning *'Have a nice day'* into *'Have a nice journey'*. Comment on this mistake by referring to similar examples between English and your language.

(7) The English noun phrase *'tennis player'* has different equivalents, as shown below. Is there a one-to-one correspondence between orthographic words and elements of meaning across languages? Discuss.

	Tenisçi (Turkish)
	Tennisçi (Azerbaijani)
	Joueur de tennis (French)
	Tennisspieler (German)
Tennis player	Tennista (Italy)
	Plejer tat-tennis (Maltese)
	Jugador de tenis (Spanish, masculine)
	Jugadora de tenis (Spanish, feminine)
	لاعب تنس (Arabic, masculine)
	لاعبة تنس (Arabic, feminine)

References

Almanna, A. (2016). *The Routledge Course in Translation Annotation: Arabic-English-Arabic*. London/New York: Routledge.

Catford, J. C. (1965). *A Linguistic Theory of Translation*. Oxford: Oxford University Press.

Chesterman, A. (1997/2000). *Memes of Translation: The Spread of Ideas in Translation Theory*. Amsterdam/Philadelphia, PA: John Benjamins.

Dickins, J., Hervey, S., and Higgins, I. (2002). *Thinking Arabic Translation*. London/New York: Routledge.

Fromkin, V. and Rodman, R. (1974/1998). *An Introduction to Language*. Belmont, CA: Christopher P. Klein.

Jackson, H. and Amvela, E. Z. (2000). *Words, Meanings and Vocabulary: An Introduction to English Lexicology*. London/New York: Continuum.

Lieber, R. (2009). *Introducing Morphology*. Cambridge: Cambridge University Press.

Malone, J. L. (1988). *The Science of Linguistics in the Art of Translation*. Albany, NY: State University of New York Press.

Newmark, P. (1988). *A Textbook of Translation*. London/ New York: Prentice Hall.

Parker, F. and Riley, K. (1994/2010). *Linguistics for Non-linguists* (4th edn). Boston, MA: Allyn & Bacon.

Plag, I. (2002). *Word-Formation in English*. Cambridge: Cambridge University Press.

Stageberg, N. (1965/ 1981). *An Introductory English Grammar*. New York: Holt, Rinehart and Winston.

Taylor, C. (1998). *Language to Language: A Practical and Theoretical Guide for Italian/English Translators*. Cambridge: Cambridge University Press.

Vinay, J. P. and Darbelnet, J. (1958/1995). *Stylistique comparée du français et de l'anglais. Méthode de traduction*. Paris: Didier. Trans. and ed. J. C. Sager and M. J. Hamel, *Comparative Stylistics of French and English: A Methodology for Translation*. Amsterdam/ Philadelphia, PA: John Benjamins.

Syntax

5

In this chapter, the structure of phrases, clauses, and sentences are studied. This involves the identification of word-level categories (nouns, verbs, adjectives, adverbs, etc.) and phrasal categories (noun phrases, verb phrases, adjective phrases, adverb phrases, etc.). Further, transformation processes and constituent tests are discussed in a direct link to translation.

After studying this chapter, you should be able to (1) relate traditional grammar knowledge to modern linguistic approaches; (2) differentiate word-level categories from phrasal categories; (3) identify parts of speech, basic grammatical functions, and complex sentence structures; (4) reorder the elements of the clause without affecting its meaning; (5) identify whether a group of words function as a unit or not; (6) deal with translating tense, aspect, voice, gender, and the like across languages; and (7) disambiguate certain structural ambiguity by resorting to constituent analysis.

In your opinion, will changing the structure and information of a sentence affect the overall meaning? Discuss with illustrative examples.

The word 'syntax' derived from the Greek word '*syntaxis*' means 'arrangement', thus referring to the way in which lexical items (i.e. words) are arranged in a given clause or sentence. To put this differently, syntax is the branch of linguistics that focuses on the study of the structures and information of sentences along with the relationship of their parts. In English, for instance, in a sentence of the following kind

The teacher asked the students many questions yesterday.

we have a 'subject' and 'predicate', to borrow terms from traditional grammar, as modelled below:

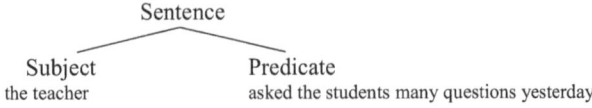

Sentence

Subject — Predicate

Subject
the teacher

Predicate
asked the students many questions yesterday

DOI: 10.4324/9781003228028-6

Speakers of some creole languages, such as Tok Pisin, tend to use the letter *'i'* as a predicate marker when the subject is a third person, as in:

What about your language or the languages that you are familiar with? Is any predicate marker used?

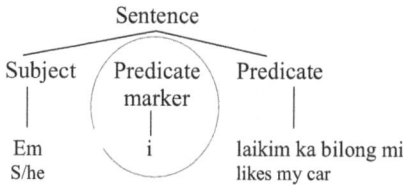

Now, let us compare the sentence *'The teacher asked the students many questions yesterday'* with the following sentence which has the same structure to see if they have the same meaning or not.

> The students asked the teacher many questions yesterday.

Although these two sentences have the same syntactic structures (Subject, Verb, Indirect Object, Direct Object, and Adverb of Time), they have different meanings. This is because each noun phrase (known as an 'argument' in semantics) fills a different semantic role (for more details, see the next chapter). To explain, let us identify the semantic role assigned to each noun phrase used in the previous sentences by raising the following questions:

- Who was the Asker in the first sentence?
- Who was the Asker in the second sentence?
- Who was the Addressee in the first sentence?
- Who was the Addressee in the second sentence?
- What was asked in the first sentence?
- What was asked in the second sentence?

In your opinion, why is the word *'yesterday'* without a semantic role?

(1) The teacher $_{\text{Asker}}$ asked the students $_{\text{Addressee}}$ many questions $_{\text{something Asked}}$ yesterday (Adjunct without a semantic role).

(2) The students $_{\text{Asker}}$ asked the teacher $_{\text{Addressee}}$ many questions $_{\text{something Asked}}$ yesterday (Adjunct without a semantic role).

The noun phrase *'the teacher'* in the first sentence fills a verb-specific semantic role of Asker, while in the second sentence it fills a verb-specific semantic role of Addressee. The noun phrase *'the students'* fills a verb-specific semantic role of Addressee in the first sentence, while it fills a verb-specific semantic role of Asker in the second sentence. However, the noun phrase *'many questions'* fills a verb-specific semantic role of something Asked in both sentences. Now, let us change the first sentence to the passive and compare the two versions.

> Active: The teacher asked the students many questions yesterday.
> Passive: The students were asked many questions yesterday by the teacher.

Here, although we have different syntactic structures, we have the same meaning. This is because the noun phrases *'the teacher'*, *'the students'*, and *'many questions'* in both versions fill the semantic roles of Asker, Addressee, and something Asked, respectively.

We can conclude that in addition to 'phonological rules' (how words are pronounced) and 'morphological rules' (how morphemes can be combined to form words), language users need to fall back on other rules to speak and understand a language, such as 'syntactic rules' and 'semantic rules'.

In your opinion, is it enough to rely on the four rules mentioned here to speak and understand a language? Discuss.

- 'Syntactic rules' refer to the rules that explain how words can be combined into sentences, thus telling us that while the sentence *'The teacher asked the students many questions yesterday'* is correct, the sentence **'The asked many questions teacher the yesterday students'* is not.
- 'Semantic rules' refer to the rules that explain how different combinations give different meanings, as in:

The teacher asked the students many questions yesterday.
The students asked the teacher many questions yesterday.

Syntactic categories

Traditionally, syntactic categories (also known as 'grammatical categories') are classified into two main types:

(1) 'Word-level categories' (e.g. noun, verb, adjective, adverb, preposition).
(2) 'Phrasal categories' (e.g. noun phrase, verb phrase, adjective phrase, adverb phrase, preposition phrase).

Identify the word-level categories employed in the following sentence: *'She'll travel to Doha with her dad tomorrow.'*

Lexical items (i.e. words) are classified into certain categories (also known as 'parts of speech'), such as noun (N), verb (V), pronoun (Pro), adjective (Adj), adverb (Adv), auxiliary (Aux), preposition (P), determiner (Det), conjunction (Conj), degree word (D), and qualifier (Qual). These lexical items can be classified into 'lexical' and 'grammatical'. Grammatical words can be further sub-classified into 'specifiers' and 'non-specifiers', as summarized here:

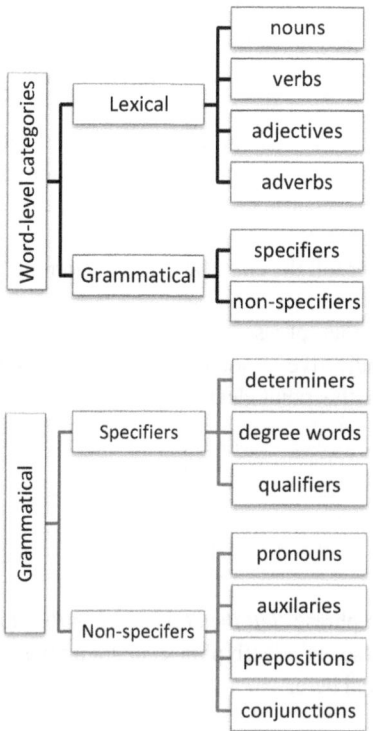

Specifiers

- **Determiners**, such as *'the'*, *'a'*, *'an'*, *'this'*, *'that'*, *'no'*, *'many'*, and *'much'*, are followed by nouns, thus functioning as the specifiers of the nouns.
- **Qualifiers**, such as *'often'*, *'never'*, *'seldom'*, *'perhaps'*, and *'always'*, function as the specifiers of the verbs.
- **Degree words**, such as *'very'*, *'almost'*, *'slightly'*, *'extremely'*, *'completely'*, *'too'*, *'quite'*, *'more'*, and *'so'*, are normally used before the adjectives, thus serving as specifiers of the adjectives.

Note that a determiner can be followed by an adjective that should be followed by a noun. What about the phrase 'the poor' in a sentence of the following kind? *'The government should help the poor'.*

Word-level categories in any language are categorized according to their shared morphological and syntactic properties, thus having certain characteristics. For example, nouns in English:

- can be pluralized, as in *'book'* > *'books'*;
- can be preceded by the definite article *'the'*, as in *'book'* > *'**the** book'*;
- can be preceded by the indefinite article *'a/an'*, as in *'book'* > *'**a** book'*.

What about your
language or the
languages that you
are familiar with?
How would you
distinguish, for
example, nouns or
verbs? Discuss.

Similarly, phrases are classified into certain categories, such as noun phrase (NP), verb phrase (PV), adjective phrase (AdjP), adverb phrase (AdvP), and preposition phrase (PP). It is worth noting that every phrasal category, such as a noun phrase, verb phrase, adjective phrase, adverb phrase, or preposition phrase, should contain at least a word-level category of the same basic type, such as a noun, verb, adjective, adverb, or preposition, respectively. To explain, let us consider the following sentence.

Note that the term
'phrase' here may
include just one tiny
word, such as the
pronoun 'I'.

The best teacher left the class early in the morning.

To begin with, the noun phrase *'the best teacher'* contains, in addition to a determiner and adjective, a noun, i.e. *'teacher'*. A tree diagram can be drawn here to make this point clear:

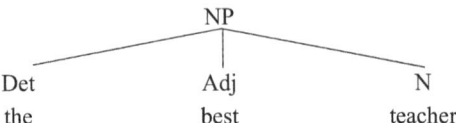

Regarding the verb phrase *'left the class early in the morning'*, it contains a verb, a noun phrase, an adverb phrase, and a preposition phrase, as syntactically represented here:

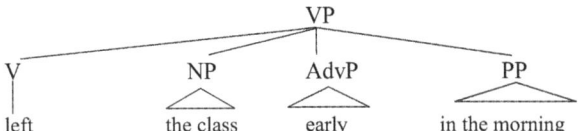

The preposition phrase *'in the morning'* is made up of a preposition *'in'* and a noun phrase *'the morning'*, which contains a determiner *'the'* and a noun *'morning'*, as shown below:

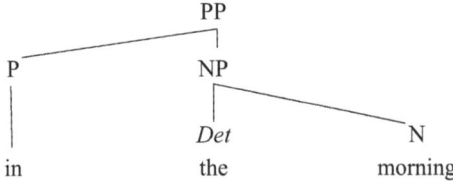

Phrase structure rules

Phrase structure (PS) rules, which are closely associated with the early stages of transformational grammar proposed by Noam Chomsky in 1957, are a type of rewriting rule used to describe the sentence or phrase structure of a particular language. They are used in syntax to break down sentences into their constituents, i.e. syntactic categories, including both (1) word-level categories (e.g. nouns, verbs, adjectives, adverbs, conjunctions, pronouns, prepositions, determiners, qualifiers, degree words, and auxiliaries) and (2) phrasal categories (e.g. noun phrase, verb phrase, adjective phrase, adverb phrase, and preposition phrase). To explain, let us break down the following sentence into its constituents:

My brother put it on the table.

S	$\longrightarrow$	NP-VP	My brother	put it on the table
NP	$\longrightarrow$	Det-N	my	brother
VP	$\longrightarrow$	V-NP-PP	put	it	on the table
NP	$\longrightarrow$	Pro	it
PP	$\longrightarrow$	P-NP	on	the table
NP	$\longrightarrow$	Det-N	the	table

Break down the following sentence into its constituents: *'My eldest brother bought a new car two days ago.'*

As stated earlier, words cannot be arranged in a random order to make meaningful phrases or sentences. To illustrate, while the noun phrase *'a beautiful girl'* is acceptable in English, **'girl beautiful a'* is not. This left-to-right sequence of the words used in the noun phrase is governed by what is called in the literature 'phrase structure rules' (or PC rules for short). According to Parker and Riley (1994/2010: 50), these PC rules specify three types of information:

What about languages, such as Arabic or Farsi? Is it also a left-to-right sequence? Discuss.

(a) Which word-level categories are permitted in a given phrase. It is an NP which can rewrite as a determiner (Det) followed by an adjective (Adj), which is, in turn, followed by a noun (N), as in: *a beautiful girl*: NP → Det-Adj-N.
(b) The left-to-right ordering of the words used. It is *'a beautiful girl'* but not **'girl beautiful a'* or **'beautiful a girl'*.
(c) Whether any of these words are optional or not. The adjective *'beautiful'* in this noun phrase is optional as it can be syntactically deleted. We can say *'a girl'*, as in a sentence of this kind: *'I saw a girl'*. By so doing, the evaluatively active noun phrase *'a beautiful girl'* becomes a non-evaluative noun phrase *'a girl'*, thereby modifying the language user's attitude towards the girl (for more details on attitudes see Chapter 9 of this book).

How would you define the term 'attitude'?

Tree diagram

To figure out the underlying syntactic structures of any phrase or sentence, a tree diagram can be used to represent these syntactic structures visually. To put this differently, a tree diagram can be used to represent what is going on structurally in a sentence or phrase. Unlike normal trees which are drawn bottom up, a tree diagram is drawn top down, thus expressing

different categories, such as phrasal categories (NP, VP, AdjP, AdvP, and PP) and word-level categories (N, V, Adj, Adv, P, Det, Pro, Qual, Deg, Aux, and Conj). To explain, let us consider the following sentence:

My close friend visited me at home yesterday.

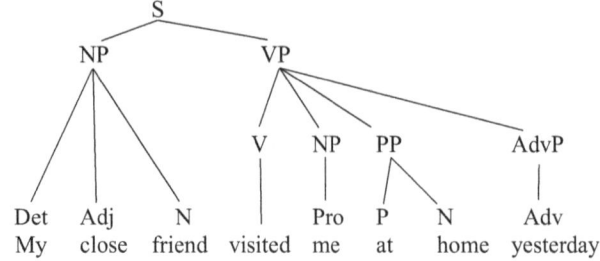

This means that every sentence should contain two phrases: a noun phrase and verb phrase regardless of what is mentioned and what is not.

To finish off this section, let us consider the following sentence:

The rich should help the poor.

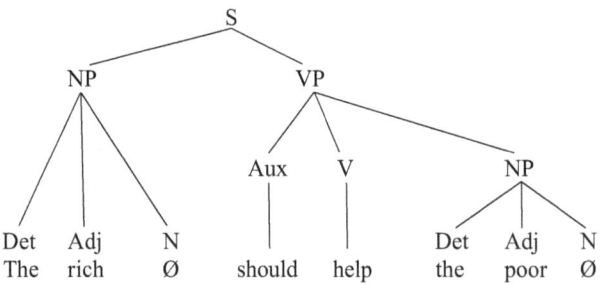

As we can see, the adjectives *'rich'* and *'poor'* in the above example function as heads in the noun phrases *'the rich'* and *'the poor'*, respectively, as there is an implicit noun in these two noun phrases. This should be given full consideration by the translators as there is an implicit noun that should be reflected in the target text implicitly or explicitly, depending on the syntax of the target language. In Arabic, for instance, such a sentence lends itself to على الأغنياء أن يساعدوا الفقراء where plural nouns reflecting the same idea are used. A translation of this sentence into German: *'Die Reichen sollten den Armen helfen'* also reflects the same idea.

Verb group

Now let us focus on the structure of the verbal elements. To do so, extra attention is paid to what is called the 'verb group' (Vgrp for short). To start with, consider the following sentences:

Identify the main phrases of the following sentence: *'Visiting relatives can be boring'.*

How would you translate such a sentence into your own language?

(1) The man _{asked} his daughter to close the door.	(no Aux + V)
(2) She _{goes} to school by car every day.	(no Aux + V)
(3) My youngest brother _{is working} on a new project these days.	(Aux + V)
(4) The wall _{was painted} by my brother some days ago.	(Aux + V)
(5) Many emails _{have been sent} to me by different universities recently.	(Aux + Aux + V)
(6) They _{might have left} it at home.	(Aux + Aux + V)

As one may observe, in all these sentences, the verb group (Vgrp) contains a lexical verb (*'ask'*, *'go'*, *'work'*, *'paint'*, *'sent'*, and *'left'*) as a head. These lexical verbs, which may or may not be preceded by an auxiliary, appear last in the Vgrp. Building on this, Vgrps can be classified into two groups:

(1) Simple Vgrps, i.e. a lexical verb without an auxiliary, as in sentences (1) and (2).
(2) Complex Vgrps, i.e. a lexical verb preceded by one auxiliary or more, as in sentences (3), (4), (5), and (6).

> What about your language or the languages that you know? Can verb groups be classified into 'simple' and 'complex'?

Added to this, when there is more than one auxiliary, only the first one is tensed. Otherwise, the lexical verb is tensed. Complex Vgrps in English can have up to four auxiliaries, which should be in the following order:

(1) Modal verbs, as in *'can'*, *'could'*, *'may'*, *'might'*, etc.
(2) Perfect aspect, as in *'have'*, *'has'*, *'had'*.
(3) Progressive aspect, as in *'is'*, *'am'*, *'are'*, *'was'*, *'were'*, etc.
(4) Passive voice, as in *'be'*, *'being'*, *'been'*, etc.

With this in mind, the sentence *'My close friend visited me at home yesterday'*, discussed earlier, can be reconsidered here:

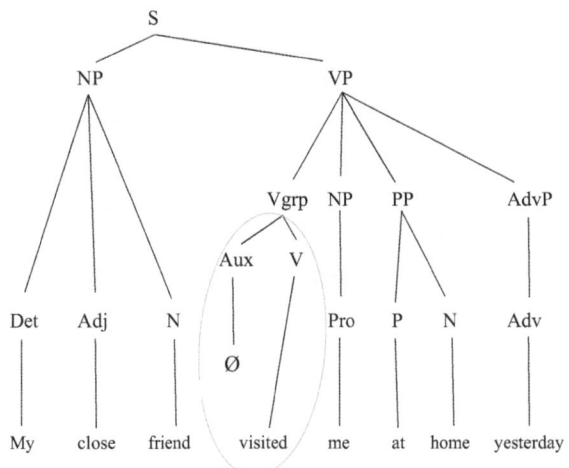

Inflection

Do you agree that 'inflection' varies from one language to another in terms of importance?

As indicated in the previous chapter, there are eight inflectional morphemes in English:

- Plural '*–s*' attached to nouns, as in '*girl*' > '*girls*'.
- Possessive '*–s*' attached to nouns, as in '*man*' > '*man's*'.
- Comparative '*–er*' attached to adjectives, as in '*big*' > '*bigger*'.
- Superlative '*–est*' attached to adjectives, as in '*small*' > '*smallest*'.
- Present '*–s*' or '*–es*' attached to verbs, as in '*like*' > '*likes*'.
- Past '*– ed*' attached to verbs, as in '*call*' > '*called*'.
- Past participle '*–ed*' or '*–en*' attached to verbs, as in '*drive*' > '*driven*'.
- Present participle attached to verbs, as in '*read*' > '*reading*'.

These inflectional affixes are attached to nouns, adjectives, and verbs, as modelled below:

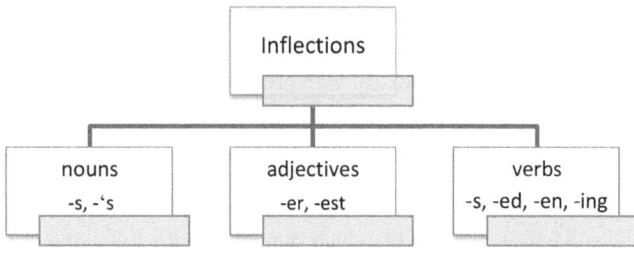

Do you agree that the definition of 'finite verbs' and 'finite clauses' differs from one language to another?

As any English finite clause should have a tense (past or non-past), aspect (simple, progressive, perfect, or perfect progressive), and voice (active or passive), another branching point Infl (short for inflection) is needed to indicate the tense, aspect, and voice of the clause or sentence. In the current widespread practice, there are two ways to represent this in a tree diagram:

(1) The Infl node is considered as a daughter of the Vgrp, as shown here:

Which tree diagram do you prefer? And why?

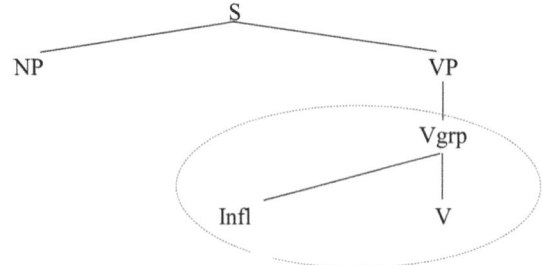

(2) The Infl node is considered as a daughter of the S, as shown here:

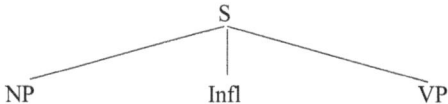

Connecting the dots (1): Syntactic ambiguity and translation

We have seen that in finite clauses we can indicate the subject of the clause along with its predicate. Similarly, we can indicate the phrases used to form such a clause. To illustrate, the following example can be considered here:

The dog ate our lunch last night.

Here, it is not a hard task to identify the subject (*'dog'* modified by the determiner *'the'*) and the predicate (*'ate our lunch yesterday'*). Further, we can indicate that the predicate is made up of a verb (*'ate'* in the past tense), direct object (*'lunch'* modified by the determiner *'our'*) and an adverb of time (*'last night'* answering the question 'When did the dog eat our lunch?'). Added to this, several phrases can be identified in the above finite clause, including *'the dog'* (a noun phrase) and *'ate our lunch yesterday'* (a verb phrase). Inside the verb phrase, two phrases can be identified: *'our lunch'* (a noun phrase) and *'last night'* an adverb phrase). However, it is not always as easy as in the above example. What about a sentence of the following kind, adapted along with the pictures from Almanna and Al-Shehari (2019: 10):

The man saw a little girl with the binoculars.

This sentence is ambiguous as it has two interpretations:

(a) The girl was seen by the man with the help of the binoculars.

Analyse this sentence syntactically: *'It is the dog that ate our lunch last night'*?

Draw two tree diagrams to syntactically represent the two interpretations.

(b) The man saw the girl who was holding the binoculars.

What about translating it into your language?

Translating this sentence into Arabic, for example, as رأى الرّجلُ الفتاةَ بالنّاظور, we have only one interpretation (first interpretation) where the man used the binoculars to see the girl. This indicates that the binoculars are not with the girl, but with the man. To have the second interpretation in Arabic, one needs to add a relative clause that contains a process of doing expressed by the verb حمل *'to carry'*, as in رأى الرّجلُ الفتاةَ التي كانت تحمل ناظوراً, i.e. *'The man saw the girl who was carrying the binoculars'*. This indicates that what is syntactically ambiguous in one language might not be ambiguous in another language. However, translators should approach ambiguous sentences carefully while translating to reflect the intended meaning.

Connecting the dots (2): Reordering sentence constituents through translation

Words within sentences can be structured into larger syntactic units called constituents. To illustrate this operation, consider the following sentence:

The woman was speaking very angrily to me.

What about your language? Is it acceptable to start with the equivalent of *'very angrily'*?

In the above sentence, there are eight words (*'the'*, *'woman'*, *'was'*, *'speaking'*, *'very'*, *'angrily'*, *'to'*, *'me'*). Some of these words, such as *'the'* and *'woman'*, *'very'* and *'angrily'*, and *'to'* and *'me'* go together, thus being structured into larger syntactic units. Building on this, *'the woman'*, *'very angrily'*, and *'to me'* form some of the sentence constituents. To prove this, constituent tests can be used. To begin with the adverb phrase *'very angrily'*, for instance, it:

● can be fronted, as in *'Very angrily, the woman was speaking to me'* (transposition: fronting test);
● can be backgrounded, as in *'The woman was speaking to me very angrily'* (transposition: backgrounding test);
● can be substituted with the word *'so'*, as in *'The woman was speaking so to me'* (replacement/substitution test);

- can be used as an answer to a question of the following kind: 'How was the woman speaking to you?' *'Very angrily'* (stand-alone test).

Now, let us prove that the noun phrase *'the woman'* is a larger unit by applying certain constituent tests. The noun phrase *'the woman'*:

- can be used as an answer to a question of the following kind: 'Who was speaking very angrily to you?' (stand-alone test);
- can be replaced with the pronoun *'she'*, as in *'She was speaking very angrily to me'* (substitution test);
- can be inserted in a group of words that functions as a unit in a cleft structure, as in *'It is the woman who was speaking very angrily to me'* (movement: clefting test).

As shown above, there are several constituent tests that can be used to prove that certain words hang together to form a larger unit called 'constituent'. The main constituent tests include the 'movement test', which can be sub-classified into 'fronting', 'clefting', the 'passive', and so on, the 'substitution/replacement test', the 'ellipsis/fragment test', the 'co-ordination test', the 'modification test', and the 'stand-alone test', as shown here:

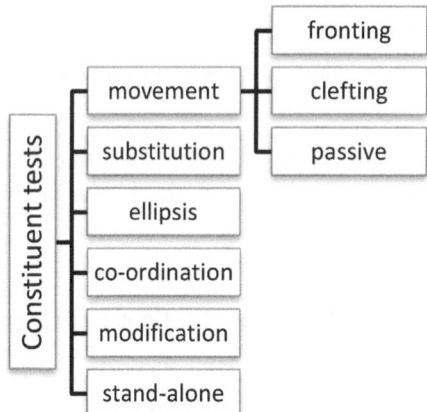

At times, for the sake of readability, acceptability, idiomaticity, authenticity, and well-formedness, the translator reorders these constituents selected and ordered in the original text, thus adopting slightly or completely a different style. To explain, let us translate this English simple sentence into Maltese:

ST	I received an email from my sister yesterday.
TT1	Oħti bagħtitli email ilbieraħ.
Back translation	My sister sent me an email last night.
TT2	Irċevejt email mingħand oħti lbieraħ.
Back translation	I received an email from my sister yesterday.
TT3	Ilbieraħ, oħti bagħtitli email.
Back translation	Yesterday, my sister sent me an email.

In the original sentence, there are three noun phrases filling three semantic roles: Actor/Sender filled by *'my sister'*, Recipient filled by *'I'*, and Theme/something Sent filled by *'an email'*, as shown here:

Actor/Sender	Recipient	Theme/something Sent
my sister	me	an email

Although we have three different translations/styles, the three semantic roles are accurately reflected in the three translations. In the first translation, while the Actor/Sender, *'Ohti'* meaning *'my sister'*, is fronted, the Recipient is backgrounded. In the second sentence, however, the Recipient is given a front seat while the Actor/Sender is given a back seat. In the third translation, the adverb of time *'Ilbierah'* meaning *'yesterday'* is fronted.

At other times, the translator, for a variety of different reasons, decides to opt for 'mystification', i.e. hiding the Agent, as shown in this example quoted from Farghal (2023: 31):

Think of some of these reasons that motivate the translator to hide the agent.

ST (Arabic)	قتلت القوات الإسرائيلية ثلاثة شبان فلسطينيين في القدس الشرقية هذا الصباح.
Back translation	The Israeli troops killed three Palestinian youths in East Jerusalem this morning.
TT (English)	Three Palestinian youths were killed in East Jerusalem this morning.

Here, as can be observed, the translator opted for a passive construction where the Agent, i.e. *'the Israeli troops'*, was not mentioned in the target text.

Connecting the dots (3): Syntactic parsing and translation

What is the difference between 'syntactic parsing' and 'semantic parsing'?

Syntactic parsing refers to the act of analysing the units of the original text (e.g. sentences, clauses, and phrases). Before embarking on translating any sentence/paragraph/text, the translators need to identify (depending on their level, and the level of the text, of course) the type of each sentence (simple, compound, complex, or compound complex; nominal versus verbal, etc.), the type of each clause (finite or non-finite), the subject of each finite clause (one word or a group of words), the tense of each finite clause (past, present, or future), the aspect of each finite clause (simple, progressive, perfect, or perfect progressive), the voice of each finite clause (active or passive), the adverbs and adjectives used in each clause, and the like.

Syntactic parsing is one of the steps that should be taken by translators according to a model proposed by Bell (1991). Building on linguistic and psycholinguistic perspectives, Bell (1991: 20) states that the translation process mainly happens within 'memory' in the sense that the transformation process involves five main phases:

(1) Visual recognition of the lexical items used in the original text where the translators identify technical terms, new terms, difficult terms, and the like.

(2) Syntactic parsing in which translators start analysing the text at hand syntactically by asking themselves several questions, such as 'How many sentences are there?', 'What is the type of each sentence? Is it simple, compound, complex, or compound complex?', 'Where is the subject of each sentence/clause?', 'Where is the main verb of each sentence/clause?', 'What is the tense/aspect/voice, etc.?', and so on.

(3) Mechanisms of lexical search in which translators mentally start looking for the equivalent of each lexical item – here the translation unit is mainly lexical items and occasionally expressions.

(4) Semantic and pragmatic processing in which translators try to activate semantic and pragmatic processes in order to produce a translation draft.

(5) Encoding the draft semantically, pragmatically and lexico-grammatically in the target language (for more details, see Almanna 2014: 52–4).

> Note that Almanna (2014) modifies the fifth step to read 'encoding the draft semantically, pragmatically, lexico-grammatically, and stylistically in the target language.

To explain, let us syntactically analyse the following sentence taken along with its translations from the official website of the United Nations:

The UN _{subject/noun phrase/determiner + noun} has evolved _{auxiliary + main verb (present, perfect, active)} over the years _{time marker indicating the whole period of evolving} to keep pace with a rapidly changing world _{purpose clause/non-finite clause introduced by 'to''}

Spanish	La ONU ha evolucionado a lo largo de los años para seguir el ritmo de un mundo que cambia rápidamente.
Arabic	وتطورت الأمم المتحدة على مر السنين لمواكبة عالم سريع التغير.

As we can see, the main components of the original sentence were given full consideration by the translators after having taken into consideration the differences between the interfacing languages. To elaborate, unlike English, Arabic, for instance, does not have a grammatical category of aspect. However, by virtue of the phrase على مرّ السنين 'over years', the emphasis is placed on the whole period that started in the past (unspecified, as we cannot specify the starting point, but predictable as it is based on our personal knowledge) and is seen as relevant to another point in the present (specified as we can specify the endpoint, which is the moment of writing). With this in mind, we have a scene characterized by being partially bounded, and this was reflected in the target text (for more details, see the next section). In the following example, the translator decided to change the passive into active without changing the semantic roles assigned to each noun phrase. By doing so, more emphasis is placed on the Actor/Asker, and not on the person being asked.

English	I was asked a difficult question by the teacher.
German	Der Lehrer stellte mir eine schwierige Frage.
Back translation	The teacher asked me a difficult question.

In this sentence, we have an example of modulation, i.e. changing the style by laying more emphasis on the Actor/Sender (*my sister*):

English	I received an email from my sister yesterday.
Maltese	Oħti bagħtitli email ilbieraħ.
Back translation	My sister sent me an email last night.

Is this modulation optional or obligatory?

Instead of opting for *'Irċevejt email mingħand oħti lbieraħ'* meaning *'I received an email from my sister last night'*, the translator decided to opt for modulation, but without changing the semantic roles assigned to each noun phrase, as shown here:

Actor/Sender	Recipient	Theme/something Sent or Received
my sister	me	an email

Connecting the dots (4): Translating tense and aspect

Both 'tense' and 'aspect' refer to time; both of them "convey temporal information about a described event or state of affairs" (Almanna 2016: 65). However, tense refers to when an event, situation, or action happens, thus locating the described event or state of affairs on the timeline: past, present, or future (Kearns 2000/ 2011: 176; Almanna 2016: 65). Aspect, by contrast, refers to how a described event, situation, or action happens. In some languages, such as English, there are four types of aspect, namely 'simple', 'perfect', 'progressive', and 'perfect progressive' (cf. Kreidler 1998; Celce- Murcia and Larsen- Freeman 1999; Kearns 2000/ 2011; Almanna 2016; Griffiths 2006). To elaborate, consider the grammatical categories associated with the verb *'to teach'* in the following sentences:

Note that 'simple aspect' is also known as 'zero aspect'.

Can you identify the tensed words in these four examples?

Example	Tense	Aspect
I $_{teach}$ in the morning.	Present	Simple
I $_{am\ teaching}$ right now.	Present	Progressive
I $_{have\ taught}$ at this university for 10 years.	Present	Perfect
I $_{have\ been\ teaching}$ at this university for 10 years.	Present	Perfect progressive

It is worth noting that some languages do not have verb tenses and aspects to indicate when and how an event or action occurs. Examples of these languages are Indonesian, Malay, Mandarin Chinese, and many creole languages. In these languages, people rely on certain words to indicate periods of time. Some other languages, such as Arabic, have only tenses. Therefore, translating those grammatical categories from a language that has both tense and aspect to a language that does not have or has only one cannot be achieved without difficulty. To make this point clear, consider the verb *'merokok'* in Malay meaning *'to smoke'*. The form of the verb is the same in the past, present, and future, as shown in the following examples:

Do you know any other languages that do not have grammatical categories of 'tense' and 'aspect'?

Aspect + tense	Malay	English
simple + present	Saya merokok.	I smoke.
simple + past	Saya sudah merokok. Or: Saya telah merokok.	I smoked yesterday.
progressive + present	Saya sedang merokok.	I am smoking.
simple + future	Saya akan merokok.	I will smoke.

One may observe that in Malay the words *'sudha'* or *'telah'* meaning *'already'* can be used to indicate that the event or action occurred in the past, thus resulting in a 'level shift', to borrow Catford's (1965) term. In this regard, Almanna (2018) holds that when we translate from a language that has only a grammatical category of tense, such as Arabic, to a language that has both tense and aspect as grammatical categories, such as English, one needs to understand the 'contextual tense' rather than adhering to the 'morphological tense' or 'structural tense'. To explain, consider the following three sentences that have almost the same forms:

How would you define the 'contextual tense'? And how is it identified?

Example	Morphological tense	Structural tense	Contextual tense
لم أزره أمس Lit. I did not visit him yesterday.	Present	Past	Past $_{simple}$
لم أزره لغاية أمس. Lit. I did not visit him till yesterday*.	Present	Past	Past $_{perfect}$
لم أزره قطُّ. Lit. I never visited him*.	Present	Past	Present $_{perfect}$

In these three sentences, the same form, i.e. لم أزره, is used. However, the meaning is different as the emphasis in the first sentence by virtue of the lexical time أمس *'yesterday'* is placed on the completion of the process of doing expressed by the verb زار *'to visit'* in the negative; therefore, it is equivalent to the simple past in English, i.e. *'I did not visit him yesterday'*. In the second sentence, by the effect of the phrase لغاية أمس *'till yesterday'*, the emphasis is put on the whole period that started in the past (unspecified as we cannot specify the starting point) and is seen as relevant to another point in the past (specified as we can specify the end point, i.e. yesterday); therefore, it is equivalent to the past perfect in English, i.e. *'I had not visited him yesterday'*. As regards the third sentence, by virtue of the word قطُّ, i.e. *never*, the emphasis is placed on the whole period that started in the past (unspecified, but predictable as it is in our scope of prediction) and is seen as relevant to another point in the present; therefore, it is equivalent to the present perfect, i.e. *'I have never (ever) visited him'*.

On this subject, Almanna (2022) suggests certain cognitive categories that can be used by translators to help them figure out the contextual tense. These categories are explained in detail in Chapter 12 of this book, so it here suffices to mention them briefly. They are 'point of emphasis', 'plexity', 'extent of causation', 'pace of events', 'time lapse', 'state of dividedness', 'state of boundedness', and 'degree of extension'.

Connecting the dots (5): Translating gender

Think of some examples of gender discrimination.

Following Scott (1986: 1054), Castro (2010: 106) defines the term 'gender' as "the combination of socio-cultural roles assigned to people in a systematic and structural way according to their sex". Therefore, to overcome gender discrimination, we need to make every possible effort to change those practices that involve gender discrimination in a particular society. Linguistic discrimination, as an example of gender discrimination, reflects, in one way or another, what is going on in a particular society. So, if there is some kind of discrimination in a given society, this discrimination is reflected in the language used by those people practising discrimination. Language, as Castro (Ibid.) puts it, "is not merely a reflection of reality/ society, but a factor that contributes to its construction. The linguistic representation of men and women therefore has a socio-cognitive dimension: representation contributes to the construction of social roles". Building on this, the way men and women are represented across languages/cultures becomes a rich site for examining issues such as gender discrimination, in particular linguistic discrimination.

Do you agree with Castro's definition of language?

Over the last four decades, a great number of studies on linguistic representation have been conducted in different languages (see, for example, Hellinger and Bussmann 2001; Castro 2010). These studies conclude that women and men are represented differently in different languages: more emphasis is placed on men, thus foregrounding them in the scene and making them visible. In this regard, Castro (2010: 107) holds that "language is sexist and androcentric, in that it renders women invisible and in that it stereotypes gender roles, in a way that is presented as natural, normal and commonsensical". Such gender discrimination is reflected linguistically on different levels. On the lexical level, it is reflected by virtue of certain linguistic markers added to certain words, thus having (1) a sexist language where women become invisible, i.e. they are backgrounded in a given scene and (2) an androcentric language where more emphasis is placed on men, i.e. they are foregrounded in a given scene. On the discoursal level, gender discrimination is reflected through ideological stereotypes of men and women. By way of explanation, consider the following example:

Building on Castro's (2010) view that 'language' is sexist and androcentric, can we classify translation in general into sexist and non-sexist, and androcentric and non-androcentric? If yes, what determines the type of translation in your opinion?

The teacher asked some of the students to leave the class yesterday.

	Translation	**Back translation**
TT1	طلبَ المُدرِّسُ من بعضٍ الطّلاب أن يغادروا الصّفَ أمس.	The male-teacher asked some of the male students to leave the class yesterday.
TT2	طلبَتِ المُدرِّسةُ من بعضٍ الطّالباتِ أن يغادرن الصّفَ أمس.	The female-teacher asked some of the female students to leave the class yesterday.
TT3	طلبَ المُدرِّسُ من بعضٍ الطّالباتِ أن يغادرن الصّفَ أمس.	The male-teacher asked some of the female students to leave the class yesterday.
TT4	طلبَتِ المُدرِّسةُ من بعضٍ الطّلاب أن يغادروا الصّفَ أمس.	The female-teacher asked some of the male students to leave the class yesterday.

Here we have four different translations. In TT1, we have an example of an 'androcentric translation' where more emphasis is placed on men. In the TT2, by contrast, we have an example of a 'non-sexist translation', where there is an attempt to include women, thus making them visible – in our mind's eye, we can see women. In TT3, despite the translator's attempt to include women in his/her translation, we have an example of an 'androcentric translation' as men, by virtue of the grammatical form and content specification used by the translator, are characterized by being-able-to-do, thus presupposing authority, while women are characterized by being-able-not-to-do, thereby presupposing submission. By contrast, in TT4, women are characterized by being-able-to-do while men are characterized by being-able-not-to-do; therefore, it is an example of a 'non-androcentric translation'. In what follows, some of the more frequent problems that arise when one translates between a language that has a grammatical gender category, such as Arabic or Spanish, and a language that does not have one or has many neutrals, such as English, can be summarized.

One of those problems is that the sex of the referent is not made explicit in the source text while in the target text it should be made explicit. To explain, a sentence of the following kind *'My friend called me yesterday'* can be translated into Arabic and Spanish in the following way:

	Translation	**Back translation**
Spanish	Mi amigo me llamó ayer.	My male friend called me yesterday.
Arabic	اتّصلَ بي صديقي أمس.	My male friend called me yesterday.

Here we have an example of a sexist translation where the word *'friend'* referring to both sexes in English is translated into Arabic as صديق and into Spanish as *'amigo'*, both referring to a male friend. Semantically, the denotative meaning of the word *'friend'* in English is wider and less specific compared with its counterparts in Arabic and Spanish; therefore, we have an example of 'divergence' (Malone 1988) or 'particularization' (Dickins

Provide more than one translation to the above sentence into your own language. Then comment on each type of translation by referring to the classification proposed in this book.

Note that translating *'amigo'*, for example, into *'friend'* results in what is called 'convergence' or 'generalization'.

et al. 2002; for more details, see Chapter 5 of this book). Cognitively, in our mind's eye, we can see only a male friend in the target texts, thus backgrounding females from the scene and laying more emphasis on males.

Another problem arises when we translate from a language that has two grammatical gender categories (male or female) into a language that has three (masculine, feminine, or neutral). To explain, the word سيّارة, i.e. car, in Arabic is feminine, but in German it is neutral and, accordingly, the indefinite article that precedes its equivalent, i.e. *'Auto'*, should be *'das'* and neither *'die'* nor *'der'*. Consider this example:

Arabic	السّيارةُ في حالةٍ جيدة.
German	Das Auto ist in einem gutem Zustand.
English	The car is in good condition.

To finish off this section, let us discuss some techniques that can be resorted to by translators to step away from examples of linguistic discrimination. To avoid the use of the forms or specific markers of each gender, thus avoiding examples of a 'sexist translation', translators can opt for what is called 'generalization' (also known as 'neutralization') where those forms or specific markers assigned to each gender can be eliminated, as shown in the following example:

> **What is the difference between 'generalization' used here and 'generalization' suggested by Dickins et al. (2002)?**

ST: Arabic	ذهبتُ إلى مركز الشّرطةِ أمس لأشتكي ضد أحد رجال الشّرطة.
Back translation	I went to the police office yesterday to complain against one of the policemen.
TT1: sexist translation	I went to the police office yesterday to complain against one of the policemen.
TT2: non-sexist translation	I went to the police office yesterday to complain against one of the police officers.

Here, by opting for the lexical item *'officers'* in place of *'men'*, we have an example of generalization where the specific marker assigned to each gender is eliminated, thus resulting in a 'non-sexist translation'.

> **What is the difference between 'particularization' suggested by Dickins et al. (2002) and 'specification' suggested by Castro (2010)?**

Another technique that can be opted for by translators is called 'specification', referring to the act of specifying both linguistic genders when referring to people, thereby reflecting in the target text the sex of the person mentioned (feminine for women, masculine for men, and both linguistic genders when referring to both sexes, or when the sex of the referent is unknown). Castro (2010: 112) believes that the goal of this strategy "is to counteract the historical and permanent invisibility of women in language". Examples of this strategy may include:

● *'s/he'* or *'he/she'* in place of *'he'*;
● *'female teachers'* or *'male teachers'* in place of *'teachers'*.

The third technique suggested by Castro is called 'linguistic disruption'. It refers to the act of "incorporating into the translated text substantial changes that include semantic alterations, linguistic innovations, new ways of spelling words, the use of bold type, capitals, italics and quotation marks etc. in order to make women visible". Compensation, as a strategy discussed by many scholars in translation studies, can be used to avoid examples of sexism. To make this point clear, let us consider the following example:

Arabic	طلبَتِ المُدرّسةُ من الطَّلبةِ أن يسلّموا الواجب في غضون يومين.
Back translation	The female-teacher asked the students to submit their assignments within two days.
TT1: without compensation	The teacher asked the students to submit their assignments within two days.
TT2: with compensation	The teacher asked her students to submit their assignments within two days.

In TT2, by means of the use of the possessive adjective 'her', the gender of the teacher is specified, thus resulting in a 'non-sexist translation' where women become visible.

Finally, if the translator fails to avoid any example of sexism used in the original text, s/he can draw the reader's attention to those examples of sexism by opting for features such as a footnote, endnote, or translator's comment.

Connecting the dots (6): Transformation and translation

A transformation can be defined as a process where a word-level category (e.g. noun, adjective, adverb) or a phrasal category (e.g. noun phrase or adjective phrase) is moved from one position to another (Parker and Riley 1994/2010: 63). Let us begin with 'yes–no questions' in English to make this point clear. To change a sentence of the following kind *'He will visit them soon'* to a 'yes–no question', a transformation known as 'inversion' is required. By means of this inversion, the auxiliary *'will'* is moved from the Infl (short for 'inflection') position, i.e. after the subject indicated by the symbol 'e' (short for 'empty') to a position to the left of the subject, as in:

Will he visit them soon?

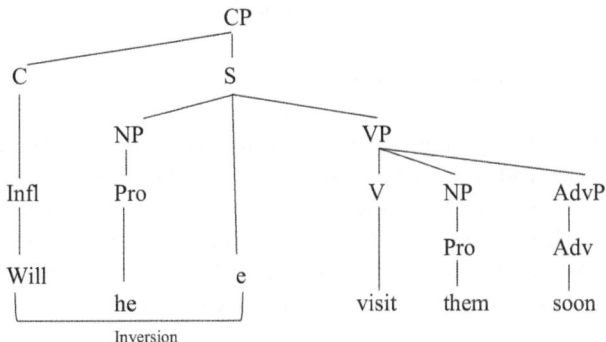

Inversion

Building on this discussion, how would you define 'inversion'?

Do you agree with Almanna's observation? Discuss.

In this connection, Almanna (2018: 45) holds that "in all types of questions (be it a 'yes–no question' or 'wh-question'), there should be a process of saying/asking", as modelled here:

He ₛₐᵧₑᵣ asked _process of saying_: "Will he visit them soon?" _Content_

By 'mode of narration', we refer to the type of speech: 'direct speech' or 'indirect speech'.

Syntactically speaking, what is called 'content' or 'verbiage' is labelled CP (short for 'complementizer phrase'). CPs are usually phrases that start with complementizers, labelled (C), such as *'that'*, *'if'*, or *'whether'*.

When the mode of narration is direct, the auxiliary is moved by applying the inversion transformation to occupy the C position (see below). However, when the mode of narration is indirect, as in:

He asked if she would visit them soon.

there will be no inversion, as the C position is occupied by the complementizer *'if'*, and the auxiliary remains in its Infl position, as shown in the following tree:

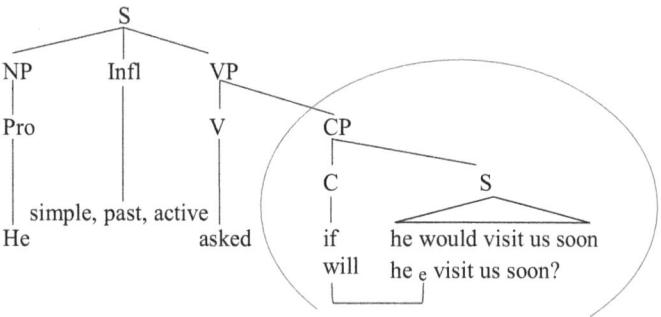

What about other languages that do not have a developed system of auxiliaries? How would they form a 'yes–no question'?

The question that may arise here is: How do we form 'yes–no questions' in English from sentences that contain no auxiliary?

Do insertion

To form 'yes–no questions' from sentences that contain no auxiliary, what is traditionally known as 'Do-support' needs to be inserted to make 'inversion' possible (O'Grady et al. 1997: 210; Almanna 2018: 55). To illustrate, the following sentence can be considered:

He read the novel last night.

In this sentence, there is no auxiliary, which carries grammatical properties such as tense and aspect, and the verb *'to read'*, which is in the past tense, does not itself permit 'inversion', but rather requires what is traditionally known as 'Do-support', i.e. *'do'*, *'does'*, *'did'*, depending on the tense and subject. As the sentence is in the past tense, *'did'* is inserted before the verb (Step 1), thus making 'inversion' possible (Step 2), as in:

Step one (insertion): He did read the novel last night.

Step two (inversion): Did he _ e _ read the novel last night?

Wh-movement

In English, a 'wh-question' is formed by:

(1) moving the 'wh-phrase' from its normal position (indicated by the symbol e that stands for the word 'empty') to a position at the beginning of the sentence;
(2) moving the auxiliary (if any) from the Infl position to the left of the subject.

To explain, the following example may be considered:

He can play football very well. (deep structure)

What can he _ e _ play _ e _ very well? (surface structure)

How can he _ e _ play football _ e _ ? (surface structure)

As we can see, in addition to the inversion transformation that moves the auxiliary *'can'* in the above example from the Infl position to the left of the subject, another transformation called 'wh-movement' is used that moves the 'wh-phrases' *'football'* and *'very well'* from their normal positions (indicated by the symbol e) to a position at the beginning of the sentence.

However, it is worth mentioning that in some languages, such as Arabic, Farsi, Indonesian, and some other languages, only the 'wh-movement' transformation is needed without the inversion transformation, as shown below in Arabic, Farsi, and Indonesian, respectively:

What about your language or the languages that you know? What do you need to form a 'wh-question'?

She travelled to France yesterday.	سافرتْ إلى فرنسا أمس.
When did she travel to France?	متى سافرتْ إلى فرنسا _ e _ ؟
She travelled to France yesterday.	(او) ديروز به فرانسه سفر كرد.
When did she travel to France?	(او) كى _ e _ به فرانسه سفر كرد؟
She travelled to France yesterday.	Dia bepergian ke Perancis kemarin.
When did she travel to France?	Kapan dia bepergian ke Perancis _ e _ ?

Due to this difference between languages such as Arabic, Farsi, and Indonesian that require only the 'wh-movement' transformation and English that requires an 'inversion' transformation in addition to the 'wh-movement' transformation, translation students at an early stage of their studies face problems in translating interrogative sentences from those languages into English, often resulting in ungrammatical sentences, such as *'When she travelled to France?'* in place of *'When did she travel to France?'*. This should be given adequate consideration by both students and instructors.

Connecting the dots (7): Translating voices

Voice is a grammatical category of verbs that is related to what thing or person is acting (active) and what thing or person is being acted upon (passive). When a verb is used to describe what an entity (thing or person) is doing, it is active. However, when it is used to describe what is done to an entity (thing or person), it is passive (e.g. Swan 1995; Crystal 1997; Almanna 2016). According to Swan, not all verbs can be expressed in the passive voice. For example, *'die'*, *'go'*, *'arrive'*, and *'have'* are all inherently active. This is related to whether a verb is transitive or intransitive. To explain, in the following sentence

The girl ate the apple yesterday. (deep structure)

there is somebody who ate the apple that can be called 'Eater', a verb in the past tense where the emphasis is placed on the completion of the act of eating, and something eaten, i.e. the apple. To change this active sentence to passive in English, we need to (1) move *'the apple'*, which is something eaten, from its position to a position at the beginning of the sentence; (2) either delete or move *'the girl'*, that is, the 'Eater', to be grouped with the verb phrase after being preceded by the preposition *'by'*; (3) insert the verb *'to be'* before the main verb; and (4) convert the main verb to the past participle, as shown here:

The apple [1] was [3] eaten [4] by the girl [2] yesterday.

As such, when the sentence begins with the Actor or Doer of the act (*'the girl'*) followed by the verb (*'ate'*) and then the object or person that the action is performed on (*'the apple'*), the sentence is in the active voice. However, when it begins with the object or the person that the action is performed on (*'the apple'*) followed by the verb group (*'was eaten'*), then it is in the passive voice. Two tree diagrams can be represented here to show the differences:

In your opinion, what are the main reasons for using the passive voice?

Note that in verbs like *'to die'*, *'to disappear'*, *'to arrive'*, etc., there is no flow of energy from one participant to another; that is why they are called 'intransitive'.

Active: The girl ate the apple yesterday.

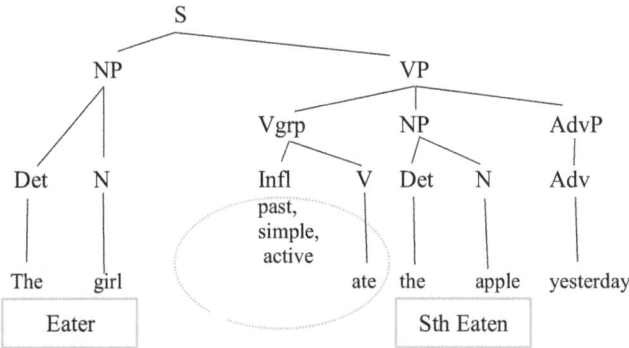

Passive: The apple was eaten by the girl yesterday.

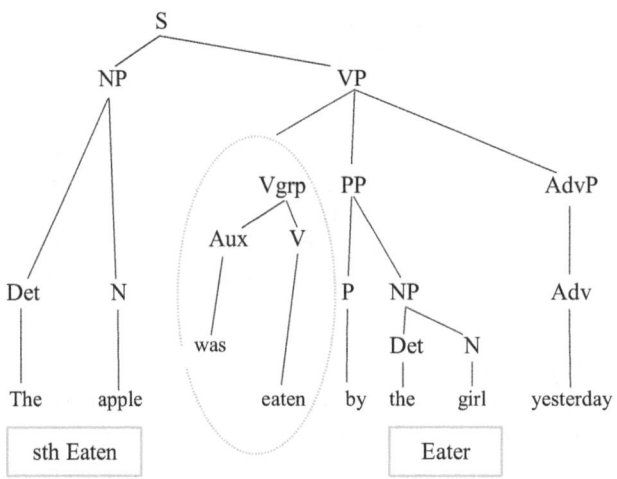

In translating from language *A* to language *B*, meaning is given a front seat; therefore, translators need to do their best to maintain the meaning; only later can they think of other issues, such as style. Building on this, the semantic roles assigned to each noun phrase should be given prime consideration by translators to produce an accurate translation and create a similar mental image in the minds of the target language readers (for more details, see the next chapter). To make this point clear, the following English sentence in the active voice can be translated into a French sentence in the passive voice to discuss the semantic roles assigned to each noun phrase.

Do you agree with this claim? Discuss.

English	The teacher sent many emails to his students yesterday.
French	Plusieurs emails ont été envoyés aux étudiants par leur enseignant hier.
Back translation	Many emails were sent by the teacher to his students yesterday.

Here, we have three noun phrases, namely '*the teacher*' filling a semantic role of Actor and a verb-specific semantic role of Sender; '*many emails*' filling a semantic role of Theme and a verb-specific role of something Sent/Received; and '*his students*' filling a semantic role of Recipient and a verb-specific role of Receiver. In the target text, French, those three noun phrases fill the same semantic roles; therefore, we have the same meaning, but a different style. In this regard, Hatim and Mason (1997: 225) rightly comment that most languages have a variety of potential resources for constructing different types of clauses, such as active clauses, passive clauses, and agentless clauses, and these "variations in structure of the clause are said to relate to different world views and to relay different ideological slants". Therefore, in the actual act of translating between languages/cultures, translators are usually influenced, whether consciously or subconsciously, by their own accumulated value system, beliefs, background, assumption, commitment, sense of belonging, and so on; hence their employment of certain linguistic devices, such as 'agency', 'transitivity', 'cohesive device', 'over-lexicalization', 'style-shifting', 'evaluativeness', and 'modality' (e.g. Hatim and Mason 1997; Farghal 2008; Almanna 2013).

At the syntactic level, 'agency', in addition to 'modality', can be employed by translators to superimpose a certain directionality/narrativity on the text at hand, thus promoting or elaborating a particular narrative/story. Agency refers to whether the Agent of the transitivity process expressed by a particular action is foregrounded in attention either in an active construction (fronted) or a passive construction (delayed and grouped with the verb phrase) or backgrounded in attention, that is, it is not mentioned. To show how removing the Agent of the action can twist the message to varying degrees, the following headlines published by *BBC News* (23 October 2017; also discussed in Almanna and Al-Shehari 2019) may be considered:

English	Russian radio presenter Felgengauer stabbed in neck.
Arabic	إسرائيلي يطعن مذيعة روسية داخل غرفة أخبار محطة إذاعة إيكو موسكوفي.
Back translation	An Israeli stabs a Russian broadcaster inside the Echo Muscovy Radio station newsroom.

In the English version, the Agent of the process of doing expressed by the act of stabbing is backgrounded in attention. By so doing, not only is the focus of attention shifted towards the Affected Participant (also known as the 'Patient'), but we no longer have an indication about the Agent of the

Do you agree that 'meaning' is related to 'deep structures' whereas 'style' is related to 'surface structures'?

Do you agree with Hatim and Mason's (1997) claim? What about issues such as one's style, language preference, and the like?

Narrativity is defined here as directionality superimposed by the language user on the text/story at hand.

process of doing, which affects informativeness and accessibility. By contrast, in the Arabic version, the Agent is foregrounded in attention (fronted), thus laying more emphasis on the Agent/Stabber. In the Arabic version, the nationality of the Agent is mentioned (for more details on the translation of this example, see Chapter 7 of this book).

Exercises and discussion

Exercise 1: Mark the following statements (T) if they are true and (F) if they are false.

(1) An adjective cannot stand alone; it should be followed by a noun.	
(2) In some languages or creoles, a predicate marker is used between the subject and the predicate.	
(3) To form a 'yes–no question' from a sentence that contains a complex verb group, a 'Do-support' needs to be inserted to make 'inversion' possible.	
(4) In a sentence of the following kind, *'The man who taught me last year resigned two days ago'*, the subject is complex, thus resulting in a complex sentence.	
(5) When a verb is used to describe what an entity (thing or person) is doing, then it is in the passive form.	
(6) In a sentence of the following kind, *'Sign here, please'*, there is only a verb phrase.	
(7) Syntactic rules refer to the rules that explain how different combinations give different meanings.	
(8) In the following sentence, *'I used to play football well'*, there is no specifier.	
(9) All languages have a grammatical category of 'tense', but not all of them have a grammatical category of 'aspect'.	
(10) When the lexical verb is preceded by an auxiliary, then we have a complex verb group.	

Exercise 2: Draw tree diagrams for the following sentences before translating them into your own language.

(1) The blind should be given priority.
(2) Some emails have been received by me lately.
(3) Clean your room.
(4) Ask me if you have a question.
(5) The king delivered an important speech yesterday.

Exercise 3: The following sentences are ambiguous. Your task is to (1) identify their different interpretations, (2) draw a tree diagram for each interpretation to illustrate the difference in meaning, and then (3) translate them into your own language to see whether they are ambiguous or not.

(1)   Visiting friends can be boring.
(2)   Flying planes can be dangerous.
(3)   The boy hit the girl with the hat.
(4)   The mother of the boy and the girl will visit us soon.
(5)   I pushed the car in the garage.
(6)   I met the young men and women.
(7)   I sent a gift to my friend from Oman.
(8)   The thief threatened the man with the knife.
(9)   The teacher said on Tuesday he would give us a mock exam.
(10)   The chicken is ready to eat.

Exercise 4: Change the following sentences into the passive. Then draw a tree diagram for each version before translating them into your language.

(1)   Our teacher has sold his car recently.
(2)   One of my close friends explained an important topic yesterday.
(3)   The company has hired many workers recently.
(4)   My eldest brother bought an expensive flat last week.
(5)   She has sold her car recently.

Exercise 5: Draw tree diagrams for the following sentences outlining the CP structure. Then, translate them into your own language.

(1)   The teacher said that the exam would be easy.
(2)   My wife asked me if I was going to visit my mother that night.
(3)   The gentleman told us that he was writing a number of important essays that night.
(4)   The students complained that they had not received their certificates yet.
(5)   I wondered if we could spend the whole night in that wonderful hotel.
(6)   My father said: "I want to visit Egypt one day".
(7)   She wanted to know if I was with her at the university.
(8)   Her father asked her whether she had done her homework.
(9)   The man assured us that it would be cheap.
(10)   My mom explained that she had been extremely busy at that time.

Exercise 6: The following text in five languages is taken from the 'Universal Declaration of Human Rights'. Comment on (1) translating tense and aspect, (2) translating gender, and (3) translating voice after translating it into your language if it is not one of the languages below.

English	Everyone charged with a penal offence has the right to be presumed innocent until proved guilty according to law in a public trial at which he has had all the guarantees necessary for his defence.
Spanish	Toda persona acusada de delito tiene derecho a que se presuma su inocencia mientras no se pruebe su culpabilidad, conforme a la ley y en juicio público en el que se le hayan asegurado todas las garantías necesarias para su defensa.
French	Toute personne accusée d'un acte délictueux est présumée innocente jusqu'à ce que sa culpabilité ait été légalement établie au cours d'un procès public où toutes les garanties nécessaires à sa défense lui auront été assurées.
Russian	Каждый человек, для определения его прав и обязанностей и для установления обоснованности предъявленного ему уголовного обвинения, имеет право, на основе полного равенства, на то, чтобы его дело было рассмотрено гласно и с соблюдением всех требований справедливости независимым и беспристрастным судом.
Arabic	كلُّ شخص متَّهم بجريمة يُعتبَر بريئًا إلى أن يثبت ارتكابُه لها قانونًا في محاكمة علنية تكون قد وُفِّرت له فيها جميعُ الضمانات اللازمة للدفاع عن نفسه.

Discussion and research points

(1) Go through any translated text from English into your own language to identify certain examples where certain sentence constituents were reordered through translation. Then discuss whether such a reordering affects the quality of translation.

(2) Select any English text that has some ambiguous sentences and translate it into your language. Then comment on the local strategies adopted by you to deal with such ambiguous structures.

(3) Influenced by the American linguist Noam Chomsky (1957), Nida (1964) stresses that the deep structures of language do not change, but what changes is only the surface structure. Do you agree?

(4) In your opinion, why do some English learners produce sentences, such as 'Where you found it?' in place of 'Where did you find it?'?

(5) Will reordering sentence constituents always promote or elaborate a different narrative/story?

References

Almanna, A. (2013). *Quality in the Translation of Narrative Fictional Texts from Arabic into English for the Purposes of Publication: Towards a Systematic Approach to (Self-)Assessing the Translation Process.* Unpublished PhD thesis. Durham: University of Durham.

Almanna, A. (2014). *Translation Theories Exemplified from Cicero to Pierre Bourdieu.* Munich: Lincom Europa Academic Publishers.

Almanna, A. (2016). *Semantics for Translation Students: Arabic-English-Arabic.* Oxford: Peter Lang.

Almanna, A. (2018). *The Nuts and Bolts of Arabic–English Translation: An Introduction to Applied Contrastive Linguistics.* Newcastle upon Tyne: Cambridge Scholars Publishing.

Almanna, A. (2022). "A Configurational System-based Approach to Translating Tenses from Arabic to English", *BJTLL: British Journal of Translation, Linguistics and Literature*, Vol. 2, pp. 1–14.

Almanna, A. and Al-Shehari, K. (2019). *The Arabic–English Translator as Photographer.* London/New York: Routledge.

Bell, R. T. (1991). *Translation and Translating: Theory and Practice.* London/New York: Longman.

Castro, O. (2010). "Non Sexist-Translation and/in Social Change: Gender Issues in Translation". In. Boéri, J. and Maier, C. (eds.), *Compromiso social y traducción/Interpretación Translation/Interpreting and Social Activism* (pp. 106–20). Granada: ECOS.

Catford, J. C. (1965). *A Linguistic Theory of Translation.* Oxford: Oxford University Press.

Celce-Murcia, M. and Larsen-Freeman, D. (1999). *The Grammar Book: An ESL/EFL Teacher's Course* (2nd edn). Boston, MA: Heinle and Heinle Publishers Inc.

Chomsky, N. (1957). *Syntactic Structures.* The Hague: Mouton.

Crystal, D. (1997). *The Cambridge Encyclopedia of Language* (2nd edn). Cambridge: Cambridge University Press.

Dickins, J., Hervey, S., and Higgins, I. (2002). *Thinking Arabic Translation.* London/New York: Routledge.

Farghal, M. (2008). "Extrinsic Managing: An Epitaph to Translational Ideological Move", *STJ: Sayyab Translation Journal*, Vol. 1, pp. 1–26.

Farghal, M. (2023). "Extrinsic Managing as Translatorial Censorship". In Almanna, A. and House, J. (eds.), *Translation Politicised and Politics Translated* (pp. 21–45). Oxford: Peter Lang.

Griffiths, P. (2006). *An Introduction to English Semantics and Pragmatics.* Edinburgh: Edinburgh University Press.

Hatim, B. and Mason, I. (1997). *The Translator as Communicator.* London/New York: Routledge.

Hellinger, M. and Bußmann, H. (eds.) (2001). *Gender across Languages: The Linguistic Representation of Women and Men, Vol. 1.* . Amsterdam: John Benjamins Publishing Company.

Kearns, K. (2000/ 2011). *Semantics.* Basingstoke/ New York: Palgrave Macmillan.

Kreidler, C. W. (1998). *Introducing English Semantics*. London/New York. Routledge.

Malone, J. L. (1988). *The Science of Linguistics in the Art of Translation*. Albany, NY: State University of New York Press.

Nida, E. (1964). *Towards a Science of Translation, with Special Reference to Principles and Procedures Involved in Bible Translating*. Leiden: E. J. Brill.

O'Grady, W., Dobrovolsky, M., and Katamba, F. (1997). *Contemporary Linguistics*. London: Longman.

Parker, F. and Riley, K. (1994/2010). *Linguistics for Non-Linguists*. Boston, MA: Pearson.

Scott, J. W. (1986). "Gender: A Useful Category of Historical Analysis", *The American Historical Review*, Vol. 91(5), pp. 1053–75.

Swan, M. (1995). *Practical English Usage*. Oxford: Oxford University Press.

Semantics

6

This chapter is an introduction to semantics and its main areas and concepts. It discusses such areas and notions as 'denotation' versus 'connotation', 'signifier' versus 'signified', 'reference' versus 'sense', 'compositional meaning' versus 'unitary meaning', 'lexical relations', 'semantic roles', 'semantic principles', and 'frame semantics' in a direct link to translation.

After studying this chapter, you should be able to (1) identify semantic roles and verb-specific semantic roles assigned to each noun phrase; (2) identify 'supplementary features' and 'diagnostic features'; (3) identify the different relationships that a word has with other words; (4) differentiate between 'compositional meaning' and 'unitary meaning'; (5) differentiate between 'connotative meaning' and 'denotative meaning'; and (6) differentiate between 'generalization' and 'particularization'.

Semantics is one of the branches of linguistics that refers to the study of the meaning of linguistic units, such as morphemes, words, expressions, phrases, and so on. For example, *'to buy'* and *'to purchase'* technically refer to the same thing, but semanticians try to analyse any shade of meaning that they might have. Unlike pragmatics, semantics concentrates on "what the words conventionally mean, rather than on what a speaker might want the words to mean on a particular occasion" (Yule 1985/1996: 114). In semantics, several notions can be studied, such as 'signifier' versus 'signified', 'reference' versus 'sense', 'denotation' versus 'connotation', 'semantic principles', and 'semantic roles' (for more details, see Almanna 2016)

Signifier versus signified

What is conjured up in your own mind when you hear the word *'Muslim'*?

Each sign is made up of two main components, namely 'signifier' and 'signified'. While the signifier is the physical form of the sign that can be seen, smelt, tasted, touched, heard, etc., the signified is what is conjured up in one's mind while seeing, touching, hearing, or tasting something (cf.

DOI: 10.4324/9781003228028-7

Bazzi 2009: 16; Farghal and Almanna 2015: 128; Almanna and Al-Shehari 2019: 16). To explain, the word *'dog'* is a sign composed of two elements: the three letters D, O, G in the linguistic system, i.e. the signifier, and what is conjured up in our mind, i.e. the signified. It is worth mentioning that people are different in terms of their socio- cultural experiences, accumulated value systems, orientations, personal knowledge, sense of belonging, and the like; therefore, what is conjured up in the language user's mind, i.e. the signified, is determined by what s/he knows about the signifier.

In the linguistic system (signifier)	In the real world (signified)
Dog (English)	
Perro/Perra (Spanish)	
Chien/Chienne (French)	
Cane/Cagna (Italian)	
Hund (German)	
Anjing (Indonesian)	
Kelb (Maltese)	
Köpek (Turkish)	
كلب (Arabic)	

As shown above, there is a relationship between the signifier and the thing that it refers to, i.e. the signified. If the relationship between the signifier and signified is direct and without any semantic load or overtone, then the meaning understood is denotative. Otherwise, if the relationship is not direct or with an overtone, then the meaning understood is connotative. By way of example, let us discuss the denotative and connotative meanings of *'butterfly'* and *'stomach'* in a sentence of the following kind:

> At the beginning of an exam, I always have butterflies in my stomach.

The lexical item *'butterfly'* without any semantic load refers to a type of insect with a long thin body and two wings that flies mostly during the day. The word *'stomach'* denotatively refers to that part of the body just below the chest where food is digested. In the sentence above, however, the meanings of these two words are not related directly to the denotative meaning of each word. Rather, the relationship between the signifier and signified in each word in such a sentence is not direct. The phrase *'to have butterflies in one's stomach'* has an overtone, i.e. to be nervous or worried, that cannot be figured out by relying on the denotative meaning of each word. Rather, these words should be treated as a unit by activating the idiom principle (see the discussion on the idiom principle in this chapter).

> In your own words, try to define 'denotative meaning' and 'connotative meaning'.

Reference versus sense

When hearing the word *'car'*, is the mental image conjured up in your mind 'static' or 'dynamic'?

Reference refers to the relationship between words or expressions (technically known as 'referring expressions') within the linguistic system and objects (technically known as 'referents') in the real world. When you hear or read, for instance, the word *'car'*, and you are familiar with its meaning in English, you will have a mental image of it, representing a road vehicle, typically with a steering wheel, an engine, four wheels, and seats to carry a small number of people, as in the following diagram:

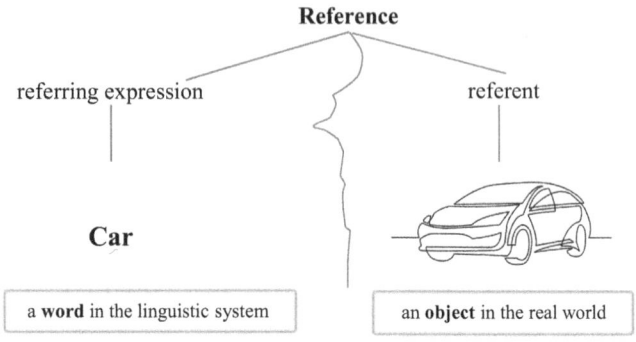

This theory (known as 'naming theory') does not work with abstract words that do not refer to anything in the real world, such as *'happiness'*, *'sadness'*, *'beauty'*, *'courage'*, *'cowardice'*, and so on. Hearing or reading these words does not conjure up any mental image in our mind.

With this in mind, to understand the meaning of the word, *'happiness'*, for instance, we need to identify its relationships with other words such as *'sadness'*, *'happy'*, and *'sad'*. These relationships are studied in semantics under what is called 'sense', which refers to the relationship that a lexical item has with other lexical items within the linguistic system.

How would you define 'sense' in semantics?

In another area of semantics: 'lexical semantics', the focus of attention is shifted towards the study of word meaning and the lexical relations that a word has with others. In this area, lexical relations, such as 'synonymy', 'antonymy', 'hyponymy', 'hyperonymy', 'polysemy', 'homonymy', and 'homophony' are given full consideration. Consider the following examples:

Provide as many examples as you can for these sense relations in your own language.

- Synonymy: *'big'*, *'huge'*, *'large'*, etc.
- Antonymy: *'big'* and *'small'*; *'short'* and *'tall'*, etc.
- Hyponymy (part-whole): *'hand'* and *'body'*; *'room'* and *'house'*, etc.
- Hyperonymy (whole-part): *'body'* and *'leg'*; *'room'* and *'window'*, etc.
- Co-hyponymy (part-part): *'hand'* and *'leg'*; *'window'* and *'door'*, etc.
- Homophony *'one'* and *'won'*; *'two'* and *'too'*; *'ate'* and *'eight'*, etc.
- Polysemy: the word *'eye'* that has many meanings, such as *'an eye of a person'*, *'an eye of needle'*, etc.

- Homonymy: the word *'spring'* in this sentence *'I saw a spring spring like a spring near the spring in the spring'*.

What is the relationship between *'basketball'* and *'sport'*?

Connecting the dots (1): Lexical relations and translation

Antonymy and modulation

An antonym is a lexical item that means the opposite of another lexical item, such as *'hot'* versus *'cold'*, *'short'* versus *'tall'*, *'expensive'* versus *'cheap'*, and *'male'* versus *'female'*. Antonyms can be all types of words: verbs, nouns, adjectives, adverbs, and even prepositions. In modern semantics, antonymy is divided into the following three main types:

(1) 'Gradable antonyms' (also known as 'non-binary antonyms') refer to gradable adjectives and adverbs, such as *'tall'* versus *'short'*, *'ugly'* versus *'beautiful'*, or *'fast'* versus *'slow'*. They are gradable because they can be used in a comparative degree (*'taller than'*) or superlative degree (*'the tallest'*). Translating, for example, *'I am shorter than my sister'* into French as *'Ma soeur est plus grande que moi'* meaning *'My sister is taller than me'* results in an 'optional modulation'.

Is there any difference between *'My sister is taller than me'* and *'I am shorter than my sister'*? Discuss

(2) 'Non-gradable antonyms' (also known as 'binary antonyms' or 'complementary pairs') refer to non-gradable adjectives, as in *'alive'* versus *'dead'*, *'single'* versus *'married'*, *'right'* versus *'wrong'*. They "are opposite ends of a scale that do not have various intermediate terms – somebody is either alive or dead; s/he cannot be alive and dead at the same time" (Almanna 2016: 106). Opting for the negation of the opposite or the other way round in translation results in an 'optional modulation', as in the following examples:

One way of capturing the relation set up by non-gradable antonyms is to use 'meaning postulates', i.e. using such a formula: 'if somebody is dead, then s/he is not alive'.

English	He did not close the door.
German	Er ließ die Tür offen.
Back translation	He left the door open.
Maltese	ħalla l-bieb miftuħ.
Back translation	He left the door open.
Thai	khao poet pratu thing wai.
Back translation	He left the door open.
Turkish	Kapıyı açık bıraktı.
Back translation	S/he left the door open.
Arabic	ترك البابَ مفتوحًا.
Back translation	He left the door open.

(3) 'Relational antonyms' (also known as 'converses' or 'converseness') refer to pairs of words that "share the same/some semantic features, but the focus or direction is reversed", as in *'send'* versus *'receive'*, *'buy'* versus *'sell'*, *'husband'* versus *'wife'*, or *'father'* versus *'son'* (for more examples see Almanna 2016: 106). Translating the English verb *'to receive'* into Maltese as *'baght'* meaning *'to send'* without changing the semantic roles assigned to each noun phrase (see the section on semantic roles in this chapter) results in an 'optional modulation', as shown in this example:

What about translating this sentence into the passive?

English	I received an email from my sister yesterday.
Maltese	Oħti baghtitli email ilbieraħ.
Back translation	My sister sent me an email yesterday.

Had the translator opted for a translation of the following kind *'Irċevejt email minghand oħti lbierah'* meaning *'I received an email from my sister yesterday'*, s/he would have avoided this optional modulation.

Hypernymy and hyponymy

Hypernym (also known as 'superordinate') is a more general word that embraces a group of more specific words. Hyponym, by contrast, is a word whose meaning is included in that of a more general word. Thus, the word *'sport'* is a more general word that embraces a group of more specific words, such as *'football'*, *'tennis'*, *'gymnastics'*, *'boxing'*, and *'marathon'*, as shown below:

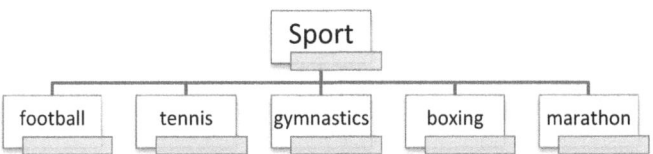

What is the relationship between *'football'* and *'tennis'*?

The denotative meaning of the lexical item *'sport'* is wider and less specific because it embraces words whose denotative meanings are narrower and more specific. The relationship between the words *'sport'* and *'tennis'*, for example, is called a hypernymy-hyponymy. This hypernymy-hyponymy relationship is "so widespread in all languages that one can say the entire fabric of linguistic reference is built up on such relationships" (Dickins et al. 2002: 55). Due to the differences between the interfacing languages and cultures, translators sometimes find themselves in a situation where they opt for generalization (translation by a general word; hypernym) or particularization (translating by a more specific word; hyponym). To make this point clear, let us have a look at the following examples:

How would you define 'generalization' in your own words?

Language pair	Hypernym	Hyponym
English–German	you	du/Sie
German–English	kochen	cook/boil/simmer
French–English	promenade	walk/ride/sail
Russian–English	рука	hand/arm
Tok Pisin–English	er	he/she
Maltese–Arabic	ziju	خال/عمّ
Arabic–English	جنين	embryo/foetus
English–Arabic	cousin	ابن عمّ/ابن خال/ابن عمّة/ابن خالة/بنت عمّ/بنت خال/بنت عمّة/بنت خالة

In the following example quoted from Baker (1992: 28), the Spanish translator opted for the lexical item *'giraba'* meaning *'to revolve'* whose denotative meaning is wider and less specific when it is compared with the verb *'to orbit'* in English. Here, we have an example of generalization, involving translating by using a more general word.

English	A well-known scientist (some say it was Bertrand Russell) once gave a public lecture on astronomy. He described how the earth **orbits** around the sun and how the sun, in turn, **orbits** around the center of a vast collection of stars called our galaxy.
Spanish	Un conocido científico (algunos dicen que fue Bertrand Russell) daba una vez una conferencia sobre astronomía. En ella describía cómo la Tierra **giraba** alrededor del Sol y cómo éste, a su vez, **giraba** alrededor del centro de una vasta colección de estrellas concida como nuestra galaxia.
Back translation	A well-known scientist (some say that it was Bertrand Russell) once gave a lecture on astronomy. In it he described how the earth **revolved** around the sun and how the latter in its turn **revolved** around the centre of a vast collection of stars known as our galaxy.

Translating the verb *'orbit'* into Arabic as يدور *'revolve'* results in an example of generalization. What about your own language?

It is worth noting that *'daba'* is not the correct form of the verb to be used. Instead, one can use *'impartió'* (more formal) or *'dio'*. Further, the word *'concida'* should be spelt *'conocida'*.

Generalization (or particularization if it is done the other way round) can be obligatory or optional, as shown in the translation of the following two examples:

Obligatory generalization

English	You need to boil the water first.
German	Sie müssen das Wasser zuerst kochen.

Comment on translating the English verb *'to need'* into German as *'müssen'*, i.e. *'must'*.

Here we have an example of obligatory generalization due to the differences between English and German. The denotative meaning of the verb *'to boil'* in English is narrower and more specific when it is compared with the verb *'kochen'* in German. Cast in more technical terms, the word *'kochen'* is a hypernym as it embraces a group of words in English, such as *'to cook'*, *'to boil'*, and *'to simmer'*.

Optional generalization

English	Cybercrimes can be classified into three types, namely: (1) Cybercrime targeting persons. (2) Cybercrimes against property. (3) Cybercrimes against governments.
Arabic	يمكن تصنيف الجرائم الإلكترونية إلى ثلاثة أنواع، هي (1) الجريمة التي تستهدف الأشخاص. (2) الجريمة التي تستهدف الأموال. (3) الجريمة التي تستهدف الحكومات.
Back translation	Cybercrimes can be classified into three types, namely: (1) Crimes targeting persons. (2) Crimes against property. (3) Crimes against governments.

Here, the translator decided to opt for a more general word, i.e. *'crime'*, when translating the more specific word *'cybercrime'*, thus resulting in optional generalization. This optional generalization that can be easily avoided does not affect the overall meaning as it is clear from the context and co-text that we are talking about cybercrimes.

Synonymy

Synonymous words are two or more words or expressions of the same language that have the same, or nearly the same, meaning, in some or all senses, such as *'fall'* and *'autumn'*, *'get'* and *'obtain'*, and *'small'* and *'tiny'*. Any synonymous words are examples of both 'mutual entailment' and 'co-hyponyms'. However, they are rarely fully identical in all contexts (cf. Palmer 1976: 60; Kreidler 1998: 97; Almanna 2016: 102). On this subject, Palmer (1976) holds the view that "no two words have exactly the same meaning" for the following five reasons (pp. 60–4; also discussed in Almanna 2016: 102–3):

(1) Some synonymous words and expressions belong to different dialects of the language, as in *'sweater'* and *'jumper'*, *'cookie'* and *'biscuit'*, *'period'* and *'full stop'*, *'flat'* and *'apartment'*, *'trousers'* and *'pants'*, *'diaper'* and *'nappy'*, and the like.

'Mutual entailment' (or 'entailment' for short) refers to the relationship between two words or sentences where the meaning of one word entails the meaning of the other, as in *'The man was assassinated'*, which entails *'The man is dead'* and *'The man is not alive'*.

(2) Some synonymous words and expressions are used in different styles or registers, as in *'find out'* and *'discover'*, *'get'* and *'obtain'*, *'go up'* and *'increase'*, *'say sorry'* and *'apologize'*, *'so'* and *'therefore'*, and the like.

(3) Some synonymous words and expressions differ in their evaluative and/or connotative meanings, as in *'a stupid student'* and *'less able student'*, *'fat'* and *'overweight'*, *'stateman'* and *'politician'*, *'strong-minded'* and *'stubborn'*, *'slim'* and *'skinny'*, and the like.

(4) Some words and expressions are close in meaning or their meanings overlap, as in, for example, the adjective *'funny'* and its synonyms, such as *'humorous'*, *'comical'*, *'hilarious'*, and *'hysterical'*. Their meanings overlap since we can have a set of synonyms for each lexical item.

(5) Some synonymous words and expressions are collocational restricted. In English, for instance, the adjectives *'quick'* and *'fast'* are synonyms, but native speakers say a *'quick shower'*, not a *'fast shower'* and *'fast food'*, not *'quick food'*.

In translating the phrase *'fast food'* from English into Arabic, it lends itself to وجبة سريعة *'fast meal'*. What about your own language?

To translate accurately, the translator needs to activate the mechanism of differentiating between the word used in the original text and its synonyms, on the one hand, and among the words that can be used in the target text on the other hand. Let us here discuss the word *'well-known'* used in the following example before translating it into Arabic:

> I received an email from one of the well-known universities some days ago.

Think of some examples of synonyms in English that require extra attention from you when translating them into your language.

Firstly, we need to differentiate between the word *'well-known'* and its synonyms in English. Is there any difference between *'well-known'* and synonyms such as *'famous'*, *'infamous'*, and *'notorious'*? According to the online Cambridge Dictionary, *'well-known'* and *'famous'* are interchangeable, i.e. known and recognized by many people, while *'infamous'* and *'notorious'* mean famous for something bad.

Secondly, we need to activate the mechanism of searching for an equivalent expression by raising the following question: How do Arabs describe a university known and recognized by many people? Two words emerge here: مشهور and معروف.

Thirdly, we need to find out the differences, if any, between these two words. While مشهور means known by many people, معروف means known by one person or many. As such, both can be used here, as shown below:

English	I received an email from one of the well-known universities some days ago.
Arabic	تسلّمت إيميلًا من إحدى الجامعات المعروفة/المشهورة قبل أيام

Polysemy and homonymy

Polysemy refers to a lexical item that has two or more related meanings. The noun *'head'*, for example, has multiple related meanings, such as a *'head of a person'*, *'head of a department'*, *'head of a lettuce'*, *'head of a nail'*, and so on, so it is an example of a polysemous word. Like polysemy, homonymy also refers to a word with two or more different meanings. However, in the case of homonymy, the word has multiple unrelated meanings. The word *'bank'*, for example, has multiple unrelated meanings. It means:

(1) a financial institution where money is kept safely for its customers;
(2) the ground along the side of a river or canal;
(3) (as a verb) to expect or trust somebody to do something, or for something to happen.

Do you have a homonymous word that can cover all ranges of meanings of the word *'bank'* in your own language?

Translating a homonymous word, such as *'bank'*, from English into a language that makes a distinction between the range of meanings of the homonymous word used in the original text results in particularization, which involves translating by using a more specific word, as shown here:

English	Once she approached the bank, she called her sister.
Arabic (TT1)	ما أن اقتربتُ من **المصرف**، حتى اتّصلت بأختها.
Arabic (TT2)	ما أن اقتربتُ من **ضفة النّهر**، حتى اتّصلت بأختها.

How would you define the term 'shift in coherence' in your own words?

To translate accurately, you, as a translator, need to be fully aware of these related or unrelated meanings of the lexical item used in the original text. In translating the polysemous word *'glava'* meaning *'head'* from Croatian to English, an inexperienced translator might opt for *'head'*, thus resulting in a 'shift in coherence' to use Blum-Kulka's (1986/2004) term. By way of example, let us discuss this sentence taken from Tudor (2017: 24):

Croatian	Knjiga je podijeljena u sedam glava.
English	The book is divided into seven heads.

Here, the translator was not fully aware of the range of meanings of the polysemous word *'glava'* in the target language, thus opting for translating it literally into *'head'* in place of *'chapter'*. In this regard, Baker (1992: 253) rightly comments that a "polysemous item in the source text will rarely have an equivalent item with the same range of meanings in the target language".

In the following example, however, the translator (Arberry 1955/1996) opted for the word *'confound'* in place of translating the word تلبسون derived from the verb ألبس or لبس meaning to dress somebody or, literally, cover somebody with clothes:

Arabic	يا أهل الكتاب لِمَ تلبسون الحق بالباطل وتكتمون الحق وأنتم تعلمون (آل عمران،71)
English	People of the Book! Why do you confound the truth with vanity, and conceal the truth and that wittingly? (Arberry 1955/1996)

In this verse, the polysemous word تلبسون is used by Allah while addressing the people of the Torah and Bible to mean to mix or to mingle the truth with falseness. Being fully aware of this, the translator produced a coherent translation.

Connecting the dots (2): Diagnostic components and translation

Any lexical item in any language has certain components. These components are classified by Nida (1975) in his book: *Componential Analysis of Meaning* into two main types: 'supplementary components' and 'diagnostic components'.

Can you identify the 'diagnostic components' shared by words like *'chair'*, *'arm-chair'*, *'stool'*, *'wheelchair'*, and *'folding chair'*?

(1) 'Supplementary components' refer to all those additional features that a lexical item shares with other semantically related words. These components, as Nida (1975: 112) explains, "may be very important for an extensive definition of a meaning but which are not diagnostic in specifying basic differences".
(2) 'Diagnostic components', on the other hand, refer to those components that "serve to distinguish the meaning of a certain lexeme from other lexemes in a particular domain or field". In other words, these components are responsible for making a distinction among those words that are semantically related.

By way of illustration, let us analyse the following lexical items: *'child'*, *'boy'*, *'girl'*, *'man'*, and *'woman'*. These lexical items are semantically related words as they all are in the same semantic domain: 'human race'. [HUMAN] as a supplementary feature is shared by all of them; therefore, this feature cannot be used to distinguish them. We need other features, such as [MALE] and [ADULT], to distinguish them from one another, as shown below:

Lexeme	HUMAN	MALE	ADULT
child	+	+/−	−
boy	+	+	−
girl	+	−	−
man	+	+	+
woman	+	−	+

These diagnostic components should be given full consideration by translators. In this regard, Almanna (2016: 17) holds:

> In the actual act of translating any text from language *A* to language *B*, translators are sometimes required to analyse some lexical items and contrast them with other semantically related lexical items in an attempt to be fully aware of the distinctive features of the lexical item at hand. It also helps the translators draw a comparison between the lexical item used in the original text and the one to be used in the target text, thus putting a finger on the similarities and differences between them.

Now, let us translate the following example from Arabic to English to make this point clear:

Arabic	سألت الأمُ الطبيبَبصوت قلق: هل الأمر سيءٌ جدًّا؟
English	The mother asked the doctor with a worried voice: "Is it very bad?".

The Arabic word صوت has more than one equivalent word in English, including *'sound'*, *'voice'*, *'volume'*, and *'vote'*. The diagnostic feature that distinguishes the lexical item opted for by the translator, i.e. *'voice'*, from the other semantically related words is that [OF HUMAN BEING]. Being fully aware of the supplementary and diagnostic features of the lexical items available, the translator translated the word صوت into *'voice'*, thus resulting in an example of 'divergence' or 'particularization', as discussed in the previous section. Suffice it to say that divergence occurs when the denotative meaning of the lexical item in the original text is wider and less specific than its equivalent in the target text. Now, let us do it the other way round. Let us translate the lexical item *'voice'*, in this example extracted from the novel *The Secret Garden* by Frances Hodgson Burnett (1994: 3) into Arabic and German:

How would you define 'divergence'?

Translate this text into your language.

ST (English)	She saw her mother coming into the garden, with a doctor. They did not notice the child, who listened to their conversation.
	"It's very bad, isn't it?" her mother asked the doctor with a worried voice.
TT1 (Arabic)	رأت أمها قادمة من الحديقة مع طبيب. لم يلحظا الطفلة التي استمعت لحديثهما.
	سألت الأم الطبيب بصوت قلق: الأمرُ سيءٌ جدًّا، أليس كذلك؟
Back translation	She saw her mother coming from the garden with a doctor. They did not notice the child who listened to their conversation.
	The mother asked the doctor in a worried voice: "It is very bad, isn't it?"

TT2 (German)	Sie sah ihre Mutter mit dem Arzt aus dem Garten kommen. Sie bemerkten das Kind, das ihrem Gespräch lauschte nicht.
	Die Mutter fragte den Arzt mit besorgter Stimme: "Es ist sehr schlimm, oder?"
Back translation	She saw her mother with the doctor from the garden coming. They noticed the child who listened to their talk not.
	The mother asked the doctor with worried voice: "It is very bad, or?"

In translating from English into Arabic and German, we have an example of 'convergence' as the denotative meaning of the lexical item *'voice'* used in the original text is narrower and more specific when compared with its equivalents صوت (in Arabic) and *'Stimme'* (in German). In Arabic, the word صوت refers to *'voice'*, *'sound'*, *'vote'*, and *'volume'*. In German, however, the word *'Stimme'* refers to *'voice'* and *'vote'* only as there are other words, such as *'Laut' and 'Lautstärke'*, to refer to *'sound'* and *'volume'*, respectively.

> Is there any difference between 'convergence' and 'generalization'?

Connecting the dots (3): Semantic roles and translation

Semantic roles (also known as 'thematic roles', 'theta roles', and 'thematic cases') are classified in this section into verb-specific semantic roles, i.e. semantic roles that are derived from the verb itself, as shown here:

> How would you define 'semantic roles' in your own words?

Verb-specific semantic role		verb
Player	from	to play
Eater	from	to eat
Buyer	from	to buy
Sayer	from	to say
Traveller	from	to travel

> Note that adding the suffix '–er' to the verb may refer to something else, as in *'liver'* from the verb *'to live'*. In such a case, you can use *'inhabitant'* as a verb-specific semantic role.

Now, let us identify the verb-specific semantic roles assigned to each noun phrase in the following example:

The teacher gave one of his students a gift two days ago.

In this sentence, there are three noun phrases, namely *'the teacher'*, *'one of his students'*, and *'a gift'*, that fill different verb-specific semantic roles, as follows:

● the teacher	fills a verb-specific semantic role of Giver.
● one of his students	fills a verb-specific semantic role of Receiver.
● a gift	fills a verb-specific semantic role of something Given.
● two days ago	is an adverb of time answering the question 'when'.

It is worth mentioning that what was given was first with the teacher and then with the student, as shown in this picture quoted from Almanna (2018: 11):

We can also notice that what was given was not affected, but it was moved from the 'Source' (*the teacher*) to the 'Goal' (*the student*).

Now, let us compare these four sentences expressing the same idea to answer the following questions:

(a) Who was the sender?
(b) Who was the receiver?
(c) What was sent?

I sent an email to my supervisor two days ago.
I sent my supervisor an email two days ago.
My supervisor received an email from me two days ago.
An email was sent by me to my supervisor two days ago.

The sender in all these sentences is the speaker indicated by the pronoun '*I*' or '*me*', the receiver is '*the supervisor*', and the thing that was sent or received is '*an email*'. This means that these sentences have the same semantic load although they have different syntactic structures.

When translating between languages, the first thing that the translator should think of is to reflect the message intended by the author in the target text, then s/he comes to think of other issues, such as the style (Almanna 2016: 128). Changing the semantic role assigned to the noun phrase by accident or on purpose will create slightly or completely different mental images and messages. By way of example, let us translate the following sentence into several languages to see if the translators managed to deal

> What about if the student had opened the gift and used it later? Would it have been affected? Discuss.

> Do you agree with this claim? Discuss.

with the verb-specific semantic roles assigned to each noun phrase used in this simple sentence or not:

The man was killed by the police yesterday morning.

Arabic	قتلت الشّرطةُ الرّجلَ أمس صباحًا.
Back translation	The police killed the man yesterday morning.
German	Die Polizei tötete den Mann gestern morgen.
Back translation	The police killed the man yesterday morning.
French	La police a tué l'homme hier matin.
Back translation	The police killed the man yesterday morning.
Maltese	Ir-raġel inqatel mill-pulizija lbieraħ filgħodu.
Back translation	The man was killed by the police yesterday morning.

In the original sentence, there are two noun phrases, namely *'the man'* and *'the police'*. These two noun phrases fill two different semantic roles and verb-specific semantic roles. While the first noun phrase *'the man'* fills the semantic role of an 'Affected Participant' and a verb-specific semantic role of 'somebody Killed', the second noun phrase *'the police'* fills a semantic role of an 'Agent' and a verb-specific semantic role of 'Killer'. Having taken into consideration language preferences and the differences between the interfacing languages, the translators opted for different styles, but with the same meaning. It is the same meaning because we have the same semantic roles assigned to each noun phrase, as shown below:

Killer	Process	Somebody killed	Circumstance
The police	killed	the man	yesterday morning
الشرطة	قتلت	الرّجل	أمس صباحًا
Die Polizei	tötete	den Mann	Gestern morgen
La police	tué	l'homme	hier matin
Il-pulizija	qatlu	Ir-raġel	lbieraħ filgħodu

Unlike simple and compound sentences, complex sentences can be analysed at different levels, as shown in the following example:

He said that he would sell his flat and travel to London to live there.

In the above sentence, two main verb-specific semantic roles can be identified, 'Sayer' and 'something Said', as shown below:

He (Sayer)	said (verbal process)	something Said (content)

Inside 'something Said' (also known as '*that*-clause' and 'complementizer clause'), there are three clauses, namely:

Side notes:

Translate this sentence into your own language without changing the semantic roles.

Note that 'yesterday morning' is an adverb of time answering the question 'when', thus having no semantic role.

Is there any difference between 'Seller' and 'Seller-to be' as verb-specific semantic roles?

- he [Seller-to be] would sell his flat [something Sold]*
- (he [Traveller-to be] would) travel to London.
- (he) [Inhabitant-to be] to live there.

It is worth noting here that as it is not asserted that (1) he sold his flat, (2) he travelled to London, and (3) he lived there, the scope of intention is greater than the extent of causation (for more details and examples of these two terms, see Chapter 12 of this book). This should be reflected when translating between languages, as shown in the translations below:

Translate this complex sentence into your own language.

Arabic	قال إنه سيبيع شقته ويسافر إلى لندن ليعيش هناك.
Back translation	He said that he would sell his flat and travel to London to live there.
German	Er sagte dass er seine Wohnung verkaufen und nach London reisen würde, um dort zu leben.
Back translation	He said that he would sell his flat and travel to London in order to live there.
French	Il a dit qu'il vendrait son appartement et se rendrait à Londres pour y vivre.
Back translation	He said that he would sell his flat and travel to London to live there.
Thai	เขาว่าจะขายแฟลตแล้วเดินทางไปอยู่ที่ลอนดอน khao wa cha khay flaet laew doenthang pai yu thi London.
Back translation	He said [that he] would sell the flat and travel to stay in London.
Turkish	Dairesini satacağını ve orada yaşamak için Londra'ya gideceğini söyledi.
Back translation	S/he said that he would sell his flat and go to London to live there.
Persian	او گفت که آپارتمانش را می‌فروشد و به لندن سفر می‌کند تا آنجا زندگی کند.
Back translation	He said he would sell his flat and travel to London to live there.

Apart from the differences between the interfacing languages in terms of word order requirements (from English to German) and dealing with tenses/aspects (from English to Arabic), the semantic roles filled by each noun phrase along with the scope of intention and extent of causation were accurately reflected by the translators, thus maintaining the same mental images in the minds of the target language readers.

To see how changing the semantic roles assigned to any noun phrase may twist the message to varying degrees, let us have a look at two *BBC News* items (28 November 2019) on the same topic (one in English and one in Arabic):

English	The International Committee of the Red Cross (ICRC) has helped repatriate 128 rebels from Saudi Arabia to Yemen.
Arabic	أعلنت اللجنة الدولية للصليب الأحمر عودة 128 من المتمردين الذين كانوا محتجزين في السعودية إلى اليمن.
Back translation	The International Committee of the Red Cross announced the return of 128 rebels who had been held captive in Saudi Arabia to Yemen.

Here, the International Committee of the Red Cross (ICRC) fills different verb-specific thematic roles. In English, it fills a verb-specific semantic role of 'Helper' that indicates its involvement as an active participant in the process. However, in Arabic, there is no reference to such participation as it fills a verb-specific semantic role of 'Announcer' in a verbal process.

Connecting the dots (4): Semantic principles and translation

In semantics, meaning can be classified into two main types, namely 'compositional meaning' and 'unitary meaning'. Compositional meaning can be figured out by following an 'open choice principle', i.e. by relying on the denotative meaning of each smaller unit (e.g. morpheme or word) used to form a larger unit (phrase, clause, or sentence), of course, in addition to the way that they are put together to form these phrases, clauses, and so on.

Unitary meaning, on the other hand, cannot be determined by relying on the denotative meaning of each morpheme or word. Rather, the larger unit should be treated as one unit by following an 'idiom principle'. As such, in semantics, there are two main principles that can be followed by language users (be they writers or speakers) to produce and understand utterances (Sinclair 1991, 1998): 'open choice principle' and 'idiom principle'.

Translators follow both principles depending on the text at hand. By way of illustration, let us translate the following short passage adapted from Almanna (2016: 140) into several languages:

> It seems that his brother is a big cheese in one of the major companies in the country. Have you met him?

Apart from *'a big cheese'*, the translator, in addition to the way in which they are put together to form larger units, can rely on the denotative and contextual meanings of each word. The noun phrase *'a big cheese'*, however, is an idiomatic expression that should be treated as one unit to be understood and then translated. It refers to an important or powerful person in a group or organization. Having understood its overall meaning, now, how would you translate it? In translating idiomatic expressions, translators try to do their best to translate accurately and idiomatically, but this is not an easy task due to the differences between the interfacing languages and cultures. There are certain local strategies that can be resorted to by translators, at

Identify the 'compositional meaning' and 'unitary meaning' in the following sentence: *'Thanks for inviting me, but ballet isn't really my cup of tea'*.

the forefront of which is an 'optimal equivalent' where the same image, function, and form are used in both languages/cultures, as in the translation of *'Necessity is the mother of invention'* into Arabic, German, and French, as shown below:

How would you translate *'Birds of a feather flock together'* into your own language?

Find more examples of 'optimal equivalents'.

```
                                    ┌─────────────────────┐
                                    │ الحاجة أم الاختراع   │
                                    │ (Arabic)            │
                                    └─────────────────────┘
┌──────────────────┐               ┌─────────────────────┐
│ Necessity is the │               │ Notwendigkeit ist die│
│ mother of invention│─────────────│ Mutter der Erfindung│
└──────────────────┘               │ (German)            │
                                    └─────────────────────┘
                                    ┌─────────────────────┐
                                    │ La nécessité est la │
                                    │ mère de l'invention │
                                    │ (French)            │
                                    └─────────────────────┘
```

Failing to reach an optimal translation, the translator can opt for an 'ideational translation' (focusing on the idea), 'functional translation' (focusing on the function of the idiomatic expression), 'idiomatic translation' (with another image), 'literal translation', 'translation by paraphrase', 'translation by omission', or 'translation by compensation', as summarized here:

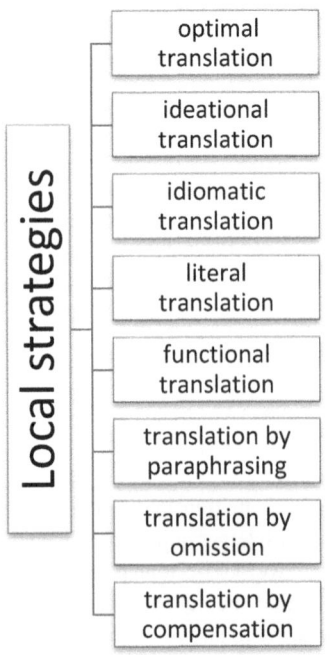

To explain, let us translate the fore-mentioned example to identify the strategies adopted by the translators when they are dealing with the idiomatic expression used in this sentence:

It seems that his brother is a big cheese in one of the major companies in the country. Have you met him?

Arabic	يبدو أن أخاه رجلٌ مهمٌ في إحدى الشّركات الكبيرة في البلاد. هل ألتقيته؟
Back translation	It seems that his brother is an important man in one of the big companies in the country. Have you met him?
Persian	به نظر می‌رسد که برادرش آدم مهمی در یکی از شرکت‌های بزرگ کشور باشد. آیا او را ملاقات کرده‌ای؟
Back translation	It seems that his brother is an important person in one of the big companies in the country. Have you met him?
German	Sein Bruder scheint ein hohes Tier in einer der bedeutendsten Firmen im Land zu sein. Hast Du ihn getroffen?
Back translation	His bother seems a high animal in one of the most important firms in the country. Have you met him?

<aside>How would you translate this sentence into your own language? Which strategy would you adopt?</aside>

In Arabic and Persian, as one may notice, the translators opted for an ideational translation where the idea is given a priority. In German, however, to describe a person in an important position in a company, one may use *'ein hohes Tier'*, literally meaning *'a high animal'*, thus resulting in a functional translation.

Connecting the dots (5): Frame semantics and translation

Frame semantics is a theory proposed and developed by Charles J. Fillmore (1977, 1982). According to this theory, the meaning of any lexical item is not static, but rather differs from one person to another. To understand the meaning of a lexical item, the denotative meaning of this lexical item needs to be linked by virtue of a frame to the socio-cultural experiences and encyclopaedic knowledge of a particular language user. So, what then is a 'frame'?

<aside>Do you agree with this claim? Discuss with illustrative examples.</aside>

A frame is defined by Almanna (2016: 24) as "a conceptual structure that provides background of beliefs, assumptions, practices against which the meaning of a lexical item can be captured". So, hearing or reading the words *'to die'* and *'to kill'*, for example, invokes in our minds different frames. The verb *'to die'* is profiled in a frame where it contrasts with the verb *'to kill'*. The verb *'to die'* invokes in our minds an *accident*-frame which has nothing to do with issues such as the intention to cause death to somebody. The verb *'to kill'*, on the other hand, evokes a *killing*-frame that has something to do with issues such as the intention to cause somebody to die – the flow of energy from the Actor to the Patient (for more details on these two verbs, see Chapter 12 of this book).

Now, let us discuss this example taken from an English documentary film titled *The Fall: Final Days of the Caliphate* subtitled by *CNN Arabic* as السقوط: آخر أيام خلافة داعش المزعومة:

ST	As they wait to be trucked to a camp for the displaced north of here, there is no bombing [PAUSE] there *IS* hunger, thirst, and misery.
TT	مع انتظار وضعهم على شاحنات تنقلهم إلى مخيّم للمشردين إلى شمال المنطقة، فإنه لا يوجد قصف، لكن هناك جوع وعطش ومعاناة.
Back translation	As they wait to be trucked to be taken to a camp for the homeless north of here, there is no bombing, but there is hunger, thirst, and misery.

In this example, the whole scene is characterized by having a force dynamic value of forcing those people who are waiting to be trucked and taken to a camp (see the discussion on force dynamics in Chapter 12 of this book for more details). The Agent, backgrounded here but predictable as it is in our scope of attention, is characterized by being-able-to-do (authority) while the Affected Participant is characterized by being-able-not-do, but to obey (submission). This force dynamic pattern was reflected by the subtitler, but s/he opted for the word المشردين that invokes in our minds a *homelessness*-frame that has almost nothing to do with wars or dangerous things, whereas in the original text the term *'displaced'* is used that invokes in our minds a *war*-frame in addition to unwillingly leaving one's house for another place, but within the same country. Had the subtitler taken into account these diagnostic and supplementary components of the lexical item, s/he would have opted for النازحين, i.e. *'displaced'*.

Approached from another perspective, the speaker while describing the scene decides to pause for a while before countering the previous proposition without using any indicator of counter-expectancy, but he relies on ideational content that can inform the reader that the proposition 'there is hunger, thirst, and misery' is in a countering relationship with the proposition 'there is no bombing'. This *let-me-remind-you*-frame that is usually associated with the use of *'but'* counters the moment of happiness invoked in the mind of the reader/listener by virtue of the existing process expressed by *'there is no bombing'*. For the sake of readability, acceptability, authenticity, and well-formedness that feed into naturalness, the subtitler decided to opt for لكن *'but'* to indicate that these two propositions are in a countering relationship. By doing so, s/he did not change the speaker's attitude (for more details on translating attitudes, see Chapter 9 of this book).

Examples of indicators of counter-expectancy in English include *'but'*, *'although'*, etc.

Exercises and discussion

Exercise 1: Mark the following statements (T) if they are true and (F) if they are false.

(1) In *'My young daughter ate a lot of rice'*, the noun phrase *'my young daughter'* fills a verb-specific semantic role of Eater and *'a lot of rice'* fills a verb-specific semantic role of 'something Eaten'.	
(2) While the noun phrase *'His father'* in *'His father bought a new flat'* fills a verb-specific semantic role of 'Buyer', *'a new flat'* fills a verb-specific semantic role of 'Direct Object'.	
(3) The words *'one'* and *'win'* are homophones.	
(4) The words *'seen'* and *'scene'* are homonymous words.	
(5) The words *'nose'* and *'eye'* are examples of co-hyponymy.	
(6) There is a relationship between the signifier and signified, and if the relationship between them is direct and without any semantic load, then the meaning understood is connotative.	
(7) When the denotative meaning of a word used in the original text is wider and less specific than its counterpart in the target text, then we have an example of 'generalization'.	
(8) When the same image, function, and form are used in both languages when translating, we have an example of 'ideational translation'.	
(9) To understand the meaning of this idiomatic expression *'To let the cat out of the bag'*, it should be treated as one unit.	
(10) Each sign is made up of two main components, namely 'signifier' and 'signified'. While the signifier is what is conjured up in one's mind, the signified is the physical form of the sign.	

Exercise 2: Read the following sentences carefully in order to label their semantic roles filled by the noun phrases in each clause. Then translate them into your own language without changing the semantic roles.

(1) I went to London.
(2) She sent me an email yesterday.
(3) The harvest has been destroyed by the flood completely.
(4) I spent many hours designing a cover for your book.
(5) My boss wrote a recommendation letter for me.
(6) My brother borrowed some money from his friend.

Exercise 3: What is the relationship between the following pairs?

(1) child – kid _____
(2) cheap – expensive _____
(3) whole – hole _____
(4) mouth – face _____
(5) mouth – body _____
(6) mouth – teeth _____

Exercise 4: Re- write the following sentences without changing the semantic roles assigned to each noun phrase. Then translate both versions into your own language.

(1) I bought a new car three days ago.

_____

(2) One of my friends received an important letter from a well-known university.

_____

(3) My young daughter ate a lot of rice in the morning.

_____

Exercise 5: Change the following sentences into the passive without changing the semantic roles assigned to each noun phrase. Then translate both versions into your language.

(1) One night, three thieves stole a lot of money from a rich man's house.
(2) They put the money in a bag and went to the forest.
(3) The thief ate his food at a hotel. Then he bought food for his two mates in the forest.
(4) He mixed a strong poison with the food.
(5) The king delivered an important speech this morning.
(6) She could not ask me any questions yesterday.
(7) The enemy launched an attack on our troops some days ago.
(8) Don't worry, our friend has paid the bill.
(9) She invited all her friends to her birthday party, but no one attended.
(10) She answered all the questions accurately yesterday.

Exercise 6: Decide whether the two lexical items in each of the following pairs are homophones or not:

(1) son – sun _____
(2) court – caught _____
(3) ate – eight _____
(4) by – bye _____
(5) tail – tale _____
(6) no – know _____

   (7) new – knew_____
   (8) sea – see _____
   (9) meet – meat _____
(10) great – greet _____

Exercise 7: Among the following pairs of antonyms, which are 'gradable' and which are 'non-gradable'?

   (1) big – small _____
   (2) smart – stupid _____
   (3) open – close _____
   (4) polite – impolite _____
   (5) strong – weak _____
   (6) sad – happy _____
   (7) alive – dead _____
   (8) legal – illegal _____
   (9) correct – wrong _____
(10) wide – narrow _____

Exercise 8: Select any political text from *BBC News* and:

(a) translate it into your own language;
(b) identify any examples of 'generalization' or 'particularization';
(c) comment on your own translation by referring to such notions as 'semantic roles', 'semantic principles', and the 'frames' conjured up in your own mind.

Discussion and research points

(1) Go through any translated book from English into your own language to identify examples of 'generalization' or 'particularization'.
(2) Select any English text that has some idiomatic expressions and translate it into your language. Then comment on your own translation by referring to the main principles of semantics.
(3) The process of doing expressed by the verb *'to kill'* was translated into a process of happening expressed by the verb *'to die'*, thus hiding the Agent. Comment on such a translation.

ST (English)	The man was killed by the police yesterday.
TT (Maltese)	Ir-raġel miet ilbieraħ.
Back translation	The man died yesterday.

(4) Is there any difference between Malone's (1988) 'divergence' and 'particularization' used by Vinay and Darbelnet (1958/1995) and later Dickins and his colleagues (2002)?
(5) How would you define 'semantic roles'?
(6) Can you rely on the denotative meaning of each word by activating the 'open choice principle' to figure out the overall meaning of the

following sentence? *'We are a luxury restaurant and if people have a bad experience, we have to carry the can.'*
(7) Do you have a homonymous word that can cover all ranges of meanings of the word *'pupil'* in your own language?

References

Almanna, A. (2016). *Semantics for Translation Students: Arabic-English-Arabic*. Oxford. Peter Lang.

Almanna, A. (2018). *The Nuts and Bolts of Arabic–English Translation: An Introduction to Applied Contrastive Linguistics*. Newcastle upon Tyne: Cambridge Scholars Publishing.

Almanna, A. and Al-Shehari, A. (2019). *The Arabic–English Translator as Photographer: A Linguistic Account*. London/New York: Routledge.

Arberry, A. J. (1955/1996). *The Koran Interpreted*. London: George Allen and Unwin.

Baker, M. (1992). *In Other Words: A Coursebook on Translation*. London/New York: Routledge.

Bazzi, S. (2009). *Arab News and Conflict*. Amsterdam/ Philadelphia, PA: John Benjamins Publishing Company.

Blum- Kulka, S. (1986/ 2004). "Shifts of Cohesion and Coherence in Translation". In Venuti, L. (ed.), *The Translation Studies Reader* (pp. 298–329). London/New York: Routledge,

Burnett, F. H. (1994). *The Secret Garden*. Oxford: Oxford University Press.

Dickins, J., Hervey, S., and Higgins, I. (2002). *Thinking Arabic Translation*. London/New York: Routledge.

Farghal, M. and Almanna, A. (2015). *Contextualizing Translation Theories: Aspects of Arabic– English Interlingual Communication*. Newcastle upon Tyne: England: Cambridge Scholars Publishing.

Fillmore, C. (1977). "Scenes-and-frames Semantics". In Zampolli, A. (ed.), *Linguistic Structures Processing* (pp. 55–82). Amsterdam: North Holland,

Fillmore, C. (1982). "Frame Semantics". In Linguistics Society of Korea (ed.), *Linguistics in the Morning Calm*. Selected Papers of SICOL-1981 (pp. 111–37). Seoul: Hanshin Publishing.

Kreidler, C. W. (1998). *Introducing English Semantics*. London/New York: Routledge.

Malone, J. L. (1988). *The Science of Linguistics in the Art of Translation*. Albany, NY: State University of New York Press.

Nida, E. A. (1975). *Componential Analysis of Meaning*. The Hague: Mouton.

Palmer, F. R. (1976). *Semantics: A New Outline*. Cambridge: Cambridge University Press.

Sinclair, J. (1991). *Corpus, Concordance and Collocation*. Oxford: Oxford University Press.

Sinclair, J. (1998). "The Lexical Item". In Weigand, E. (ed.), *Contrastive Lexical Semantics* (pp. 1–24). Amsterdam/ Philadelphia, PA: John Benjamins.

Tudor, A. (2017). *Machine Translations of Polysemous Croatian Words in Various Text Genres*. Unpublished MA thesis. Rijeka, Croatia: University of Rijeka.

Vinay, J. P. and Darbelnet, J. (1958/ 1995). *Stylistique comparée du français et de l'anglais. Méthode de traduction*. Paris: Didier. Trans. and ed. J. C. Sager and M. J. Hamel, *Comparative Stylistics of French and English: A Methodology for Translation*. Amsterdam/ Philadelphia: John Benjamins.

Yule, G. (1985/ 1996). *The Study of Language*. Cambridge: Cambridge University Press.

Discourse analysis

7

This chapter introduces a branch of linguistics which is one of the most relevant fields for students and researchers of translation: usage-based linguistics. It covers two main related areas, namely 'discourse analysis' and 'pragmatics'. In this chapter, 'discourse analysis' is discussed. You are first given a definition along with its relation to pragmatics. Then you learn about the main approaches to discourse analysis, namely (1) 'social approaches', such as 'conversation analysis' and 'critical discourse analysis'; (2) 'linguistic approaches', such as 'systemic functional linguistics', 'sociolinguistics', and 'cognitive discourse analysis'; and (3) other approaches, such as 'multi-modal texts', 'multi-voiced texts', and 'intercultural communication'.

After you have studied this chapter, you should be able to understand what discourse analysis is as well as its main approaches. In this chapter, special attention is paid to two main approaches, namely 'conversation analysis' and 'critical discourse analysis', which are discussed in a direct relation to translation.

Usage-based linguistics is a branch of linguistics that covers two main related areas, namely 'discourse analysis' and 'pragmatics'. Discourse analysis and pragmatics "have much more in common: they both study context, text and function" (Cutting 2002: 2). Firstly, they do not rely on semantic principles, such as the 'open choice principle' and 'idiom principle' to arrive at the intended meaning, but rather they rely on context. Secondly, they study whether the text (be it spoken or written) at hand is meaningful and unified for the language user or not, i.e. whether the text is cohesive and coherent ('discourse analysis') or relevant ('pragmatics'). Thirdly, they focus on the purpose of communication, i.e. what purpose or goal is the language user trying to achieve? To make all these points clear, let us discuss this exchange between son and father:

> What are the semantic principles? Explain them with illustrative examples.

Son: I went to the supermarket and lost the money.
Father. You lost the money, that's great.

> Why is *'that's great'* a finite clause?

Here, the finite clause *'that's great'* in such a situation cannot be interpreted out of its context by relying, for instance, on the denotative meaning of

DOI: 10.4324/9781003228028-8

each word used by the speaker because it is used sarcastically. Therefore, the purpose of communication and the context in which it is used should be given full consideration. One of the interlocutors (father) decided to communicate with his son indirectly, thus flouting Grice's cooperative principle and its supportive maxims, in particular the maxim of relevance (be relevant) and part of the maxim of manner (i.e. avoid ambiguity). Despite this, "the process of communication continues uninterrupted, thanks to human rationality and reasoning, which is based on the cooperative principle between producer and receiver in communication" (Farghal and Almanna 2015: 112). Had the father said, for instance, *'That's terrible'*, *'Oh my God'* or just *'What?'*, he would have been relevant and avoided ambiguity, thus observing the maxim of relevance and maxim of manner (for more details on Grice's cooperative principle, see the next chapter).

Discourse analysis

The word 'discourse' comes from the Latin word *'discursus'* meaning 'conversation' or 'speech'. Discourse, in its narrow sense, is seen by Crystal as a "continuous stretch of (specially spoken) language larger than a sentence, often constituting a coherent unit such as a sermon, argument, joke, or narrative" (1992: 25). Discourse, in its broader sense, can be defined as a "social practice" (Fairclough and Wodak 1997: 258), thus comprising discourses of social institutions such as science, education, politics, business, and religion. Discourse analysis, however, is the branch of linguistics "which deals with the various devices used by speakers and writers when they knit single sentences together into a coherent and cohesive whole" (Aitchison 1999/2003: 60). It can be defined as "the practice of exploring what kinds of speaking, writing and images are treated as 'normal' (and 'abnormal') in real situations, and proportions, combinations and purposes of discourse that are conventionally acceptable (or not) in these situations" (Hall et al. 2011: 76). Discourse analysis covers a wide range of different areas, such as 'cohesion', 'coherence', 'pragmatics', 'functional linguistics', 'register', 'speech events', and 'schema'. It examines:

> What is the difference between 'cohesion' and 'coherence'?

> Can you think of some devices that can be used by language users to knit their sentences together into a coherent and cohesive whole?

(1) issues related to the textual relations appearing on the surface of the text (i.e. cohesion);
(2) the relation between text and its context (i.e. coherence);
(3) speech acts, cooperative principle, implicature, etc. (pragmatics);
(4) agency, modality, etc. (functional linguistics);
(5) the relation between linguistic features and features of a situation, such as field of discourse, tenor of discourse, and mode of discourse (i.e. register);
(6) the relation between the text producer and the text receiver and their roles (i.e. speech event/social factors and dimensions);
(7) the relation between text interpretation and text participants' background knowledge (i.e. schema).

> What is the difference between 'text' and 'discourse'?

Approaches to discourse analysis can be classified into three main types:

(1) Social approaches that include 'conversation analysis', 'discursive psychology', and 'critical discourse analysis'.
(2) Linguistic approaches that include, 'speech act theory', 'systemic functional linguistics', 'ethnography of communication', 'interactional sociolinguistics', 'contrastive rhetoric', and 'cognitive discourse analysis'.
(3) Other approaches that include 'multi- modal texts', 'multi- voiced texts', and 'intercultural communication'.

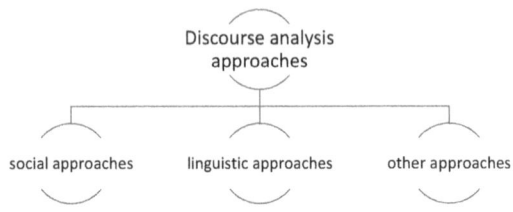

In this chapter, only 'conversation analysis' and 'critical discourse analysis' are discussed. Others, such as 'cohesion', 'pragmatics', 'appraisal', 'register', and 'cognitive discourse analysis' are discussed in different chapters of this book.

Connecting the dots (1): Conversation analysis and translation

Conversation analysis was developed out of a sociological approach to language and communication called 'ethnomethodology' in 1978 by Harold Garfinkel (for more details, see Hall et al. 2011: 87). As an approach to discourse analysis, conversation analysis focuses on "the organizational structure of spoken interaction" (Ibid.), thus studying such topics as:

(1) the speakers' decision when to speak, when not to speak, and how to speak (rules of turn-taking);
(2) the speakers' utterances and their degree of relatedness (adjacency pairs);
(3) the description of the structures used by the speakers in a particular conversation (preference organization or preference structure);
(4) the description of the structures used by the speakers and how they are related to social roles, status, politeness, intimacy, formality, etc.;
(5) conversational openings, pre-closings, and closings;
(6) discourse markers, fillers, feedback, repair, and response tokens (e.g. 'mmm', 'yeah', etc.).

What is meant by 'ethno-methodology'? Try to learn more about it.

Turn-taking is a mechanism by which speakers organize their own conversation where they try not to speak at the same time, but to speak one at a time in alternating turns (Drew and Heritage 1992: xxxiv). To take or give a turn to others, speakers use certain linguistic techniques, such as *'well'*, *'you've lost me'*, *'what do you think?'*, and *'right?'*) and non-linguistic techniques, such as facial expressions and postures.

Adjacency pairs used in a conversation (such as in the form of a greeting, question, offer, or suggestion) are exchanges consisting of two turns produced by two different speakers in a conversation. By opting for these adjacency pairs, speakers can organize their conversation in a way that would help them speak one at a time in alternating turns. Typical examples of adjacency pairs as mentioned by Thornbury and Slade (2006) include:

- greeting/greeting;
- question/answer;
- complaint/denial;
- offer/accept;
- request/grant;
- compliment/rejection;
- challenge/rejection;
- instruct/receipt.

In this regard, Cutting (2002/2008: 28–9) states that "the utterance of one speaker makes a certain response of the next speaker very likely". Utterances are then ordered into two parts: first part and second part and "categorized as a question-answer, offer-accept, blame-deny, and so on, with each first part creating an expectation of a particular second part". This is called a 'preference structure', i.e. "each first part has a preferred and a dispreferred response" (Ibid.). Consider the following example:

A: Did you call her last night? (A question that needs an answer)
B: No, I didn't. (An answer that does not require any further comment, but A can comment)
A: Why? (A question that needs an answer)
B: I couldn't. (An answer that does not require any further comment, but A can comment)
A: Is she still in London? (A question that requires an answer).
B: Yes, she'll travel next week. (This adjacency pair in the form of a question with a preferred response of an answer functions as a pre-suggestion).
A: Why don't you go to her and say sorry? She's a nice girl. (A suggestion that needs either an acceptance or rejection)
B: You really think so? (An indirect acceptance)

How would you translate words like *'well'*, *'you've lost me'*, etc. used by speakers to take a turn in a conversation?

Think of examples of these adjacency pairs in your language.

How would you define 'preference structure'?

Can *'Could you sign here, please?'* be considered a question that requires an answer?

Translate this conversation into your own language functionally.

How would you define 'expansion' in the sense that Schegloff (2007) uses the term?

The adjacency pair in the form of a question *'Is she still in London?'* with a preferred response of an answer *'Yes, she'll travel next week'* is inserted in the conversation to "prepare the ground for a further sequence" (Cutting 2002/2008: 29). A 'sequence' is defined by Schegloff (2007: 3) as a "course of action implemented through talk". In the above example, one of the speakers opts for asking a question and the other speaker decides to cooperate by resorting to what is called a preferred response of an answer. Such a sequence is called a 'pre-expansion', or more accurately a 'pre-suggestion' as it prepares the ground for an adjacency pair in the form of a suggestion-acceptance/rejection. Schegloff (2007) mentions three types of expansion, namely (1) 'pre-expansion', (2) 'insert-expansion', and (3) 'post-expansion', as in the following example:

Pre-expansion	Insert-expansion	Post-expansion
A: Do you have classes today? **B: No, I don't. How can I help you?**	A: Do you know there is a football match between Oman and Kuwait tonight? B: Yes, my close friend told me.	A: Would you like a piece of cake? B: No thanks, I'm ok
A: Could you please invigilate my exam? B: With pleasure. A: I don't know what to say. B: It's nothing.	A: Would you like to go with me? **B: What time does it start?** **A: 7:30 p.m.** B: That's great.	**A: I made it myself.** **B: Oh, really, then I must taste it.**

Do you agree with this claim? Discuss.

As far as translation is concerned, turn-taking along with the adjacency pairs used is usually maintained when translating a conversation from language *A* to language *B*. However, translators and interpreters may face a problem while rendering a conversation that contains several discourse markers. In any language, there are many markers or "language signals that can be used by speakers or writers like traffic signs to 'signpost', or guide listeners or readers through a text" (Almanna 2018: 297). These discourse markers can be 'formal', used in both spoken and written texts, such as *'actually'*, *'in fact'*, *'to elaborate'*, *'in other words'*, and *'to explain'*, or 'informal', used in spoken texts, such as *'well'*, *'you know'*, *'a kind of'*, *'a sort of'*, *'but anyway'*, and *'oh'*. In her book *Discourse Markers in Native and Non-Native English Discourse*, Müller (2005) talks of the main reasons behind using discourse markers. They can be summarized as follows:

Is there any difficulty in translating these discourse markers into your own language? Reflect on this.

- to initiate discourse (*'ok'*, *'now'*, etc.);
- to close discourse (*'ok'*, *'right'*, etc.);
- to hold the floor (*'um'*, *'eh'*, *'anyhow'*, *'anyway'*, etc.);

- to take the floor (*'hold on are you saying ...?'*, *'okay so, you mean that ...'*, *'by the way'*, *'but'*, *'well'*, *'true'*, *'well'*, *'to be honest with you'*, etc.);
- to shift the focus of attention to another topic (*'okay'*, *'well'*, *'now'*, etc.);
- to be used as fillers (*'you know'*, etc.);
- to be used as backchannels (*'oh, really?'*, *'were they?'*, etc.);
- to be used as delaying tactics (*'well'*, *'you know'*, etc.);
- to be used to avoid pausing (*'let me check'*, *'where's it?'*, *'one second'*, etc.);
- to repair discourse (*'I mean'*, etc.);
- to get the speaker involved in the topic (*'right?'*, etc.);
- to seek confirmation (*'right?'*, *'okay?'*, etc.);
- to refer to other ideas discussed earlier (*'as I told you'*, etc.);
- to sound intelligent and informed (*'you know'*, etc.);
- to indicate reactions or show interest (*'oh really'*, *'oh my God'*, *'oh yeah?'*, *'uh-huh'*, *'really?'*, *'really'*, *'that's great'*, *'I see'*, *'sounds nice'*, *'seriously?'*, *'you must be joking'*, *'you're kidding'*, *'no way!'*, etc.);
- to indicate you agree (*'that's right'*, *'I couldn't agree more'*, *'for sure'*, *'absolutely'*, etc.);
- to indicate you disagree (*'I'm not so sure about that'*, *'you really think so?'*, *'I don't see it that way'*, etc.);
- to indicate you didn't get it (*'you've lost me'*, *'sorry'*, *'I didn't catch you'*, etc.);
- to indicate you understood (*'okay'*, *'I see'*, etc.);
- to indicate the language user's attitude towards a proposition.

> Think of other reasons behind the use of these discourse markers?

> Try to translate these discourse markers from English into your own language. Is there any difficulty?

In the following exchange adapted from Salinger's *The Catcher in the Rye* (1951: 60) and translated by Karimi (2002, cited in Saffari and Hashemian 2012: 75) into Persian, the filler *'the hell'* is used to indicate that the language user is not happy with what is going on.

English	What the hell are you doing?
	Nothing
Farsi	خوب، داری چکار میکنی؟
	هیچی
Back translation	Well, what are you doing?
	Nothing.

> How would you translate the filler *'hell'* into your own language? Identify the main strategies that you may adopt.

This exchange consists of two turns produced by two interlocutors in a conversation where the second utterance *'Nothing'* depends on the first one *'What the hell are you doing?'*. In other words, the second utterance is a response to the first one; therefore, they form what is called an adjacency pair. Translating this adjacency pair into Persian, as shown in the example, is no problem at all. However, the suggested translation does not

> How would you define 'translation brief'?

communicate the intended meaning behind the original sentence whose interlocutor, by the effect of the filler *'the hell'*, clearly expresses his/her unhappiness or disgust. The translation brief given to the translator (purpose of translation, text type, genre, readership, etc.) can sometimes cause the translator to opt for omission as a local strategy, as in the above translation into Persian where Karimi decided to omit the filler in his translation. Omitting such a filler without any sort of compensation that would reflect the language user's attitude in the target text affects the quality of translation in terms of accuracy. Another strategy is to change the degree of formality, thus modifying the register, as in the following translation where Arabic is very formal to the degree that it is hardly used between friends or family members.

Arabic	ماذا تفعل بحق الجحيم؟
	لا شيء.
Back translation	What the hell are you doing?
	Nothing.

To maintain the degree of formality, one may opt for a functional translation as in the following translation suggested by a colleague:

Arabic	لخاطر الله، ماذا تفعل؟
	لا شيء.
Back translation	For the sake of God, what are you doing?
	Nothing.

Translating such a filler in a similar situation from English to French or German, for instance, causes no problem, as it lends itself to a sentence of the following kind where the language user's attitude is reflected easily by virtue of what is called the 'optimal equivalent':

'Optimal equivalent' or 'full equivalent' means the same image, function, and form are used in both languages/ cultures, as in the translation of *'Necessity is the mother of invention'* into French as *'La nécessité est la mère de l'invention'*.

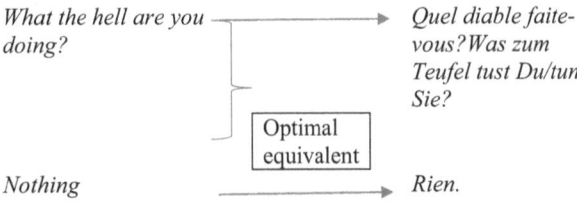

What the hell are you doing? → Quel diable faitevous? Was zum Teufel tust Du/tun Sie?

Optimal equivalent

Nothing → Rien.

Connecting the dots (2): Critical discourse analysis and translation

Critical discourse analysis is an interdisciplinary approach concerned with how 'power' is exercised through language. It is defined by Coffin (2001: 99) as an "approach to language analysis which concerns itself with issues of language, power and ideology". It "gives attention to the dynamic interplay between text production, the text itself, and text interpretation or consumption" (Coffin 2001: 99). Critical discourse analysis is "a type of discourse analytical research that primarily studies the way social power abuse, dominance, and inequality are enacted, reproduced, and resisted by text and talk in the social and political context" (van Dijk 2001: 352). Critical discourse analysts take an explicit position with a view to understanding, exposing, and, accordingly, challenging social inequality.

Critical discourse analysis relies heavily on (1) Halliday's systemic functional linguistics and (2) critical linguistics, as shown below:

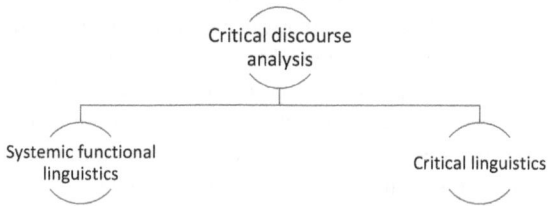

It is an approach to discourse analysis, which, through close linguistic analysis, aims at highlighting and/or demystifying any ideological move that would twist the message to varying degrees, thus producing 'realities' differently. In this respect, Hart (2013: 404), advocating Fowler (1991, 1996), holds that the "prevailing methodology in critical linguistics is sourced from Halliday's systemic functional grammar".

Fairclough and Wodak (1997: 271– 80; also discussed in Paltridge 2006: 179) talk of four main areas and/ or topics that can be studied and examined by doing critical discourse analysis:

(1) Social and political issues: How certain social and political issues are constructed and presented in discourse, how these issues are approached, and from which perspective, etc.
(2) Power relations: Who controls the conversation? Who allows whom to take part in a conversation? etc.
(3) Social relations: How people are presented in the media, and how such a representation establishes a certain relationship between the person and the public or the addressed people.
(4) Ideologies: How ideologies are reflected in discourse, how realities are presented differently, and how the same act may be praised by some people while it is denounced by others, etc.

Not only does critical discourse analysis cover "the description and interpretation of the discourse in context", but it tries to provide us with explanations for the main reasons behind it as well (Paltridge 2006: 185). To do so, analysts can study discourse critically by focusing on:

How would you define the term 'ideology'?

Find out the main differences between 'systemic functional linguistics' and 'critical linguistics'.

Think of other areas that can be examined by doing 'critical discourse analysis'.

(1) the text to discover (a) what genre (discourse type) the text at hand belongs to, (b) how the text producer adheres to the generic conversions, and (c) if not, what effect s/he is trying to achieve;
(2) the perspective from which the text is presented;
(3) the background knowledge, attitude, point of view, etc. that the text presupposes, reflects, and constructs.

Critical discourse analysis does not confine itself to analyse certain words or structures used by the text producer, but rather relates these words and structures to structures of the socio-political context. Several grammatical categories constituting systemic functional grammar can be used to analyse discourse critically. These grammatical categories include 'transitivity', 'agency', 'nominalization', 'modality', 'attribution', 'topicalization', 'selectivity', and 'presupposition'. In translation studies, these grammatical categories can also be used to explore how texts are manipulated by translators and trans-editors to superimpose a certain directionality/narrativity on the text/story at hand, particularly in the media.

> Narrativity here is defined as the directionality that you, as a language user, superimpose on the text/story at hand.

Transitivity

> Note that 'transitivity' in the sense that Halliday uses the term has nothing to do with 'transitive' and 'intransitive' verbs.

Transitivity is defined by Halliday (1976: 199) from a functional point of view as "the set of options relating to cognitive content, the linguistic representation of extralinguistic experience, whether of the phenomena of the external world or of feelings, thoughts and perceptions". In transitivity, several processes can be identified, such as a process of doing, a process of happening, a process of behaving, a process of saying, a process of sensing, a process of existing, a process of having, and a process of being. In analysing these processes, one can distinguish three main components, namely 'the process' itself typically expressed by verbs, 'participants' typically expressed by noun phrases, and 'circumstances' typically expressed by adverbs (for more details, see Chapter 9 of this book). Let us here consider the following example extracted from *The Independent* (22 September 2013; also discussed in Aslani and Salmani 2015: 85) along with its translation into Persian published in *Keyhan* (23 September 2013):

> Identify the processes in the following example and then translate it into your own language:
> 'When I was young, I used to watch TV a lot'.

English	The Syrians have long claimed that a substantial amount of Soviet-made weaponry has made its way from Libya into the hands of rebels in the country's civil war with the help of Qatar.
Persian	بسیاری از تروریست‌های سوری اعتراف کرده‌اند با کمک قطر مقادیر زیادی تسلیحات نظامی از لیبی دریافت کرده‌اند که ساخت اتحاد جماهیر شوروی سابق بوده است.
Back translation	Many Syrian terrorists have admitted that they have received a substantial amount of Soviet-made weaponry from Libya with the help of Qatar.

Here we are dealing with a process of saying expressed by the verb *'to claim'*. The Sayer in the English version is all Syrians (*The Syrians have long claimed ...*) while in the Persian version the Sayer is 'many Syrian terrorists' (*Many Syrian terrorists have admitted ...*). By virtue of the content specifications and grammatical forms used in the English version, the role of some countries, such as Qatar and Libya, in the civil war in Syria is emphasized, thereby hiding or backgrounding the role played by the Syrian government in such a civil war.

Moreover, in the English version, the Receiver of the weapons is the rebels according to the Syrians, while in the Persian version the Receiver of the weapons is Syrian terrorists according to the translator or trans-editor who describes them as terrorists.

Further, in the English version, by virtue of the framing verb *'to claim'*, the editor distances him/herself from the attributed material. However, by means of the framing verb *'to admit'* used in the Persian version, there is no explicit or overt indication as to where the translator or trans-editor stands concerning the attributed material. This textual restructuring shows how the translator or trans-editor overtly intervenes in the text to insist upon the value of the proposition that those fighters are terrorists who received a substantial amount of Soviet-made weaponry from Libya with the help of Qatar. This textual restructuring superimposes a certain directionality/ narrativity on the text/story at hand to have it meet the translator's (or the organization's) accumulated value system, sense of belonging, orientation, commitments, and so on.

Agency

Agency refers to whether the Agent or Actor of the action is mentioned or suppressed in the text. To observe how removing the Agent of the action can twist the message to varying degrees, the following headlines published by *BBC News* (23 October 2017; also discussed in Almanna and Al-Shehari 2019: 127) can be reconsidered:

Is there any difference between 'Agent' and 'Actor' as semantic roles?

English	Russian radio presenter Felgengauer [Patient] stabbed in neck
Arabic	إسرائيلي [Agent] يطعن مذيعة روسية [Patient] داخل غرفة أخبار محطة إذاعة إيكو موسكوفي.
Back translation	An Israeli stabs a Russian newsreader in the newsroom of Echo Moscovy radio station.

By virtue of the passive voice employed by the *BBC* in the English version, the focus of attention is shifted towards Felgengauer, i.e. the stabbed person filling the role of Patient (also called 'Affected Participant'; for more details on semantic roles, see the previous chapter). By doing so, the focus of attention is shifted away from the Agent. In the Arabic version, however, by the effect of the active voice, the focus of attention is shifted towards the Agent. To create distance and hostility towards the Agent, the Arabic version resorts to explicitly naming the nationality of the Agent, thus touching on the feelings of the Arabs. As regards informativeness, the English version provides us with less information as we no longer have an indication about the Agent/Killer in the process of doing expressed by the verb 'to stab'.

Nominalization

Comment on the differences between 'I breathed deeply' and 'I took a deep breath', before translating them into your language.

Do you agree with Kress and Hodge (1979) that any transformation serves two functions, namely 'economy' or 'distortion'?

Nominalization is the process of converting a verb or another part of speech into a noun, thereby transforming actions or events typically expressed by verbs or descriptions of nouns and pronouns typically expressed by adjectives into concepts, things, or people typically expressed by nouns. According to Kress and Hodge (1979: 9), any transformation – a term borrowed by them from Chomsky but used differently – contains distortion. They argue that transformations "serve two functions, economy and distortion" (Kress and Hodge 1979: 9). If this transformation serves distortion, then it is ideological. Juznic, following Halliday and Matthiessen (2004: 636), writes that nominalization can be considered as "a type of grammatical metaphor whereby processes which are congruently realized by verbs are metaphorically realized by nouns expressing the same process as those verbs" (2012: 251). On this subject, Fowler (1991: 80) comments that nominalization can be used by language users (writers, speakers, translators, trans-editors, etc.) as a strategy to hide or suppress the Agent, thus offering prime sites where ideologies can be expressed. By way of example, the following headlines in both English and Arabic taken from *BBC News* (7 April 2012; also discussed in Fattah 2020: 121) can be considered:

English	Hamas hangs Gaza prisoners, including one 'collaborator'.
Arabic	إعدام ثلاثة مدانين بقطاع غزة، أحدهم بتهمة التخابر مع إسرائيل.
Back translation	The execution of three convicts in the Gaza Strip, one convicted with collaborating with Israel.

Here, a simple comparison between the two versions shows that the Agent of the process of doing expressed by the verb 'to hang' in English is suppressed in the Arabic version, where a nominal group without an Agent is recruited. On this subject, Fattah (2020: 121) comments that the execution here is "represented as the outcome of a normal judicial process where the accused were charged, convicted and then executed by some competent authorities that are not normally newsworthy in a news headline".

Modality

Modality refers to how language users can express their own attitudes, opinions, or moods towards what happens in the world or towards the truth of an utterance. Paying little or no attention to the modal verb or modalized particle used in the original text and translating it inaccurately on purpose or by accident may well twist the message to varying degrees. To make this point clear, let us here discuss the following examples quoted from Barnes (2014: 31):

English	But if she could have looked a little further back, into the stillness and the darkness before Time dawned, she would have read there a different incantation.
French	Mais si elle avait pu voir un peu plus loin, dans le silence et l'obscurité qui précédèrent la nuit des temps, elle aurait lu là une incantation différente.
Back translation	But if she had been able to see a little further, in the silence and darkness that preceded the dawn of time, she would have read a different incantation there.

In some languages, such as Arabic, 'modality' covers (1) 'modalized verbs', (2) 'modalized prepositions', (3) 'modalized particles', and (4) 'modalized prepositional phrases'. What about your own language?

In this example, the instance of lost opportunities is expressed by *'could have'* followed by a past participle; it is used twice in English. Being fully aware of the use and function of such modals, the translator opted for *'avait pu'* and *'aurait lu'*, thereby reflecting such a lost opportunity which presupposes that the addressee is characterized by being-able-not-to-do (powerlessness).

To reflect this lost opportunity in German, one may opt for a translation of the following kind:

German	Aber wenn sie ein wenig weiter hätte schauen können, in die Stille und die Dunkelheit bevor der Morgen dämmert, dann hätte sie hier eine andere Beschwörung gelesen.
Back translation	But if she had been able to look a little further, into the silence and the darkness before the morning dawned, she would have read there another incantation.

In the following example quoted from Farghal (2008: 11), there is an example of reproducing the 'reality' differently:

English	The Head of the International Investigation Commission in the assassination of the Lebanese former Prime Minister Rafiq Al-Hariri said that some Syrian officials may have been involved in this crime.
Arabic	قال رئيس لجنة التحقيق الدولية في اغتيال رئيس الوزراء اللبناني السابق رفيق الحريري إن بعض المسئولين السوريين متورطون في هذه الجريمة.
Back translation	The Head of the International Investigation Commission in the assassination of the Lebanese former Prime Minister Rafiq Al-Hariri said that some Syrian officials are involved in this crime.

Comment on the differences between these three sentences (1) *'He said that he would send me an email'*, (2) *'He confirmed that he would send me an email'*, and (3) *'He claimed that he would send me an email'*.

Here, the translator managed to handle the source text, apart from dealing with the modal verb *'may'*. The whole meaning is manipulated by the effect of not translating this tiny word *'may'*. The use of *'may'* to express possibility in the original text excludes the event from known reality, thus being considered as part of irreality – it invokes in our minds a *not-sure-frame*. In the target text, however, by means of the content specification and grammatical form employed, the possible Syrian involvement becomes an absolute certainty, thus being part of reality.

Attribution

Attribution refers to the process of opening up space for other voices to be heard in the text; this can be achieved by virtue of certain framing verbs, such as *'to say'*, *'to claim'*, and *'to argue'*, certain angle circumstances, such as *'according to'*, *'in the words of'*, *'in the opinion of'*, and *'in the view of'* (for more details, see Chapter 9 of this book). In the following example quoted along with its translation into French from Barnes (2014: 38), there is an example of attribution.

English	"It is a lovely place, my house," said the Queen. "I am sure you would like it".
French	C'est un endroit ravissant, ma maison, poursuivit la reine. Je suis certaine que vous l'aimerez.
Back translation	"It is a lovely place, my home," continued the queen. "I'm sure you'll like it".

In the above example, there is no explicit or overt indication as to where the speaker stands concerning the attributed material. This attitude, i.e. the speaker's particular stance (acknowledgement) towards the proposition, was reflected by the translator when opting for the verb *'poursuivit'*, roughly meaning *'to continue'*. In the following example quoted from Farghal (2008: 4), the acknowledgement expressed by the verb *'to say'* in the past was translated as an example of distancing:

ST (English)	In an interview with Newsweek yesterday, the Israeli Defense Minister said that the Palestinian suicide operations constitute the main cause for the Israeli troops entering cities in the West Bank.
TT (Arabic)	ادعى وزير الحرب الصهيوني في مقابلة مع مجلة النيوزويك أمس أن العمليات الاستشهادية الفلسطينية هي السبب الرئيس في اجتياح قوات الاحتلال الإسرائيلي للمدن الفلسطينية في الضفة الغربية المحتلة.
Back translation	In an interview with the Newsweek yesterday, the Zionist War Minister claimed that the Palestinian martyrdom operations are the main cause for the Zionist troops storming Palestinian cities in the occupied West Bank.

Here, by the effect of translating the neutral verb *'to say'* into ادعى *'to claim'*, the language user's attitude towards the attributed materials was completely changed. In the target text, by virtue of the framing verb ادعى *'to claim'*, we have an example of distancing where the speaker was presented as distancing him/herself from the attributed material. Not only was this framing verb translated inaccurately, but several words and expressions (as shown below) were manipulated through this 'attitudinal translation' to have them meet the translator's (the translator here refers to all those involved in the process of translation at its macro level, such as reviser, editor, proofreader, translation quality controller, translation manager, and translation commissioner) accumulated value system, orientation, commitment, sense of belonging, and so on.

How would you define 'attitudinal translation'?

ST	TT	Back translation
Israeli Defense Minister	وزير الحرب الصهيوني	Zionist War Minister
suicide operations	العمليات الاستشهادية	martyrdom operations
Israeli troops	قوات الاحتلال الإسرائيلي	Zionist troops
entering	اجتياح	storming
cities	المدن الفلسطينية	Palestinian cities
West Bank	الضفة الغربية المحتلة	occupied West Bank

These selections are ideologically significant ideational ones as they manipulate the language user's attitude towards the proposition. While translating a sensitive text loaded with political or religious words and expressions, two strategies, which are closely related to lexical choices, rear their ugly heads: 'name-calling' and 'counter-naming'. Name-calling involves the use of offensive names and phrases as in the use of *'regime'* in place of *'government'*. Counter-naming, by contrast, refers to how the euphemized word or phrase is depreciated, as in *'Zionist War Minister'* in place of the euphemized phrase *'Israeli Defense Minister'*.

Find more examples of 'name-calling' and 'counter-naming'

Topicalization

Topicalization refers to the process of ordering words in a clause or sentence, thus laying more emphasis on some of them. To explain, let us discuss the word order of this simple sentence:

Translate this sentence into your own language twice without changing the semantic roles.

The man was killed by the police yesterday morning.

This sentence can be syntactically reordered in a variety of different ways without changing the semantic roles assigned to each noun phrase, as shown here:

- The police killed the man yesterday morning.
- Yesterday morning, the man was killed by the police.
- Yesterday morning, the police killed the man.

- It is ^{the police} who killed the man yesterday.
- It is ^{the man} who was killed by the police yesterday.

This sentence can lend itself to such translations, but these are just illustrative examples as one may come up with other versions:

Arabic	قتلت الشّرطةُ الرّجلَ أمس صباحًا.
Back translation	The police killed the man yesterday morning.
German	Die Polizei tötete den Mann gestern morgen.
Back translation	The police killed the man yesterday morning.
French	La police a tué l'homme hier matin.
Back translation	The police killed the man yesterday morning.
Maltese	Ir-raġel inqatel mill-pulizija lbieraħ filgħodu.
Back translation	The man was killed by the police yesterday morning.
Thai	เช้าวานนี้ ตำรวจฆ่าคนตาย / chao wanni, tamruat kha khon tay.
Back translation	Yesterday morning, the police killed the man.
Turkish	Polis dün sabah adamı öldürdü.
Back translation	The police yesterday morning killed the man.
Persian	پلیس این مرد را دیروز صبح کشت.
Back translation	The police killed this man yesterday morning.

Do you agree with this claim?

While translating between any language pair, translators need to consider the order of words along with the emphasis that each word carries and what order the target language prefers in a given genre, text type, and so on. In translating the complex sentence quoted from Hervey et al. (2006: 159) from English into German, for example, the translator may opt for TT1 or TT2 depending on the translation brief and the order that the target language prefers.

ST	What annoys me most is that they never even say hello.
TT1	Was mich am meisten ärgert, ist, dass sie niemals grüßen.
Back translation	What annoys me most is that they never greet.
TT2	Am meisten ärgert mich, dass sie niemals grüßen.
Back translation	Most annoying to me is that they never greet.

Here, although TT1 is very close to the English sentence that employs a 'pseudo-cleft' structure (also known as a 'wh-cleft' structure), native speakers of German would rather opt for a syntactically simpler structure, as in TT2.

The above occurs at the sentence level. While translating or trans-editing a text, due to the differences between the interfacing languages/cultures as well as the conventions of each communicative event, several examples of re-segmentation can take place. These instances of re-segmentation include, for example, reordering the clauses and sentences, breaking up sentences, joining sentences, and re-paragraphing. This results in emphasizing what is not emphasized in the original text and de-emphasizing what is emphasized therein. However, at other times, emphasizing, as opposed to de-emphasizing, is employed by those involved in the process of translation to superimpose a certain directionality/narrativity on the text at hand, thus promoting or elaborating a different narrative/story/product. To make this point clear, let us consider these two *Reuters News* items touching on the same topic (one in English and the other in Arabic; 7 April 2015):

> Following Somers and Gibson (1994), a narrative can be defined as a story of a set of events ordered in sequence, both spatially and temporally.

English	The United States is speeding up arms supplies and bolstering intelligence sharing with a Saudi-led alliance bombing a militia aligned with Iran in neighboring Yemen, a senior U.S. diplomat said on Tuesday.
Arabic	قال أنتوني بلينكين نائب وزير الخارجية الأمريكي يوم الثلاثاء إن الولايات المتحدة تعجل بإمدادات الأسلحة للتحالف الذي تقوده السعودية ضد المقاتلين الحوثيين المعارضين للرئيس اليمني عبد ربه منصور هادي.
Back translation	Anthony Blinken, the U.S. Deputy Secretary of State, said on Tuesday that the United States was expediting arms supplies to the Saudi-led coalition against Houthi fighters opposed to Yemeni President Abed Rabbo Mansour Hadi.

Here, a process of saying expressed by the verb *'to say'* in the past is used in both versions. Due to the differences between the interfacing languages, the verb قال *'to say'* is placed at the beginning of the sentence. However, the speaker in the verbal process is clearly identified in the Arabic version as أنتوني بلينكن *'Antony Blinken'* while it is left implicit in the English version, *'a senior U.S. diplomat'*. Not only this, but the tension between the two countries (Saudi Arabia and Iran) is explicitly expressed by *Reuters* in its English version while it is reduced in its Arabic version. In the phrase *'a militia aligned with Iran'*, for instance, the word *'Iran'* in the English version is given a front seat while in the Arabic version the word is backgrounded in attention. Such reordering, along with some additions and omissions, promotes a slightly different narrative.

> The term *'frame'* can be defined as a conceptual structure that provides background on beliefs, assumptions, and practices against which the meaning of a word can be understood.

Selectivity and presupposition

Selectivity refers here to the process of selecting a lexical item or expression that is profiled in a given frame where it contrasts with other semantically related words and expressions. Language users (writers, speakers, translators, trans-editors, etc.) carefully select their own words with the potential to persuade their readers and cause them to (dis)believe in what they (dis)believe. To make this point clear, let us consider the following example taken from *BBC News* (2 December 2015) and translated into Arabic and German:

English	One of the workers died at the scene, while the other was rushed to a nearby hospital where he succumbed to his injuries. Their two colleagues were unharmed.
Arabic	وقتل أحد المستخدمين فورا فيما نقل الآخر إلى مستشفى محلي حيث فارق الحياة. ولم يصب الموظفان الآخران في الحادث.
Back translation	And one of the workers was killed immediately, while the other one was taken to a local hospital, where he died. The other two employees were not injured in the accident.
German	Einer der Arbeiter starb noch vor Ort, während der andere in ein nahe gelegenes Krankenhaus gebracht wurde, wo er seinen Verletzungen erlag. Ihre beiden Kollegen blieben unverletzt.
Back translation	One of the workers died at the scene, while the other was taken to a nearby hospital where he succumbed to his injuries. Their two colleagues remained unharmed.

Here, as one may notice, in English, a process of happening expressed by the verb *'to die'* is used. While this process was translated into Arabic as a process of doing expressed by قتل *'to kill'*, it was translated into German as a process of happening expressed by the verb *'sterben'*, i.e. *'to die'*. It is worth noting that each verb used here has a certain profile in a given semantic frame. The verb *'to die'* is profiled in a frame where it contrasts with the verb *'to kill'*. While the verb *'to die'* is characterized by having a monadic personation type, i.e. it requires only one participant, the verb *'to kill'* is characterized by having a dyadic personation type, i.e. it requires at least two participants: 'Agent' and 'Patient'. The verb *'to die'*, to elaborate, invokes in our minds an *accident*-frame that has nothing to do with issues such as the intention to cause death to somebody. On the contrary, by resorting to the verb *'to kill'*, a *killing*-frame is activated that has something to do with issues such as the intention to cause somebody to die (causativity) – flow of energy from the Agent to the Patient (transitivity). In the Arabic version, by virtue of the lexical item فورا, i.e. *'immediately'*, the pace of events is sped up, thus indicating that there is no time lapse between the act of shooting, backgrounded in attention but it can be predicted as it is in our scope of attention, and passing away, foregrounded in attention.

Presupposition refers to "an implicit assumption about the world or background belief relating to an utterance whose truth is taken for granted in discourse" (Farghal and Almanna 2015: 104). The following example extracted from *The Independent* (22 September 2013; also discussed in Aslani and Salmani 2015: 84) along with its translation into Persian published in Keyhan (23 September 2013) can be considered here:

English	Assad had a message for the American people that they should not get involved in another Middle Eastern conflict.
Persian	اسد خطاب به مقامات آمریکایی تأکید کرد، پیام من به آمریکایی‌ها این است که ورود به هرگونه جنگ و درگیری در خاورمیانه تجربه خوبی برای آنها نیست.
Back translation	Assad said to American officials, "My message to Americans is that entering any kind of war and conflict in the Middle East is not a good experience for them".

Here, by means of the content specification and grammatical form utilized by the translator, the intended meaning is manipulated: The use of the lexical item *'another'* presupposes that they had already got involved in a conflict, or maybe more than one conflict, in the Middle East, but this presupposition cannot be retrieved from the Persian translation. Further, while the addressee in the original text is *'American people'*, the addressee in the target text is مقامات امریکایی, i.e. *'American officials'*. This presupposes that Assad's message is serious, on the one hand, and on the other hand, that Syria will not be an easy prey, but it will fight fiercely, and that America will suffer the disastrous sequences of such a conflict against Syria.

Presuppositions are "background assumptions that are pegged to certain lexical items or structures which are called presupposition-triggers (e.g. definite expressions, iteratives, cleft structures, etc.)" (Farghal and Almanna 2015: 104–5). When one of these presupposition-triggers is used in the original text, the presupposition can be easily captured. Consider the following example translated from Arabic into English by Husni and Newman (2008: 85–6):

ST	عاد من جديد يسترق النظر إليها عله يجد شيئاً في ملامحها يضيء ما اعتراه من حيرة وذهول.
Back translation	He began sneaking looks at her, hoping to find something in her features that [would] illuminate the bewilderment and astonishment that he had experienced.
TT	Once again he glanced over at her, and noticed something in her features that shed light on what had baffled him.

Here, the experienced Arabic translator understood that the in-text participant was looking at her, which is presupposed by the presupposition-trigger من جديد *'once again'*. This presupposition was reflected in the target text. However, the translators failed to deal with the clause of

Do you agree that there is an example of a shift in transitivity in the translation of this example as the process of having expressed by the verb *'to have'* a message was translated into a process of saying something? Does this have ideological implications? Discuss.

Identify the presupposition in these two sentences *'I used to smoke heavily'* and *'I'm looking for another job'*. Then translate the sentences into your own language.

purpose introduced by علّ meaning *'in the hope of'* when opting for the additive connector *'and'*. To explain, in the source text, it is not asserted that the in-text participant found something in her features; therefore, the scope of intention is greater than the extent of causation (see Chapter 12 for more details). In the TT, however, by opting for the additive connector *'and'*, the translators imposed different specifications on the scene, thereby emphasizing the completion of the act of noticing at a specific point in the past.

Let us finish off this section by discussing the translations of the following sentence taken from the beginning of Trump's Speech on Jerusalem (6 December 2017) to see how not paying extra attention to the existential presupposition employed by Trump may twist the message to varying degrees:

ST (English)	My announcement today marks the beginning of a new approach to conflict between Israel and the Palestinians.
TT1 (Arabic)	إن إعلاني اليوم يمثل بداية لنهج جديد تجاه الصراع بين الإسرائيليين والفلسطينيين.
Back translation	Indeed, my announcement today represents the beginning of a new approach to the conflict between the Israelis and Palestinians.
TT2 (German)	Meine heutige Ankündigung markiert den Beginn einer neuen Herangehensweise an den Konflikt zwischen Israel und den Palästinensern.
Back translation	My announcement today marks the beginning of a new approach to the conflict between Israel and the Palestinians.
TT3 (French)	Mon annonce d'aujourd'hui marque le début d'une nouvelle approche du conflit entre Israël et les Palestiniens.
Back translation	My announcement today marks the beginning of a new approach to the conflict between Israel and the Palestinians.
TT4 (Thai)	คำประกาศในวันนี้ของผม ถือเป็นจุดเริ่มต้นของแนวทางใหม่ต่อความขัดแย้งระหว่างชาวอิสราเอลกับปาเลสไตน์ / kham prakat nai wanni khongphom thuepen chutroemton khong naewthang mai to khwamkhatyaeng rawang chaw Isarael kap Palestine.
Back translation	My announcement today is accounted for the beginning of a new approach to the conflict between Israel and Palestinians.
TT5 (Persian)	اطلاعیه امروز من نشان‌دهنده آغاز رویکردی جدید به درگیری میان اسرائیل و فلسطینیان است.

What about if the translator identifies the presupposition, but decides not to reflect it in the target text? Can it be considered an example of an 'ideological move'? Discuss.

Translate this text into your own language. Then comment on your own translation by referring to the presupposition.

Back translation	My announcement today represents the beginning of a new approach to the conflict between Israel and Palestinians.

In the original text, the phrase *'Israel and the Palestinians'* presupposes that the conflict is between Israel as a state and the Palestinians as a group of people. This is an example of 'existential presupposition', typically expressed by a noun phrase that presupposes the existence of the entity named by the language user (Yule 1985/1996: 20). This presupposition, which was reflected in TT2 (German), TT3 (French), TT4 (Thai), and TT5 (Persian), cannot be retrieved in TT1 (Arabic). In TT1, Trump's attitude towards the above-mentioned conflict was manipulated by the translator, thus presenting both of them as two groups of people.

> In your own opinion, what motivates the Arabic translator to manipulate Trump's attitude towards the conflict?

Exercises and discussion

Exercise 1: Mark the following statements (T) if they are true and (F) if they are false.

(1) 'Sociolinguistics' is one of the social approaches to discourse analysis.	
(2) Adjacency pairs are exchanges consisting of two turns produced by two different speakers in a conversation.	
(3) *'Could you open the window?'* is a question that needs an answer.	
(4) According to Schegloff (2007), there are three types of 'expansion'. They are 'pre-expansion', 'insert-expansion', and 'post-expansion'.	
(5) 'Discourse analysis' is one of the branches of 'usage-based linguistics'.	
(6) One of the main reasons behind using 'discourse markers' is to change the topic.	
(7) Social relations, that is, how people are presented in media, for example, is one of the areas that can be examined by doing critical discourse analysis.	
(8) Discourse can be studied critically by focusing on, for example, the issues, attitudes, points of view, and background knowledge that the text presupposes, reflects, and constructs.	
(9) Transitivity according to Halliday (1976) refers to transitive and intransitive verbs.	
(10) Critical discourse analysis is an interdisciplinary approach concerned with how people exercise 'power' while using language.	

Exercise 2: The process of doing expressed by the verb *to kill* was translated differently from English into Arabic, as shown below. Comment on the translations by referring to issues such as 'transitivity', 'agency', 'topicalization', 'selectivity', and 'presupposition'.

ST	In breaking news by the French News Agency, dozens of Palestinian civilians were killed in an Israeli air attack on the Gaza Strip.
TT1	في خبر عاجل لوكالة الأنباء الفرنسية، **مات** عشرات الفلسطينيين المدنيين في هجوم جوي إسرائيلي على قطاع غزة.
Back translation	In breaking news by the French News Agency, tens of Palestinian civilians **died** in an Israeli air attack on the Gaza Strip.
TT2	في خبر عاجل لوكالة الأنباء الفرنسية، **قتل** عشرات الفلسطينيين المدنيين في هجوم جوي إسرائيلي على قطاع غزة.
Back translation	In breaking news by the French News Agency, tens of Palestinian civilians **were killed** in an Israeli air attack on the Gaza Strip.
TT3	في خبر عاجل لوكالة الأنباء الفرنسية، **استشهد** عشرات الفلسطينيين المدنيين في هجوم جوي إسرائيلي على قطاع غزة.
Back translation	In breaking news by the French News Agency, tens of Palestinian civilians **died as martyrs**, in an Israeli air attack on the Gaza Strip.

Exercise 3: Translate the following conversation between Mark and Allie into your own language. Then comment on your translation by touching on issues such as turn-taking, adjacency pairs and their forms, preferred and dispreferred responses, any examples of expansion along with their types, and the discourse markers used and their functions.

Allie: Thank you very much, Mark.
Mark: Ah, you're welcome. I'm really sorry for the coffee.
Allie: That's ok. It's late. I'll have a meeting at 12.30.
Mark: We can take a taxi.
Allie: Ok. Do you like the shirt?
Mark: Well, yeah. It's exactly the same as the other one.
Allie: The same? It's completely different.
Mark: Sorry.
Allie: Typical man.
Mark: Allie, can I ask you something?
Allie: Yeah, what?
Mark: Would you like to have dinner with me tonight?
Allie: Tonight?
Mark: Yes, you see, it's my birthday.
Allie: Oh. Happy Birthday! I'm sorry I can't have dinner tonight. I'm busy.
Mark: Oh ... How about Friday night?
Allie: Friday? Well. Ok.

> **Mark:** Do you know a good restaurant?
> **Allie:** Let me think. Do you like Italian food?
> **Mark:** I love it.
> **Allie:** Well, there is a new Italian restaurant. We can go there.
> **Mark:** Good idea. Taxi.

Exercise 4: Select any journalistic text and:

(a)   translate it into your own language;
(b)   comment on your translation by referring to such notions as 'transitivity', 'modality', and 'attribution'.

Discussion and research points

(1)   Select any conversation and analyse it by referring to:
    (a) turn-taking;
    (b) adjacency pairs and their forms;
    (c) preferred and dispreferred responses;
    (d) any examples of expansion along with their types;
    (e) the discourse markers used and their functions.

(2)   In their book titled *Language and Ideology*, Kress and Hodge (1979) hold the view that ideology cannot be separated from language since, by using language, people express their different viewpoints which emerge from their ideological backgrounds. Do you agree with this? Discuss.

(3)   Go through any translated book from English into your own language to identify examples of ideological moves.

(4)   Go through any translated book from your own language into English to identify examples of 'name-calling' and 'counter-naming'.

(5)   Select any English political text and translate it into your language. Then comment on your own translation by referring to such notions as 'agency', 'topicalization', 'selectivity', and 'presupposition'.

References

Aitchison, J. (1999/ 2003). *Linguistics* (6th edn). London: Teach Yourself.

Almanna, A. (2018). *The Nuts and Bolts of Arabic–English Translation: An Introduction to Applied Contrastive Linguistics*. Newcastle upon Tyne: Cambridge Scholars Publishing.

Almanna, A. and Al-Shehari, A. (2019). *The Arabic–English Translator as Photographer. A Linguistic Account*. London/New York: Routledge.

Aslani, M. and Salmani, B. (2015). "Ideology and Translation: A Critical Discourse Analysis Approach towards the Representation of Political News in Translation", *International Journal of Applied Linguistics & English Literature*, Vol. 4(3), pp. 80–8.

Barnes, M. (2014). "Ideology in Translation: CS Lewis': The Lion, the Witch and the Wardrobe". Unpublished MA thesis. Johannesburg: University of the Witwatersrand.

Coffin, C. (2001) "Theoretical Approaches to Written Language – A TESOL Perspective". In Burns, A. and Coffin, C. (eds.), *Analysing English in a Global Context: A Reader. Teaching English Language Worldwide* (pp. 93–122). London: Routledge.

Crystal, D. (1992). *Introducing Linguistics*. London: Penguin English.

Cutting, J. (2002). *Pragmatics and Discourse: A Resource Book for Students*. London: Routledge.

Drew, P. and Heritage, J. (eds.) (1992). *Talk at Work*. Cambridge: Cambridge University Press.

Fairclough, N. (1999). "Linguistic and Intertextual Analysis within Discourse Analysis". In Jaworski, A. and Coupland, N. (eds.), *The Discourse Reader* (pp. 183–211). London: Routledge.

Fairclough, N. (2006). *Language and Globalization*. London: Routledge

Fairclough, N. and Wodak, R. (1997). "Critical Discourse Analysis". In van Dijk, T. (ed.), *Discourse Studies: A Multidisciplinary Introduction* (Vol. 2, pp. 258–84). London: Sage.

Farghal, M. (2008). "Extrinsic Managing: An Epitaph to Translational Ideological Move", *STJ: Sayyab Translation Journal*, Vol. 1, pp. 1–26.

Farghal, M. and Almanna, A. (2015). *Contextualizing Translation Theories: Aspects of Arabic–English Interlingual Communication*. Newcastle upon Tyne: Cambridge Scholars Publishing.

Fattah, A. (2020). "Ideological and Evaluative Shifts in Media Translation/ Trans-editing". In Hanna, S., El-Farahaty, H., and Khalifa, A. (eds.), *The Routledge Handbook of Arabic Translation* (pp. 115–45). London/ New York: Routledge.

Fowler, R. (1991). *Language in the News: Discourse and Ideology in the Press*. London: Routledge.

Fowler, R., (1996). "On Critical Linguistics". In Caldas-Coulthard, C. R. and Coulthard, M. (eds.), *Texts and Practices: Reading in Critical Discourse Analysis* (pp. 3–14). London: Routledge.

Hall, C. J., Smith, P. H., and Wicaksono, R. (2011). *Mapping Applied Linguistics. A Guide for Students and Practitioners*. London/ New York: Routledge.

Halliday, M. A. K. (1976). "Notes on Transitivity and Theme in English. Part 2", *Journal of Linguistics*, Vol. 3(1), pp. 199–244.

Hart, C. (2013). "Event-Construal in Press Reports of Violence in Political Protests: A Cognitive Linguistic Approach to CDA", *Journal of Language and Politics*, Vol. 12(3), pp. 400–23.

Hervey, S., Loughridge, M., and Higgins, I. (2006). *Thinking German Translation. A Course in Translation Method: German to English*. London/New York: Routledge.

Husni, R. and Newman, D. (2008). *Modern Arabic Short Stories: A Bilingual Reader.* London: Saqi Books.

Juznic, T. M. (2012). "A Contrastive Study of Nominalization in the Systemic Functional Framework", *Languages in Contrast*, Vol. 12(2), pp. 251–76.

Kress, G. and Hodge, R. (1979). *Language as Ideology*. London: Routledge and Kegan Paul.

Müller, S. (2005). *Discourse Markers in Native and Non-native English Discourse*. Amsterdam: John Benjamins.

Paltridge, B. (2006). *Discourse Analysis: An Introduction*. London: Bloomsbury.

Saffari, M. and Hashemian, M. (2012). "A Study of Translation of Fillers and Catch Phrases in Two Persian Translations of The Catcher in the Rye", *Journal of Language, Culture, and Translation*, Vol. 1(2), pp. 69–80.

Salinger, J. D. (1951). *The Catcher in the Rye*. New York: Random House, Inc.

Schegloff, E. (2007). *Sequence Organization in Interaction: A Primer in Conversation Analysis I*. Cambridge: Cambridge University Press.

Thornbury, S. and Slade, D. (2006). *Conversation: From Description to Pedagogy*. Cambridge: Cambridge University Press.

Trump, D. J. (2017, December 6). *Statement by President Trump on Jerusalem*. Whitehouse.gov. Retrieved from www.whi teho use.gov/ briefings-statements/statementpresident-trump-jerusale

Van Dijk, T. A. (2001). "Critical Discourse Analysis". In Tannen, D., Schiffrin, D., and Hamilton, H. (eds.), *Handbook of Discourse Analysis* (pp. 352–71). Oxford: Blackwell.

Yule, G. (1985/ 1996). *The Study of Language*. Cambridge: Cambridge University Press.

Pragmatics

8

> This chapter introduces a branch of linguistics which is one of the most relevant fields for students and researchers of translation: pragmatics (for an overview of the relation between translation studies and pragmatics, see House 2018a). You will first be given a definition of pragmatics and a brief historical description of the development of this field. Then, you will learn about the main concepts in pragmatics: 'deixis', 'reference' and 'inference', 'conversational implicature', 'cooperative principle' and 'conversational maxims', 'speech acts', and 'cross-cultural pragmatics'.
>
> After you have studied this chapter, you should be able to understand what 'pragmatics' is and how its various components relate to each other, how people manage to understand one another, how what they say is often much more complex than meets the eye, how what is NOT said is often as relevant as what is actually uttered, what speech acts are and how they can be analysed, and how all these pragmatic areas vary across different cultures.

Outline the main differences among 'syntax', 'semantics', and 'pragmatics' according to Morris and Peirce.

In the 1930s, Charles Morris (1938) and Charles Peirce (1931–1958) developed the semiotic trichotomy, which suggests that 'syntax' deals with the formal relations of signs to one another, 'semantics' with the relation of signs to what they denote, and 'pragmatics' with the relation of signs to their users and interpreters. Another important development that led to the establishment of something like a pragmatic approach to linguistics dates back to the late 1960s and early 1970s, starting with the work by the generatively oriented linguists George Lakoff and John Robert Ross (1967). These linguists were among the first to recognize the limitation of the 'syntactic straitjacket' and generally the limits of the generative, 'pan-syntactic' approach – whereby all of linguistic science including phonology and semantics were to fit into a syntactic framework – when it came to explaining language in use by human beings.

DOI: 10.4324/9781003228028-9

A new model slowly emerged, which attacked the old paradigm with its exclusive emphasis on syntax and structure. We can say that a 'paradigm shift' emerged, and this shift coincided with increasing knowledge about languages other than English suggesting that certain phenomena could only be described by referring to contextual concepts. We here have the beginning of the 'pragmatic turn' from the paradigm of theoretical grammar – especially syntax – to the paradigm of the language user, broadening linguistics to a discipline that caters for meaning and context as well as the way people actually use language. To invoke Chomsky's distinction between 'competence' and 'performance' (e.g. Chomsky 1965), pragmatics is clearly concerned with performance principles of language use. It is a theory of language understanding that takes context into account in order to complement the contribution that semantics and syntax can make to meaning. This implies that – contrary to Chomsky's assumptions – language structure may not be independent of the uses to which it is put. In other words, it may be possible to explain linguistic phenomena functionally, i.e. with reference to pragmatic principles and external factors such as speakers, listeners, and topics.

> What is the difference between 'competence' and 'performance' according to Chomsky?

In a famous paper entitled 'Out of the pragmatic wastebasket', Yehoshua Bar-Hillel (1971) complains that scholars who ignored the nature of certain linguistic problems tried to force bits and pieces found in the 'pragmatic wastebasket' into their syntactic or semantic theories. The notion 'pragmatic wastebasket' has to date often been quoted to refer to problems defying satisfactory syntactic and/or semantic analysis and explanation.

> How would you define 'pragmatic wastebasket'?

Apart from this origin of pragmatics, constituting a rebellion against Chomskyan linguistics, another probably even more important influence from the early 1960s onwards came from linguistic philosophers (the so-called 'Ordinary Language Philosophers') such as Austin (1962), Searle (1969), and Grice (1975). Their ideas about the phenomenon of language have had a lasting impact on the development of the new discipline of pragmatics. In 1962, Austin's book *How to Do Things with Words* was published – a book about how people communicate with each other by means of language that shaped further developments of the new discipline of pragmatics. We will deal more extensively with Austin's influence in the section on 'speech acts' below.

Context and contextual meaning

Pragmatics is the study of meaning as this meaning is communicated by a speaker (or writer) to an addressee, and how this addressee interprets this meaning. Pragmatics deals more with what human beings mean when they use language than what the words, phrases, utterances, or texts mean on their own. In pragmatics we are not only interested in what people mean in an abstract sense, but rather what they mean in a particular context, and how this context impacts on what is said. This means that we have to consider the context if we want to grasp what people mean, and

> What is meant by 'context'? And how would you define 'contextual meaning'?

What is *not* said in *'That's great'* in this exchange:
Son: *'I lost my money.'*
Father: *'That's great.'*

The meaning of the sentence *'Do you know what time it is?* varies according to the context in which it is uttered. Think of different situations to yield as many meanings as you can.

this involves looking at how speakers organize and structure what they intend to say, considering who they address, and where, when, and under which circumstances they say what they say. In short, pragmatics is the study of 'contextual meaning'. Since context involves the addressees of an utterance, pragmatics also involves looking at how addressees make inferences about what is said, so that they will be able to interpret what the speaker has intended to say. This interpretation necessarily also touches upon how things 'not' said may be as important as what is actually said. This means that pragmatics involves exploring how more is frequently said than what is actually uttered. In pragmatics, we focus on people's intended meanings, their assumptions, their purposes or goals, and the kinds of actions or acts (e.g. acts of requesting) they are performing when they speak. It goes without saying that this is an extremely difficult task, since speakers may imply things and infer others without providing explicit linguistic evidence for this. Since pragmatics makes it necessary not only to make sense of what people say, but also of what they have in mind, it also touches upon psycholinguistic and cognitive issues.

In sum, pragmatics is the study of linguistic acts and the contexts in which these acts are performed by human beings. Pragmatics involves context-dependent aspects of meaning which are systematically abstracted away from the pure semantics of logical form, and which also involves what goes on in people's minds.

Cross-cultural pragmatics

A milestone in the field of cross-cultural pragmatics is the well-known Cross-Cultural Speech Act Analysis Project (CCSARP) (Blum-Kulka et al. 1989) that began its work in the early 1980s. In this project, the realization of the speech acts 'request' and 'apology' was examined in seven different languages and language varieties, namely British, American, Australian English, German, Canadian French, Danish, and Hebrew. In this research project, a newly developed data elicitation method, the Discourse Completion Test (DCT) was used. In this test, subjects were asked to fill in blanks in a dialogic situational description in which they had to produce a particular speech act. Requests and Apologies were chosen because both these speech acts constitute face-threatening acts, i.e. acts that threaten someone's public self image, as in asking him/her to do you a favour. One of the major findings that emerged from this project is that degrees of social distance and power between participants are among the most important factors determining variation in the realization of speech acts. And these factors can also interact with other situational factors and are subject to considerable cultural variation.

Another major result of the CCSARP Project refers to findings about levels of directness of the realization of speech acts. With respect to the speech act 'request', for instance, nine different request strategies were distinguished, which are ordered according to decreasing degrees of directness.

(1) Mood derivable

The grammatical mood of the utterance conventionally determines its illocutionary force as a 'request'. But functional equivalents, such as finite forms and elliptical sentence structure, also express this directness level, as in *'Leave me alone!'*, *'No smoking in the kitchen'*, *'The menu, please'*, and the like.

How would you translate these examples into your own language?

(2) Explicit performative

The speaker's intention is explicitly named in his/her use of an illocutionary verb, as in *'I am asking you to move your car'*.

What is the difference between '*I am asking you to move your car*' and '*move your car*'? Discuss.

(3) Hedged performative

The illocutionary verb denoting the requestive intent is modified by, for example, modal verbs or verbs expressing intention, as in *'I must ask you to clean the kitchen right now'*, *'I wanted to ask you to present your paper a week later'*, etc.

(4) Locution derivable

The illocutionary intent is directly derivable from the semantic meaning of the locution, as in *'Sir, you'll have to/must/should/ought to move your car'*.

(5) Want statement

The utterance expresses the speaker's desire that the event denoted in the proposition come about, as in *'I'd like to borrow this book'*.

(6) Suggestory formula

The illocutionary force is a suggestion couched in a routine formula, as in *'How about cleaning the kitchen?'*, *'Why don't you shut up?'*, etc.

How would you translate these examples into your own language?

(7) Preparatory

The utterance contains reference to a preparatory condition for the feasibility of the request, typically one of ability, willingness, or possibility as conventionalized in a given language, as in *'Can I borrow your car?'*, *'Could you possibly lend me your car?'*, etc.

(8) Strong hint

The illocutionary force is not immediately derivable from the locution; however, the locution contains relevant elements of the intended illocutionary act. Hints are not conventionalized and thus require more inferencing activity from the hearer, as in *'Will you be going home now?'* (Intention: Getting a lift home).

(9) Mild hint

The locution contains no elements of immediate relevance to the intended illocution, thus putting increased demand on context analysis and knowledge activation on the part of the hearer, as in *'You've been busy here, haven't you?'* (Intent: Getting hearer to clean the kitchen).

In the production of speech acts, the central or head act is often internally and/ or externally modified by syntactic and lexical downgraders and upgraders and/ or so-called supportive moves, as explained in the table below and the examples that follow, quoted from House and Kádár (2021: 121ff): Can I borrow your notes?

(1) Syntactic downgraders	interrogatives, subjunctives, and conditionals.
(2) Lexical downgraders	hedges, downtoners, appealers, etc.
(3) Upgraders	expletives, intensifiers, repetitions, etc.
(4) Supportive moves	grounders, imposition minimizers, getting a precommitment, etc.

Translate these sentences into your own language.

- Interrogative: *Can I borrow your notes?*
- Subjunctive: *It might be better if you were to leave now.*
- Conditional: *I would suggest you leave now.*
- Hedge: *It would <u>somehow</u> fit better if you gave your paper next week.*
- Downtoner: *Could you <u>possibly</u> lend me your notes?*
- Appealer: *Clean up the kitchen, <u>will you</u>?*
- Expletive: *Why don't you clean up that <u>bloody</u> mess!*
- Intensifier: *The kitchen is in a <u>terrible</u> mess!*
- Repetition: *Go away, go away!*
- Grounder: *<u>I missed class yesterday.</u> Can I borrow your notes?*
- Imposition minimizer: *Can you lend me 10 pounds? <u>I'll pay you back tomorrow.</u>*
- Getting a precommitment: *Can you do me a favour?*

The CCSARP Project has had an enormous impact on the field of cross-cultural pragmatics and both its methodology and the categorial scheme suggested are still widely used today with many different languages. An important recent update is provided in House and Kádár's (2021) book titled *Cross-Cultural Pragmatics*.

In what follows, the central topics and phenomena generally treated in pragmatics, such as 'deixis', 'speech acts', 'cooperative principle', 'inference', and 'conversational implicature' are introduced and discussed in a direct link to translation.

Connecting the dots (1): Translating deixis

This subdomain of pragmatics aims to analyse and describe the characteristics of elements that vary in meaning, such as expressions like *'I'*, *'you'*, *'here'*, *'there'*, *'now'*, *'then'*, *'hereby'*, or markers of tense/ aspect whose meanings are constant but their referents vary with speakers, hearers, time and place of an utterance, style or register, or the function of the speech act in which they occur.

This variation is due to the fact that any use of language always takes place in a certain situational context at a particular time and at a particular place by human beings who usually share a lot of the perception and knowledge of the situation and general knowledge of the world. This boundness of utterances to the context in which they occur has important consequences for understanding them, and accordingly does not generally create problems whenever a minimum of common ground exists. Thus, utterances like *'I told him all that yesterday, when he was here'* is clearly comprehensible when one can identify:

- the speaker (*'I'*);
- the time of utterance to identify *'yesterday'*;
- where the utterance took place (*'here'* can be anywhere);
- who the speaker talked to (we only know it is a male person (*'him'* and *'he'*));
- a part of what was said before, i.e. what is meant exactly by *'all that'*.

So, the necessary information for disambiguating utterances like the above stems from the extralinguistic situational context and/or from the linguistic co-text.

We can say that 'contextuality' is one of the most basic features of language, and it is one of the important links between language, perception, and cognition. What is meant when something is uttered therefore depends on the linguistic form of the utterance, on features of the situation as perceived by speaker and hearer (including previous utterances between them), and on the shared general knowledge of the world.

How would you define 'contextuality'?

As the above example shows, one major device for integrating contextual information in order to achieve understanding is deixis. Deictic expressions vary in meaning depending on where, when, and by whom they are used. Deixis is classified into three main types, namely 'personal deixis' (*'I'*, *'you'*, *'my'*, etc.), 'temporal deixis' (*'now'*, *'today'*, etc.), and 'local deixis' (*'here'*, *'there'*, *'left'*, etc.), as shown here:

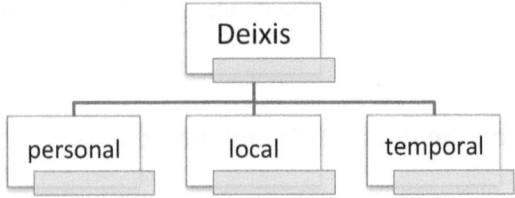

Closer examinations of the deictic systems of different languages have led to insights into the connections between its various types and its relation to other phenomena of contextuality.

Deixis can be defined as the relation of language to its point of origin. Of the three types of deixis described above, it is personal deixis which creates most problems for translators, mainly because of differences in the systems of personal deixis across languages. In the case of local and temporal deixis it is the co-text provided in a text which usually resolves meaning ambiguities, thus facilitating translation. In cases of personal deixis, however, the translator is often confronted with serious linguistic problems. Consider for instance the following English sentence:

I hope you'll learn a lot from reading this chapter.

How is the translator going to translate this sentence into languages which differentiate between 'informal' and 'formal' or 'deferential' uses of the second person singular and plural pronoun, e.g. German *du/Sie* or French *tu/vous*? Clearly, in this case the translator has to make a choice depending on the co-text and the context of this utterance. The translator also needs to know the socio-pragmatic norms holding in a particular linguaculture, because these norms determine whether the informal or the formal personal pronoun is conventionally preferred in a particular situation. A recent study of translations of the English pronoun *'you'* in IKEA catalogues into many different languages (see House and Kádár 2020) has shown how intricate translational decisions can turn out to be in the case of translating the English personal pronoun *'you'* used in both product descriptions and direct address to potential customers into many different languages. It was shown that the impersonal *'you'* (brandmark of the Swedish company IKEA) was translated equally impersonally in the German, Hungarian, Dutch, Belgian Dutch, Japanese, and Mainland Mandarin catalogues. However, in the French, Belgian French, and Hong Kong Mandarin IKEA catalogues and the catalogues for various North African countries (all former French colonies), the formal/deferential form of the personal pronoun, i.e. *'vous'*, was invariably used. Here are some examples from several IKEA catalogues.

ST	Have <u>you</u> ever had this irresistible urge to leave the world behind <u>you</u> and to have a breath, even for a moment? <u>You</u> are not alone. Not easy to achieve this? <u>You</u> might be surprised ...

| TT (Belgian French) | Vous avez déjà eu cette envie irrésistible de laisser l'agitation du monde derrière vous, de souffler et de respirer, même pour un moment? Vous n'êtes pas seul. Pas simple d'y parvenir? Vous serez peut-être étonné … |

| ST | You had that kind of moment, didn't you? When you really want to leave the bustling external world, close out the world outside, have a deep breath, even for a moment. Probably all people have these moments. You would think it is not easy to achieve, but it is not necessarily like that. |
| TT (Chinese Mandarin) | 你是否有过那样的瞬间?急切地想要将这个纷乱的世界甩在身后，关掉对外的开关，深呼吸，哪怕只是一会儿? 大概每个人都有吧!想实现却不太容易，也不尽然。 |

| ST | Have you ever felt the need to escape the crowds – logging out and catching your breath – if only for a moment? You (je) are not the only one. And it does not have to be difficult at all to realise this. |
| TT (Dutch) | Heb je wel eens zin om de drukte te ontvluchten – uitloggen en op adem komen – al is het maar voor even? Je bent niet de enige. En het hoeft ook helemaal niet moeilijk te zijn om dit te realiseren. |

As shown in these and other examples consulted, due to the differences in the systems of personal deixis across languages, it is personal deixis that requires extra effort from the translator.

Connecting the dots (2): References (c)overtly translated

Reference, as explained in Chapter 6 of this book, can be defined as an act in which a speaker uses linguistic forms to enable a hearer to identify something. These linguistic forms, or referring expressions, can be proper nouns (e.g. *'Europe'*), definite or indefinite noun phrases (*'the man'*, *'a man'*), or pronouns (*'he'*, *'it'*). The choice of a particular expression depends on what the speaker thinks his/her addressees already know, i.e. their common ground. In shared situational contexts, pronouns functioning as deictic expressions are generally sufficient for successful reference, but whenever identification becomes more difficult, more elaborate noun phrases may become necessary (e.g. *'That person with the big red nose'* rather than *'him'*). Since there is no direct relationship between entities to which words refer, a hearer's task is to 'infer' which entity the speaker intends to identify when s/he employs a particular referring expression. We can say that

What is the difference between 'referent' and 'referring expression'?

successful reference is collaborative in that both speaker and hearer need to think about what the other has in mind.

Proper names seem to have a pragmatic connection with certain objects with which they are conventionally associated. If a proper name is used referentially to identify such an object, addressees will have to make the necessary inference, for example from the name of a country to a Olympic team in the following sentence: '*Germany won two gold medals today*'.

What are the other parts of 'context'?

The physical environment as a major part of the context is often crucial when it comes to inferring how a referring expression has to be understood. So, for instance, the physical context of a restaurant and the conventional ways of speaking by the staff working there are crucial for interpreting utterances such as *'The cheeseburger just complained about the size of the bun'*. Here, as explained in Chapter 6, we cannot rely on the open choice principle to arrive at the intended meaning. In other words, we cannot rely on the denotative meaning of each word used in this sentence to know that it is not really the cheeseburger who complained, but we need to rely on the context to infer that it is the customer having ordered the cheeseburger who complained.

Covert translation versus overt translation

In referring to certain objects, names, institutions, dates, etc., it is necessary to know the particular culturally embedded meanings which these entities have for members of that linguaculture. More often than not, these meanings are not valid in other linguacultures, and it is thus up to translators to make an important choice in their translation as to whether they opt for an 'overt translation' or a 'covert translation' (House 2015, 2016, 2018b). It suffices it to say here that an 'overt translation' is one in which the translator leaves the original text as far intact as possible, respecting the original and its author, and then engages in cultural transfer, thus informing foreign readers about culturally embedded phenomena in the original culture. In a 'covert translation', however, original texts are not simply transposed from the source to the target cultural context in the medium of a new language but are often substantially transformed as they move from one language into another one. Unlike an overt translation, a covert translation lives up to the target language's expectations in terms of readability, accessibility, authenticity, idiomaticity, and well-formedness that feed into naturalness (for more details on these two types, see House 2015).

The major difficulty in translating overtly is, of course, finding linguistic-cultural 'equivalents' whenever possible. If it is not possible to find an equivalent, the translator can leave a particular term untranslated and explain it in a glossary. Here we deal with overt manifestations of cultural phenomena that are transferred only because they happen to be manifest linguistically in the original. And in these cases, inferencing is left to the reader of the translation, but s/he can always also immediately consult a glossary. A good example to exemplify this point is the translation of the Afghan-American author Khaled Hosseini's novels *The Kite Runner* and *A Thousand Splendid Suns*, where many original Pashto terms are left untranslated in the German version, such as *'namoos'*, *'nang'*, *'iftar'*, *'kolba'*, *'Ramadan'*, *'hijab'* and *'harami'*.

The very opposite situation is the case of a 'covert translation'. Here, the translator attempts to re-create an equivalent speech event. The function of a covert translation is to reproduce the function the original has had in its discourse world, and to reach functional equivalence. The translation operates only in the world of the new culture, so the translator's task is to transform the original with the potential to adapt it to the needs, knowledge, and competence levels of the target readers. To do this s/he uses a 'cultural filter' (House 2015) as a means of capturing socio-cultural differences in expectation norms and stylistic conventions between the source and target cultural context.

In terms of reference to, for instance, important dates in a particular linguaculture, the translator might choose to translate overtly by leaving the date and name intact or covertly by changing it in order to accommodate towards the feelings and sensitivities of target readers. Thus, for instance, *'Columbus Day'* (12 October 1492), triumphantly celebrated in the United States as the day America was 'discovered', is often called differently in Latin America, where the term *'Día de la Raza'* (Day of the Race) has long been in use, thus deliberately avoiding mention of Columbus. So, in translating a text where *'Columbus Day'* occurs, the translator must make a choice between an overt or a covert translation, depending on their own convictions or the assumed feelings of the readers of their translation, as well as other factors like the ideology of their employers.

Another interesting example in which the translator must make a choice between an overt translation and covert translation is the US English and Israeli term *'Terrorist attacks'*, often translated very differently by Palestinian translators and translators who hold a different opinion as *'Liberation struggle'*.

Connecting the dots (3): The cooperative principle and translation

In any conversation, we can assume that those involved are generally cooperating with each other and that for reference to work at all, collaboration is necessary. In many conversations, speakers intend to communicate much more than they explicitly say. For instance, when hearing the utterance *'Business is business'*, which at first sight seems to have no communicative value, the hearer needs to assume the speaker is cooperative and does want to communicate something. And this 'something' is more than the words uttered; it is an additionally conveyed meaning called an 'implicature'. Implicatures are prime examples of more being communicated than what is actually said. However, we can only understand this 'more' when we assume that some basic 'cooperative principle'

Do you agree that while 'speech acts' focus on conventional forms used to express different illocutionary forces in a given language, conversational implicature refers to language users' ability to figure out what is not explicitly said?

is in operation. The cooperative principle of conversation (followed by four subprinciples or maxims) as suggested by H. Paul Grice (1975) is the following:

> Make your contribution such as is required, at the stage at which it occurs, by the accepted purpose or direction of the talk exchange in which you are engaged.

The four maxims of the cooperative principle are as follows:

(1) Quantity
- Make your contribution as informative as is required (for the current purposes of the exchange).
- Do not make your contribution more informative than is required.

(2) Quality: Try to make your contribution one that is true.
- Do not say what you believe to be false.
- Do not say that for which you lack adequate evidence.

(3) Relation
- Be relevant.

(4) Manner: Be perspicuous
- Avoid obscurity of expression.
- Avoid ambiguity.
- Be brief (avoid unnecessary prolixity).
- Be orderly.

These maxims are implicit assumptions which we hold in conversation, with the basic assumption in conversation being that – unless otherwise indicated – all conversationalists adhere to the 'cooperative principle' and the various concomitant maxims. If speakers violate them, they convey more than they say via a 'conversational implicature', and hearers need to infer what is not explicitly said. By way of illustration, let us consider the following example:

A: Did you meet my parents?
B: I met your father.

In B's utterance there is an implicature that she did 'not' meet the mother.

Because implicatures are generally part of what is communicated but not said, a speaker can always deny that s/he had intended to communicate such a meaning.

As far as translation is concerned, it is important that translators give adequate consideration to these maxims that are flouted, whereby implicit messages are conveyed by way of conversational implicature. To explain, the following example extracted from Mahfouz's novel (1959/2006: 473) أولاد حارتنا, translated by Peter Theroux (1996: 368) into *Children of the Alley* may be considered:

Comment on this exchange by referring to the 'cooperative principle and its maxims:
A: *'Shall we go out tonight?'*
B: *'I sold my car'*

Arabic	قمحة منه قبل فنجان شاي قبل "لا مواخذة" بساعتين، وبعدها فإما ترضى عن محسوبك عرفه، أو تطرده من الحارة مشفوعا باللعنات.
Back translation	A grain of it before a cup of tea two hours before "excuse me", and after that either you'll be pleased with your servant, Arafa, or you send him out of the neighbourhood accompanied by your curse.
English	A grain of that in a cup of tea two hours before, well, you know, no offence, and after that, either you will be happy with your servant Arafa or you can kick him out of the alley with every curse you know.

Here, instead of explicitly referring to the act of having intercourse, the author lets one of the in-text characters mention it implicitly, thus flouting Grice's maxim of quality (speaking the truth) and maxim of quantity (employing the right amount of language). Being fully aware of this, the translator, as can be seen, decided to maintain the conversational implicature by opting for *'well, you know, no offence'*. By so doing, he invited his readers to get involved in the interpretation of the text by relying on their encyclopedic knowledge and socio-cultural experiences.

It is worth noting that flouting any maxim on purpose results in what is termed by Grice as a 'conversational implicature'.

Cultural filters

According to the Gricean 'cooperative principle', speakers' contributions to a conversation should contain information that is required at a particular point and heeding the current goal and direction of the talk. The abovementioned maxims of quantity, quality, relation, and manner are unstated assumptions which speakers are assumed to generally have in a conversation. However, these maxims are not universally valid; rather, they vary across cultures and are therefore a challenge for the translator who needs to have the relevant cross-cultural pragmatic knowledge necessary for producing a covert translation. For example, as House (2006, 2018a) has shown in a series of contrastive pragmatic discourse analyses, German and English speakers tend to vary in their interpretations of the 'cooperative principle' and the attendant maxims, which means that translators of English texts into German and German texts into English need to be aware of this and to be able to apply a 'cultural filter' if necessary. A cultural filter is a procedure used by a translator in a covert translation in order to make his/her translation compatible with the target readers' preferences and discourse norms (for more details, see House 2018b: 92ff). To explain, here are two relevant examples involving English–German translations. The first example taken from a popular science text about HIV vaccines is in English, while the second one taken from an instruction for using ovenware is in German:

English	Most vaccines activate what is called the humoral arm of the immune system.
German	Die meisten Vakzine aktivieren den sogenannten humoralen Arm des Immunsystems (nach lateinisch humor, Flüssigkeit).
Back translation	Most vaccines activate the so-called humoral arm of the immune system (after Latin *'humor'*, liquid).

This example shows that the translator applied a cultural filter to the original sentence expatiating on the content by adding an etymological explanation, thus violating the maxims of quantity and relevance as interpreted by the original English writer.

German	Kerafour ist in unabhängigen Prüfungsinstituten auf Ofenfestigkeit und Mikrowellenbeständigkeit getestet worden. Damit Sie lange Freude an ihm haben, geben wir Ihnen einige kurze Gebrauchshinweise: (1) Stellen Sie nie ein leeres, kaltes Gefäß in den erhitzten Ofen (als leer gilt auch ein nur innen mit Fett bestrichenes Gefäß).
Literal translation	Kerafour has been tested for ovenproofness in independent testing institutes. So that you can enjoy it for a long time, we give you some brief instructions for use: (1) Never put an empty cold vessel into the heated oven ('empty' also refers to a vessel which is only rubbed with fat).
English	Kerafour oven-to-table pieces have been tested for ovenproofness in independent testing institutes. So that you can enjoy it for a long time, we give you some brief instructions for use. (1) Never put an empty cold vessel into the heated oven.

In this example, the English translator apparently thought the bracket in the German original is needlessly explicit violating the Anglophone interpretation of the maxims of quantity and relevance, and consequently decided to leave it out.

Connecting the dots (4): Cross-cultural pragmatics and translation

In translation, and especially in a covert translation, knowledge about, and awareness of, cross-cultural differences in the production and reception of texts is of crucial importance for the practising translator. For example, in translation involving the languages German and English, the cultural filter necessary for a covert translation has been given substance through a series of contrastive discourse analyses (summarized in House 2006), which resulted in a number of dimensions of cross-cultural differences, as shown below:

German		English
Directness	←→	Indirectness
Orientation towards self	←→	Orientation towards other
Orientation towards content	←→	Orientation towards addressees
Explicitness	←→	Implicitness
Ad hoc formulation	←→	Routines

Given these differences in German and English cross-cultural discourse preferences, the translator needs to adapt his/her translation accordingly. While these dimensions were established for the translation pair German–English, it is both possible and desirable to undertake empirical contrastive pragmatic research comparing many other language pairs and suggesting specific parameters along which these languages differ as guidelines for the application of a cultural filter for each of these language pairs. The following excerpt is taken from an English commercial circular by an investment consultancy firm and its German translation, in which the author informs shareholders about an action they need to perform.

Think of some examples in which cross-cultural communication fails.

English	In order to avoid the possibility of accidental misdirection of your certificates, your assistance is required. We have enclosed a 'Dividend Instruction Form' for your completion; this should be returned in the pre-addressed envelope.
German	Um zu vermeiden, dass Ihre Zertifikate versehentlich fehlgeleitet werden, bitten wir Sie, das beigefügte Dividendenzustellungsformular auszufüllen und in dem ebenfalls beigefügten adressierten Umschlag zurückzuschicken.
Back translation	In order to avoid that your certificates are accidentally misdirected, we ask you to fill out the enclosed Dividend Instruction Form and to return it in the also enclosed addressed envelope.

The above covert translation into German shows that the author appears to be much more forceful, active, and direct, while the English original expresses the action to be performed more abstractly and more indirectly. The utterance in the English original seems to have the illocutionary force of a subtle suggestion whereas in the translation, it has been transformed into a request. And while the original attempts to suggest that it is not the company that wants something done, but rather that some external necessity proposes a course of action to the shareholder, the translation is much more direct and explicit in this regard. In the following example quoted from Mahfouz's novel (1973: 57) بين القصرين translated into English by Hutchins and Kenny (1990: 57) as *Palace Walk*, the author also appears to be much more forceful, active, and direct.

Arabic	وصاحت خديجة في سخرية: - تتوظف دون الرابعة عشرة! . . . وماذا تصنع إذا بُلت على نفسك في الوظيفة؟!
Back translation	And Khadija yelled sarcastically, - "You get employed before fourteen! What will you do if you urinate on yourself at work?"
English	Khadija yelled sarcastically, "You want to get a job before you're fourteen! What will you do if you wet your pants at work?"

The question ماذا تفعل إذا بُلت على نفسك في الوظيفة *'What will you do if you urinate on yourself at work?'* (literal meaning) recruited in the original text performs an illocution (pragmatic meaning) other than 'questioning'; it is the illocution of disapproval. This is an 'indirect speech act' where the relationship between the structure and its function is indirect (for more details, see the next section). The translators managed to handle this illocution of disapproval when opting for the question *'What will you do if you wet your pants at work?'*.

Connecting the dots (5): Speech acts and translation

Utterances perform actions which are generally known in pragmatics as 'speech acts'. As discussed above, the idea of a 'speech act' originates in the philosophy of language, and in particular in the work of Austin (1962), Searle (1969), and Grice (1975). Austin was the first to assume that the minimal units of human communication are not linguistic expressions, but rather the performance of certain kinds of acts such as making statements, asking for information, requiring some goods, apologizing, thanking, greeting, and so on.

In describing such speech acts, Austin (1962: 94) distinguishes between three types of acts that each utterance has:

(1) 'Locutionary act', referring to the actual act of saying something, as in *'It's hot in here'*.
(2) 'Illocutionary act', referring to the performance of an act *in* saying something as opposed to an act *of* saying something, as in *'Could you please turn on the AC?'*.
(3) 'Perlocutionary act', referring to the consequential effects of an act, as in, for example, getting the AC turned on.

It is worth noting that in this example, there are two types of meaning: 'literal meaning' (*It's hot in here*) and 'pragmatic meaning' (*Could you please turn on the AC?*).

The most well-known classification of speech acts was suggested by John Searle (1969). Much later, an interaction-based classification of speech acts was proposed by Edmondson and House (1981), which proved to be important for the analysis of speech acts embedded in discourse (see also Edmondson et al. 2023). Searle's speech act classification comprised five types of general functions performed by speech acts. They are explained below:

(1) Declaratives

These are speech acts that change the world via their utterance. In order to appropriately perform them, the speaker must have a special institutional role, in a specific context. An example is: *'I name this ship Queen Elizabeth II'*, uttered by the Queen herself.

(2) Representatives

These are speech acts that state what the speaker believes to be the case or not. In uttering a representative, speakers make words fit the world as they believe it is. Representatives comprise statements of facts, assertions, conclusions, and descriptions, as in *'The earth is flat'*, *'Searle wrote about speech acts'*, *'It is raining today'*, etc.

(3) Expressives

These are speech acts that state what the speaker feels. They are generally about the speaker's experience of psychological states such as pain, joy, sorrow, and pleasure. In uttering an expressive, speakers make words fit the world of feeling, as in *'I am very happy'*, *'My condolences!'*, *'Congratulations!'*, *'That's wonderful!'*, etc.

(4) Directives

These are speech acts which speakers use when they want someone else to do something. In uttering a directive, speakers make the world fit the words. Directives are commands, orders, requests, or suggestions and they can be positive or negative, as in *'Take me home'*, *'Can you pass the salt, please'*, *'Don't do that again'*, etc.

(5) Commissives

These are speech acts which speakers use to commit themselves to some future action. They are used by speakers to attempt to make the world fit the words. Commissives express what the speaker intends. They can be positive or negative and comprise promises, pledges, refusals, threats etc., as in *'I promise to be on time'*, *'I will never let you down again'*, etc.

In their *Pedagogic Interactional Grammar of English*, Edmondson and House (1981, and Edmondson et al. 2023) present an alternative,

> Do you agree that the Sayer of a declarative speech act should be characterized by being-able-to-do something with words?

> It is argued that in directives, if the speaker does have an authority, then the addressee has no choice of performance. Do you agree?

> Identify the speech act type according to Edmondson et al. in the following sentence: *'Why don't you call her now?'*

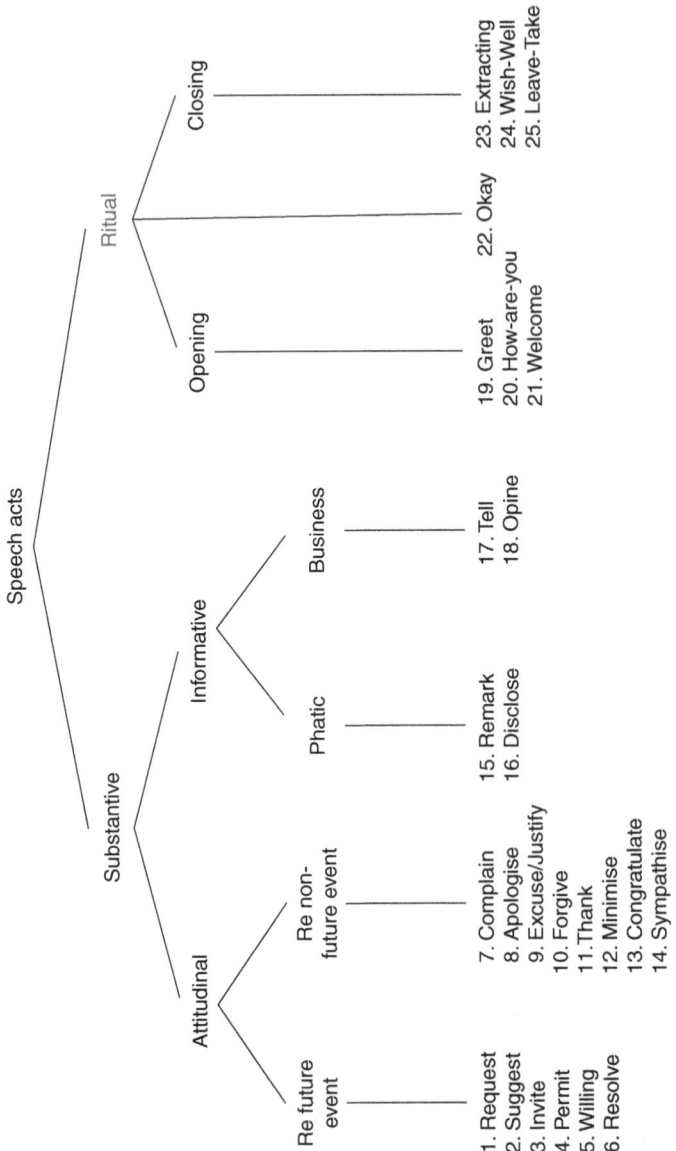

interactionally motivated classification of speech acts, as shown in the above figure.

As shown in the figure, speech acts are classified into two main types: (1) 'substantive', which can be further subclassified into 'attitudinal' and 'informative'; and (2) 'ritual', which can be further subclassified into 'opening' and 'closing' (for more details, see Edmondson et al. 2023).

Direct and indirect speech acts

Another classic distinction of speech acts is the one between direct speech acts and indirect speech acts. Whenever there is a direct relationship between a structure and a speech act function, we have a 'direct speech act', and whenever there is an indirect relationship between a structure and a function, we have an 'indirect speech act'. For example, an utterance *'It's cold in here'* can be a direct speech act if it is just a statement and an indirect speech act if it is meant as a request to close an open window. And an utterance like *'I am thirsty'* can be interpreted in an appropriate context as a remark on the speaker's situation, as a request for something to drink, or from a child as a request for attention. *'Can you give me something to drink?'* is a conventionally indirect speech act, and *'I am thirsty'* is a non-conventionally indirect speech act. In general, we can say that in uttering a direct speech act, the speaker says what s/he means, while in uttering an indirect speech act s/he means more than, or something other than, what s/he says. It has proved difficult to specify exactly what is meant by the notion of 'indirectness'. Some scholars like Searle have linked certain types of indirectness to certain forms of language through a claim for conventionality, and they suggest that certain linguistic forms are conventionally used to perform certain speech acts, such as *'Would you mind doing X'* as the standard way to realize a request. But other scholars like Sperber and Wilson (1986) who, in the spirit of Grice and his general conversational principle and maxims, emphasize the role of general pragmatic principles, in particular the 'principle of relevance', in order to account for the (cognitive) process by which any indirect meaning is encoded or decoded in context. It is entirely an empirical matter what specific forms of indirectness are used in a particular language for performing a specific speech act.

As we have seen in the above example from a commercial circular, in 'covert translation' it is often the case that a certain speech act is changed into another one. Here is another English–German example which involves both a speech act change and a concomitant change in politeness. The example features a German sign in an airport alerting passengers of an obstruction in their path:

German	Damit die Zukunft schneller kommt!
Literal translation	Such that the future comes more quickly!
English	We apologize for any inconvenience work on our building site is causing you!

Identify the speech act type according to John Searle (1969) in this sentence:
'I sentence you to two years in prison'.

Reflect on your own language to find certain linguistic forms that are conventionally used to perform certain speech acts.

Here we see a difference in perspective, i.e. a focus on the content in German and an interpersonal focus in English zeroing in on the human beings crossing the path of the building sites and realizing the speech act of 'apology' as opposed to the speech act of a 'tell' in the original. This has important implications for politeness, given the intimate relation of an apology to politeness.

Another example relates to the translation of an original English science text and its German translation, again involving cultural filtering, which here amounts to consistently changing readers' involvement in the text, thus creating a stronger distance between writer and reader and between the text and its readers.

Translate this text into your own language. Then comment on your own translation by referring to the speech act theory.

English	Suppose you are a doctor in an emergency room and a patient tells you she was raped two hours earlier. She is afraid she may have been exposed to HIV, the virus that causes AIDS but has heard that there is a 'morning-after pill' to prevent HIV infection. Can you in fact do anything to block the virus from replicating and establishing infection?
German	In der Notfallaufnahme eines Krankenhauses berichtet eine Patientin, sie sei vor zwei Stunden vergewaltigt worden und nun in Sorge, AIDS-Erregern ausgesetzt worden zu sein, sie habe gehört es gebe eine ‚Pille danach', die eine HIV-Infektion verhüte. Kann der Arzt überhaupt etwas tun, was eventuell vorhandene Viren hindern würde, sich zu vermehren und sich dauerhaft im Körper einzunisten?
Back translation	In the emergency room of a hospital a patient reports that she had been raped two hours ago and was now worrying that she had been exposed to the AIDS-Virus. She said she had heard that there was an After-Pill, which might prevent an HIV-Infection. Can the doctor in fact do anything that might prevent potentially existing viruses from replicating and establishing themselves permanently in the body?

This covert translation can be understood as being governed by the translator's goal to adapt the English original text to the assumed reception habits of a German target audience. The cultural filtering relates here in particular to the degree of direct addressee involvement. Readers of the translated text are no longer asked to imagine themselves as one of the agents of the scene presented in the text as they are in the English original. Instead, the scene in the hospital so vividly brought to life in the original text is in the translation presented, as it were, from the outside with addresses no longer asked to actively engage with what is presented.

What we can here recognize is that cultural filtering in this translation has led to the production of a very different text through changing the personal pronoun *'you'* in the original to third person reference, thus resulting in a more impersonal, more abstract, more detached, and less persuasive text.

Exercises and discussion

Exercise 1: Mark the following statements (T) if they are true and (F) if they are false.

(1) The term 'pragmatic wastebasket' refers to problems still defying satisfactory syntactic and/or semantic analysis and explanation.	
(2) Austin's book *How to do Things with Words* explains how people communicate with each other by means of language.	
(3) In pragmatics, the interpretation of what is 'not' said can be as important as what is said.	
(4) *'Why don't you call her?'* is an example of a suggestory formula.	
(5) Pragmatics is concerned with performance principles of language use rather than competence principles.	
(6) According to Searle, 'representatives' are speech acts that change the world via their utterance.	
(7) An 'overt translation' is one which hides anything that betrays the foreignness of a source text.	
(8) While the lexical item *'really'* in *'I'm really sorry'* is an expletive, the degree word *'very'* in *'The exam was very easy'* is an intensifier.	
(9) While *'now'* is an example of local deixis, and *'me'* is an example of personal deixis, *'there'* is an example of temporal deixis.	
(10) While the lexical item *'again'* is an example of iterative items, the verb *'pretend'* is an example of a counter-factual verb.	

Exercise 2: Before translating the following six sentences into your native language, how would you describe the following utterances and how would you rank their directness level?

(a) Read this brochure!
(b) Please read this brochure.
(c) Would it be too much to ask you to read this brochure?
(d) Why don't you have a look at this brochure?
(e) Would you mind reading this brochure?
(f) Would you be so kind as to read this brochure?

Exercise 3: Before translating the following sentences into your own language, identify the type of speech act according to John Searle's (1969) classification:

(a)   I thank you for the effort that you have put in thus far.
(b)   I promise I'll bring it tomorrow.
(c)   I hereby acknowledge the safe receipt of your email.
(d)   I announce you husband and wife.
(e)   I advise you not to go with them.
(f)   I admit it was my mistake not his.

Exercise 4: Write sentences in your language in which you perform the act of (a) requesting, (b) threatening, (c) congratulating, (d) thanking, and (d) advising. Then translate them into English.

Exercise 5: The following conversation between two old friends is adapted from the British Council: Learn English website (https://learn english.britishcouncil.org). Your task is to:

(a)   translate the conversation into your language, taking into account the differences between the interfacing languages/cultures;
(b)   comment on your translation by adopting a pragmatic approach.

A:	Patrick? Is that you?
B:	Selina! Hello!
A:	Well, well. Patrick Eastwood. How have you been?
B:	Good. Great, actually. How are you? I haven't seen you for ... how long?
A:	It's been ages. At least fifteen years. Wow.
B:	Yeah. Wow.
A & B:	So, what are you doing here?
A:	Sorry, you go first.
B:	OK. What are you doing here? I thought you'd moved to London.
A:	I was in London for a couple of years. But it didn't work out.
B:	Oh, I'm sorry to hear that. Are you ... OK?
A:	I'm fine! The dream job wasn't really a dream, you know? Um ... and London is great but it's so expensive. I mean, just the rent on a flat is ... uh ... madly expensive.
B:	I see.
A:	So, I came back. I've been back now for almost five months. Living back home with Mum and Dad. Which is err ... interesting. Um ... but anyway, what about you?
B:	Me? Oh, nothing new. You know me – 'Patrick the predictable'. I never left here.
A:	Oh. And is that ...?
B:	Oh, I'm very happy. I'm married now. We've just celebrated our tenth anniversary.
A:	No way! You? Married? To ...?
B:	I don't think you know her. Her name's Marigold. And we've got two kids. They're five and eight years old.

A:	Married and with two kids? Wow!
B:	Don't look so surprised!
A:	No, no ... I'm just amazed how time flies! I'm happy for you. I really am.
B:	Thanks. You should really come round to the house one day.
A:	That would be great. Let's swap numbers and ...

Discussion and research points

(1) What is the difference between *'I wanted to ask you about your friend'* and *'I want to ask you about your friend'* in terms of politeness and directness?

(2) Select any short text translated from English into your own language. Then comment on it by adopting a pragmatic approach.

(3) Do you think that directness in the realization of a speech act, such as a request, is the same as the politeness with which the speech act is realized? For example, is the direct speech act of the utterance *'Move your car!'* as uttered by a police officer necessarily impolite? If yes, why, and if not, why not?

(4) How would you define 'covert translation' and 'overt translation'? Support your answer with examples of texts which need to be translated covertly and texts that will be standardly translated overtly?

(5) Explain in your own words how and why 'pragmatics' is relevant and important for translation.

(6) Why is the notion of 'context' so important for translation?

(7) What is the difference between 'direct speech acts' and 'indirect speech acts'? Discuss with illustrative examples.

References

Austin, J. L. (1962). *How to Do Things with Words*. Oxford: Oxford University Press.

Bar-Hillel, Y. (1971). "Out of the Pragmatic Wastebasket", *Linguistic Inquiry*, Vol. 2. pp. 401–7.

Blum-Kulka, S., House, J., and Kasper, G. (eds.) (1989). *Cross-Cultural Pragmatics: Requests and Apologies*. Norwood, NJ: Ablex.

Chomsky, N. (1965). *Aspects of the Theory of Syntax*. Cambridge, MA: MIT Press.

Edmondson, W. J. and House, J. (1981). *Let's Talk and Talk about It: A Pedagogic Interactional Grammar of English*. Munich: Urban & Schwarzenberg.

Edmondson, W. J., House, J., and Kádár, D. (2023). *Expressions, Speech Acts and Discourse: A Pedagogic Interactional Grammar of English*. Cambridge: Cambridge University Press.

Grice, H. P. (1975). "Logic and Conversation". In Cole, P. and Morgan J. (eds.), *Syntax and Semantics, Vol. 3. Speech Acts* (pp. 41–58). New York: Academic Press.

House, J. (2006). "Communicative Styles in English and German", *European Journal of English Studies*, Vol. 10(3), pp. 249–68.

House, J. (2015). *Translation Quality Assessment: Past and Present.* London: Routledge.

House, J. (2016). *Translation as Communication across Languages and Cultures.* London: Routledge.

House, J. (2018a). "Translation Studies and Pragmatics". In Ilie, C. and Norrick, N. (eds.), *Pragmatics and its Interfaces* (pp. 143–63). Amsterdam: Benjamins.

House, J. (2018b). *Translation: The Basics.* London: Routledge.

House, J. and Kádár, D. (2020). "T/V Pronouns in Global Communication Practices: The Case of IKEA Catalogues across Linguacultures", *Journal of Pragmatics*, Vol. 161, pp. 1–15.

House, J. and Kádár, D. (2021). *Cross-Cultural Pragmatics.* Cambridge: Cambridge University Press.

Hutchins, W. and Kenny, O. (1990). *Palace Walk* (trans.). Cairo: The American University Press.

Lakoff, G. and Ross, J. R. (1967). "Is Deep Structure Necessary?" In McCawley, J. D. (ed.), *Syntax and Semantics: Notes from the Linguistic Underground* (Vol. 7, pp. 159–64). New York: Academic Press.

Mahfouz, N. (1959/2006). أولاد حارتنا. Cairo: Dār Al-Shurūq.

Mahfouz, N. (1973). بين القصرين. Cairo: Maktabat Misr.

Morris, C. W. (1938). "Foundations of the Theory of Signs". In Neurath O., Carnap, R., and Morris, C. W. (eds.), *International Encyclopedia of Unified Science* (Vol. 1(2), pp. 1–59). Chicago, IL: The University of Chicago Press.

Peirce, C. S. (1931–1958). *Collected Papers.* Volumes 1–6: Hartshorne, C. and Weiss, P. (eds.), Volumes 7–8: Burks, A. W. (ed.). Cambridge, MA: Belknap Press, Harvard University Press.

Searle, J. (1969). *Speech Acts.* Cambridge: Cambridge University Press.

Sperber, D. and Wilson, D. (1986). *Relevance.* London: Blackwell.

Theroux, P. (1996). *Children of the Alley* (trans., 1st edn). New York: Anchor Books.

Functional linguistics

9

This chapter introduces another branch of linguistics which is one of the most relevant fields for translators, as well as students and researchers of translation: 'functional linguistics'. The chapter discusses such areas and notions as 'register', 'cohesion', 'attitude', 'engagement', and 'graduation'. Register is analysed by referring to three variables: 'field of discourse', 'tenor of discourse', and 'mode of discourse'. These three variables are associated with three types of meanings, namely 'ideational meaning', 'interpersonal meaning', and 'textual meaning'. After introducing these linguistic areas and notions, they are discussed with a direct link to translation.

After you have studied this chapter, you should be able to (1) distinguish 'ideational meaning' from the other two types of meaning; (2) distinguish evaluative language from non-evaluative language; (3) distinguish between 'grammatical cohesion' and 'lexical cohesion'; (4) conduct a register analysis of different types of (translated) texts; (5) defend your own translation by adopting a model of translation quality assessment that uses a register-based approach to translation evaluation; and (6) comment on your translation by referring to Halliday's three types of meanings.

The basic definition of 'language', as shown in Chapter 1 of this book, is a system of communication based upon the use of words in a structured and conventional way. We use language to communicate with others in order, for instance, to thank them for doing something, promise them to do something, ask them about something, tell them what happened to us, and express our feelings. As such, we use language to do something with it (promising, complaining, denying, thanking, asking, telling, etc.) – language is used for a particular purpose to get things done. This view is consistent with the notion of systemic functional linguistics (or 'functional linguistics' for short), which was developed by M. A. K. Halliday in the 1960s (e.g. 1964) and developed further by his many disciples, most prominently by Christian M. I. M. Matthiessen (Matthiessen 1985/2014).

> Think of the communicative functions of language. What are they?

Language and meaning

Halliday (in Matthiessen 1985/2014: 25) holds that we "use language to make sense of our experience, and to carry out our interactions with other

> What is the difference between 'language' and 'meaning'?

DOI: 10.4324/9781003228028-10

people". This means that language cannot be used in isolation from what is going on outside the linguistic system. Rather, there is always some sort of interaction between the language and what is going on in the context enveloping it. To transform, as Halliday (Ibid.) puts it, our sociocultural experiences into wording, there are two steps.

(1) The experiences and interpersonal relationships are transformed into meaning (semantics).
(2) These experiences and interpersonal relationships transformed into meaning are further transformed into wording (lexicogrammar), as shown below:

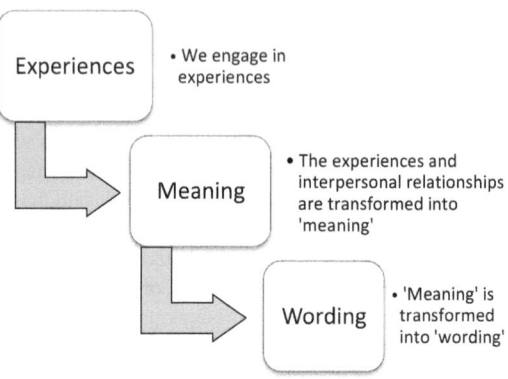

Can we say 'meaning' in the sense used by Halliday means 'style'? Discuss.

Meaning is transformed into wording, which is realized through the words, structures, conjunctions, etc. chosen by the language user. Those choices are systematically related first to the variety of language which a language user considers appropriate to a specific situation (register) and that is determined by the conventional text type (genre), which is, in turn, conditioned by the sociocultural environment, as shown in the following figure.

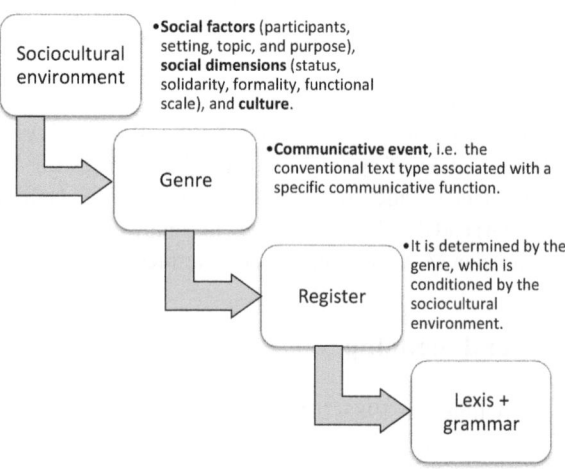

Register, as illustrated in the next section, is analysed by considering three variables:

(1) 'Field of discourse': the content and subject matter of the text.
(2) 'Tenor of discourse': the relationship between the participants.
(3) 'Mode of discourse': the form of communication (spoken, written, written to be read, etc.).

These three variables are associated with three strands of meanings (also known as 'functions' or 'metafunctions'):

(1) 'Ideational meaning' associated with the field of discourse.
(2) 'Interpersonal meaning' associated with the tenor of discourse.
(3) 'Textual meaning' associated with the mode of discourse.

> Identify the 'ideational meaning', 'interpersonal meaning', and 'textual meaning' of this sentence: *'Sadly, the tourism and money brought in by the World Cup games won't benefit the people who need it most'.*

Register–meaning relation

So, when you say, for example, *'As for the innocent girl, she was brutally killed by the thief yesterday'*, three types of meanings can be identified here:

> Translate this sentence into your own language by reflecting the three strands of meaning.

(1) 'Ideational meaning' realized by the transitivity process used: The thief ^Agent^ killed ^process of doing^ the girl ^Affected Participant^ yesterday ^circumstance^.
(2) 'Interpersonal meaning' realized by the language user's negative attitude towards the act of killing (*'brutally'*) and positive attitude towards the girl (*'innocent'*).
(3) 'Textual meaning' realized by the use of a transition marker (*'as for'*).

Now, translating the above sentence into, for example, German as *'Das unschuldige Mädchen wurde gestern von dem Dieb getötet'* meaning *'The innocent girl was killed by the thief yesterday'*, one can notice that the ideational meaning is certainly reflected in the translation. But is this enough? In the translation, the interpersonal meaning is only partially reflected as we do not have information about the language user's attitude towards the act of killing, although it can be invoked by virtue of the evaluatively active word *'unschuldig'* meaning *'innocent'*. However, the decision of not translating *'brutally'* results in a clear loss of interpersonal meaning. Further, the translator paid little or no attention to how the sentence is organized in a particular communicative event and how it hangs together as a cohesive whole (textual meaning), thus losing out on textual meaning in the translation. The example shows how we need to pay attention to all three types of meaning if we want to produce a functionally equivalent translation.

Connecting the dots (1): Register and translation

What is the difference between 'style' and 'register'?

The term 'register' can be defined as a variety of language that language users (be they writers or speakers) consider appropriate to a specific situation. In analysing discourse in general and register in particular, Halliday (1994) came up with a comprehensive model for register analysis. In contrast with the traditional grammarians, who view the concept of 'transitivity' as a reference to verbs that take objects, Halliday (1976: 199) defines transitivity from a functional point of view as "the set of options relating to cognitive content, the linguistic representation of extralinguistic experience, whether of the phenomena of the external world or of feelings, thoughts and perceptions". In analysing registers, full consideration is given to the following variables that were also mentioned above:

Identify the main components of this behavioural process:
'She cried bitterly over her mom last night'.

(1) 'Field of discourse': studying the content by focusing on transitivity processes and the circumstances used with each process, if any.
(2) 'Tenor of discourse': identifying the participants and their relations.
(3) 'Mode of discourse': identifying the channel or medium used to deliver the message, whether it is spoken, written, or written to be spoken, etc.

Field of discourse

In analysing the 'field of discourse', the content or subject matter, i.e. what has been said by the language users (speakers or writers), is examined. To this end, transitivity processes are given serious consideration. In studying these different types of processes, three main components should be considered: (1) the 'process' itself normally expressed by a verbal group; (2) the 'participants' determined in advance by the writer/speaker, which are typically realized by a nominal group; and (3) the 'circumstances' associated with the process, typically expressed by an adverb or a preposition phrase, as explained in this example:

Is there any difference in 'meaning' if we say:
'It is my father and his colleagues who travelled to the UK two weeks ago to attend a conference there'?

My father [participant] travelled [process] to the UK [circumstance: 'place' answering the question 'where'] with his colleagues [circumstance: 'company' answering the question 'with whom'] two weeks ago [circumstance: 'time' answering the question 'when'] to attend a conference there [circumstance: 'reason' answering the question 'why'].

In this chapter, following Almanna (2018), these processes are classified into eight processes:

(1) Process of doing (*He is eating right now*).
(2) Process of happening (*The ball disappeared in the corridor*).
(3) Process of behaving (*She laughed from ear to ear*).

(4) Process of sensing (*My sister saw him in the street*).

(5) Process of saying (*He said that he would travel to the UK soon*).

(6) Process of being (*My father is an English teacher*).

(7) Process of having (*I have three brothers*).

(8) Process of existing (*There are two books on the table*).

While translating from language *A* to language *B*, we might be confronted with transitivity shifts. These shifts occur due to a variety of different reasons, such as the differences between the interfacing languages, the translation brief, text type preference, or the translator's competence. By way of example, let us consider the following article taken from the Universal Declaration of Human Rights 1948 in three languages, namely English, French, and Arabic, to see if there is any type of shift:

English	Everyone has the right to recognition everywhere as a person before law.
French	Chacun a le droit à la reconnaissance en tous lieux de sa personnalité juridique.
Back translation	Everyone has the right to recognition everywhere of their legal personality.
Arabic	لكلّ إنسان، في كلّ مكان، الحقُّ بأن يُعترَف له بالشخصية القانونية.
Back translation	Every human being, everywhere, has the right to be recognized as a legal person.

Here, a 'process of having' expressed by the verb *'to have'* is used to describe people's right to be recognized as having legal personality. This was reflected in the three languages. However, in the French translation, the translator confused the two semantically related French words *'personnalité'* meaning personality and *'personne'* meaning *'person'*. So, in place of using *'personne juridique'*, which is a standardized phrase in French legal terminology, s/he used *'personnalité juridique'*, thus skewing the coherence of the text.

Sometimes while translating between languages, the process itself along with its components is reflected, but its content is manipulated on purpose or by accident, as in the following example quoted from *Casablanca* by Michael Curtiz (1942):

ST (English)	Rick: The problems of the world are not in my department. I'm a saloonkeeper.
TT (Spanish)	Rick: Los problemas del mundo no son de mi incumbencia. Regento un cabaret.
Back translation	Rick: The world's problems are none of my business. I run a cabaret.

How many processes are there in a sentence of the following kind? *'Some weeks ago, she decided to travel to the UK to study law, but yesterday she changed her mind?'*

How would you define 'transitivity shift'?

In this example, there are two processes of being in the original text. However, in the target text, the second process of being, *'I'm a saloonkeeper'*, becomes a process of doing, *'Regento un cabaret'*, meaning *'I run a cabaret'*. As can be seen, in addition to this shift in the type of the process from a process of being to a process of doing, the content of this short passage is manipulated, thus weakening the relationship between the source text and target text – this is one of the norms proposed by Chesterman 1997, which is called a 'relation norm', i.e. there should be a relationship between the source text and the target text; otherwise, it is not a translation.

Tenor of discourse

'Tenor', as mentioned above, refers to the relationship between the participants; it can be realized through evaluative words, modality, mood, and the like. According to House's (1977/1981, 1997, 2015) translation evaluation model, tenor covers "the addresser's temporal, geographical and social provenance as well as his intellectual, emotional or affective stance (his 'personal viewpoint')" (1997: 109). Bayar (2007: 140), echoing Halliday's (1978) views, states that tenor "regulates the degree of formality between participants in the text or between the text sender and the text receiver or both". At this level, the reader, according to Bayar (2007), "can infer the social status and/or relations obtaining between in-text participants and between the text sender and receiver". She (Ibid.) emphasizes: "Selections in the text are thus made consistently with such status and relations". By analysing the tenor of the text, one can infer what the author and the audience of the text is like, as well as the relationship between the author and his/her audience. So, the tenor of a given text, according to Bell (1991: 186–8) can be signalled along four overlapping categories: (1) 'personalization' as opposed to 'impersonalization', (2) 'accessibility' as opposed to 'inaccessibility', (3) 'social distance' as opposed to 'standing', and (4) 'formality' as opposed to 'informality'.

(Im)personalization

'Personalization' refers to the presence of the speaker/writer, on the one hand, and listener/reader, on the other hand, in the text. To create a feeling of solidarity and/or intimacy, to provoke the intended reader and get them involved in the situation by letting them feel they are, as it were, physically present in that situation, writers opt for personalization. Such personalization can be achieved via many techniques, including the use of:

- the first person pronoun *'I'*, referring to the writer;
- the second person pronoun *'you'*, referring to the reader;
- the pronoun *'we'*, referring to both the writer and the reader;
- directives, for instance, *'see the next section'*;
- rhetorical questions;
- other questions put in the mouth of the reader or an imagined participant.

'Impersonalization', on the other hand, is related to objectivity whereby writers try to distance themselves from their readers, laying more emphasis on the message itself, rather than the participants (Bell 1991: 187). Impersonalization can be achieved by opting for:

- the pronoun *'it'* as a subject instead of *'I'*;
- passive structures in place of active structures;
- abstract nouns, among others.

In a similar vein, House (1981: 73–4) writes that impersonalization can be detected by tracing certain syntactic means, such as:

- the complexity of noun phrases;
- presence of over-correctness;
- absence of contractions and elliptical clauses.

(In)accessibility

'Accessibility', as opposed to 'inaccessibility', refers to the amount of information that is presumably shared by the writer and the intended reader. So when writers assume that the information in their minds is universally known and thus supposedly shared by a great number of readers, they feel that less needs to be expressed explicitly in the text, and thus the text becomes less accessible (cf. Bell 1991: 188). So, the notion of accessibility versus inaccessibility is very much related to explicitness versus implicitness.

Politeness: Social distance versus standing

'Politeness' is defined here as a means utilized by participants to show their awareness of others' face, whether negative or positive. Showing awareness of the public self-image of another person who is "socially distant is often described in terms of respect or deference", whereas showing awareness of the face of another person who is "socially close is often described in terms of friendliness, camaraderie, or solidarity" (Yule 1985/ 1996: 60). In touching on the tenor of discourse, Bell (1991: 187) holds that politeness can be studied in two different ways:

- One is horizontal, measuring "the distance between the social groups" (i.e. social distance).
- The other is vertical, reflecting a "power relationship connected with status, seniority and authority" (i.e. standing).

(In)formality

'Formality', as opposed to 'informality', refers to the attention the language user pays to "the structuring of the message" (Bell 1991: 186). Extra attention, as Bell (Ibid.) elaborates, "leads to more care in writing and this marks the text as possessing a higher degree of formality and signals a more distant relationship between sender and receiver(s)".

How the register of a text might be changed through translation can be seen in the following example quoted from Gu and Wang (2021: 388):

Chinese	我也深知中国的稳定和发展来之不易 … 13年来, 中国所取得的巨大成就说明稳定是至关重 要。
Back translation	I too deeply know that China's stability and development didn't come easy … 13 years on, China's massive achievements indicate that stability is vital.
English	I know so well the stability and development of this country have not come by easily … The tremendous achievements we have scored over the past 13 years have fully proven that stability is of vital importance.

Here, the writer opted for impersonalizing the second part of the passage *'13 years on, China's massive achievements indicate that stability is vital'*, thereby emphasizing the distance between him/her and the intended readers. By contrast, the translator decided to personalize it by opting for the inclusive plural pronoun *'we'*, thus reducing the distance between the text producer and text receiver, on the one hand, and creating solidarity and intimacy between them on the other hand. But not only this, the translator also added the evaluatively active word *'fully'* before the verb *'to prove'*, which is an example of 'endorsement' that indicates that the translator decided to intervene in the text so as to insist upon the value of the proposition *'stability is of vital importance'*. The result is that the writer's attitude is changed through translation, which also contributes to shifting the register. To reinforce this point, let us consider how the following sign used in a public swimming pool in Liverpool is translated into German:

ST	Please vacate the swimming pool
TT1	Die Badezeit ist zu Ende
Back translation	Bath time is over
TT2 (literal)	Bitte verlassen Sie das Schwimmbad
Back translation	Please vacate the swimming pool

The above example shows how the attention is shifted from focusing on actions performed by human beings, as in the process of doing expressed by the verb *'to vacate'* that requires people to do something, towards the message itself expressed by *'Bath time is over'*. This results in shifting the register, in particular its tenor and the interpersonal meaning. In the English original, to elaborate, the distance between the text producer and text receiver is reduced, thus creating solidarity and intimacy between them. In the German translation (TT1), however, the distance between them is emphasized by impersonalizing the text.

Mode of discourse

'Mode of discourse' refers to the channel used by language users to carry their message in a particular medium. The medium can be written or spoken. The spoken mode can be subdivided into spontaneous versus non-spontaneous, while the written one can be subdivided into written to be spoken, written to be spoken as if not written, and written not necessarily to be spoken (e.g. to be read, to be read as if heard or as if overheard) (cf. Gregory and Carroll 1978: 37–47; Bell 1991: 191; Al-Rubai'i 1996: 69). However, writers, in particular literary writers, sometimes tend to mix written and spoken modes of discourse in their writing in an attempt to bring about a realistic illusion. In this regard, Leech and Short (1981; also discussed in Al-Rubai'i 2005: 10–12) stress that there are five notions of realism that may help in bringing out such a realistic illusion: verisimilitude, credibility, authenticity, objectivity, and vividness. Al-Rubai'i (1996: 68) states that writers can relate written modes of discourse to spoken ones by:

- making use of dialectal features;
- utilizing the features of spoken language, e.g. elisions, fillers, and corrections;
- indicating the character's way of speaking, e.g. *'she said in a low voice'*;
- using graphological devices, such as italics, capitalization, dashes, dots, or quotation marks.

Consider the following short passage taken from Mahfouz's novel أولاد حارتنا (1959/1986: 126–7) translated by Philip Stewart (1997: 110) into English as *Children of Gebelawi*:

Arabic	كوني محضر خير يا ست هانم. فقالت هدى هانم بصوت متهدج من الغضب: قطع الطرق لا يكون بالنهار والشمس طالعة. فقالت تمر حنة بامتعاض: الله يسامحك يا ست هانم، الحق على جدنا الذي أغلق على نفسه الأبواب.
Back translation	Contribute positively, madam. Madam Hudaa said in a voice that was trembling with anger: "Banditry cannot happen during the day and the sun is rising". Tamerhinna said wryly: "May God forgive you, Madam. Blame is on our grandfather who closed the doors on himself".
English	Use your good influence, madam. Hudaa spoke in a voice that trembled with rage: You aren't going to get away with daylight robbery. Henna said angrily: God forgive you, madam! The truth is with our Ancestor who has locked the gates on himself.

Here, Mahfouz tries to indicate the character's way of speaking by using certain phrases, such as بصوت متهدج من الغضب *'in a voice trembling with anger'* and بامتعاض *'wryly'*, in addition to employing dialectal features, such as هانم as well as culture-specific expressions, such as الله يسامحك *'May God forgive you'*. As such, the mode of discourse here is written to be spoken. This should be reflected in the target text should you wish to maintain the register.

Connecting the dots (2): Appraisal and translation

According to Martin and White (2005: 33), 'appraisal' can be defined as the "interpersonal system at the level of discourse semantics". The interpersonal system gives issues such as "mood, modality, forms of address, pronoun choice and 'evaluative epithets'" full consideration with a view to identifying the meaning that can be expressed by these grammatical and lexical categories (Munday 2012: 14). However, it is worth noting that "much of appraisal is expressed by lexical choices and there are few grammatical structures that can be seen as having evolved with a primarily evaluative function" (Thompson 2004: 75). Although appraisal theory belongs to the interpersonal metafunction of Halliday's systemic functional grammar, these three metafunctions – ideational metafunction (a function for relating experience), interpersonal metafunction (a function for creating interpersonal relationships), and textual metafunction (a function for organizing information) – work hand in hand in creating certain patterns of meaning (Eggins 1994/ 2004: 111; Halliday and Matthiessen 2004: 599). The three metafunctions construct three types of meanings: 'representations', 'exchange', and 'messages' (Thompson 2004: 30). However, the relationship between participants, whether characterized by solidarity (intimate or distant), status (superior, inferior, or equal), or formality (formal or informal), and so on, is determined by the superordinate effect of the interpersonal metafunction.

> Note that the word 'metafunction' can be replaced with 'meaning' or 'function'.

Appraisal theory has been developed by Martin (1992a, 1992b, 1995a, 1995b) and White (1998, 2000, 2003) since the early 1990s; its categories "have been put to the test in numerous contexts and, as a consequence, modifications (an ongoing process) have been made" (Coffin and O'Halloran 2006: 84). Appraisal theory comprises three main sematic systems, as shown and explained below:

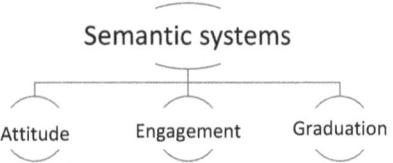

Semantic systems

Attitude   Engagement   Graduation

(1) 'Attitude', referring to one's feeling and opinion about something or somebody (e.g. *'Your email **pleased** me'*).

(2) 'Engagement', referring to the sources of an attitude and how language users position themselves concerning the attributed material, whether acknowledging it (e.g. *'Somebody **said** ... '*), endorsing it (e.g. *'Somebody **made** it **clear** ... '*), or distancing themselves from it (e.g. *'Somebody **claimed** ... '*).

(3) 'Graduation', referring to how an attitude is graded (e.g. *'She is a **very** clever girl'*).

Attitude

'Attitude' refers to one's feeling or opinion about something or somebody. If it is about something, then we have an example of 'appreciation' that can be subdivided according to Martin and White (2005) into 'reaction', 'composition', or 'valuation'. However, if it is about somebody, then we have an example of 'judgement', which has something to do with such notions as ethical versus unethical, honest versus dishonest, normal versus abnormal, and so on. Judgement is categorized by Martin and White (2005) into two main groups: 'social esteem' and 'social sanction'. Social esteem, i.e. how special (normality), capable (capacity), and resolute (tenacity) people are, involves admiration or criticism. Social sanction, i.e. how truthful people are (veracity) or how ethical people are (propriety), however, involves praise or condemnation. Below are illustrative examples.

> Identify the type of 'judgement' in this sentence:
> *'She is naughty'.*

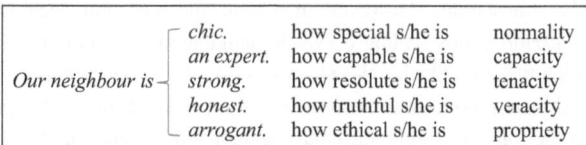

	chic.	how special s/he is	normality
	an expert.	how capable s/he is	capacity
Our neighbour is	*strong.*	how resolute s/he is	tenacity
	honest.	how truthful s/he is	veracity
	arrogant.	how ethical s/he is	propriety

However, when the attitudinal assessment is concerned with emotions such as **happiness** versus **unhappiness** (emotions that have something to do with 'affairs of the heart', such as happiness, sadness, love, and hate), **satisfaction** versus **dissatisfaction** (feelings of peace, fear, confidence, and trust), or **security** versus **insecurity** (feelings that have something to do with achievement and frustration, whose source is the activities we are engaged in), then we have an example of 'affect', as shown in the following three sentences:

I ^{feel} tired. (by virtue of the process of sensing expressed by the verb *'to feel'* we have an example of 'affect' as we are talking about our feelings)

She is a ^{strong} girl. (by virtue of the evaluative word *'strong'* we have an example of 'judgement' as we are evaluating somebody's character)

It is a ^{boring} lecture. (by virtue of the evaluative word *'boring'* we have an example of 'appreciation' as we are evaluating something, i.e. the lecture)

To translate appropriately, that is, reflecting the language user's attitude, evaluatively active words should be paid extra attention in translating from language *A* to language *B*. To explain, let us translate the following simple sentence into German, French, Turkish, Arabic, and Persian.

English	His lecture was terribly boring.
German	Sein Vortrag war furchtbar langweilig.
Back translation	His lecture was terribly boring.
French	Son cours était terriblement ennuyeux.
Back translation	His class was terribly boring.
Turkish	Onun dersi çok sıkıcıydı.
Back translation	His/her lecturer was very boring.
Arabic	كانت محاضرته مملة.
Back translation	His lecture was boring.
Persian	سخنرانی‌اش به‌شدت کسل‌کننده بود.
Back translation	His lecture was extremely boring.

In English, due to the presence of the evaluatively active word *'boring'*, the language user's negative attitude towards the lecture can be easily figured out. This negative attitude is further emphasized through the use of the adverb *'terribly'*. This negative attitude was also reflected in the German, French, Turkish, and Persian translations. However, in Arabic, the translator decided not to translate *'terribly'*, thus scaling down the language user's attitude. Had s/he opted for a translation like كانت محاضرته مملة جدًا *'His lecture was very boring'*, s/he would have produced an accurate translation. To reinforce this point, let us discuss the following authentic example quoted from Gu (2020: 183) where the Chinese premier refuted what had been hinted by the journalist that the cause of the widespread corruption in China is one-party rule.

ST (Chinese)	我看不出这个反腐败的问题一个党执政，多党轮流执政 有什么太大的关系[...]关键是法制，尤其要坚决地执法，- 中国在这方面已经取得了很大的成绩。
Back translation	I don't see that this anti-corruption issue has anything significant to do with one-party rule or multi-party rule … the key is the rule of law, especially to strictly enforce the law. China has in this respect achieved great results.
TT (English)	I do not see a very significant link or clear logic between fighting corruption on the one hand and exercising one-party rule or multi-party rule … in my view the key is for us to work to build our legal system and also to exercise very strict law enforcement in our country. So in fact, we have already made significant result and accomplishment.

In this example, as the back translation shows, the hint that the cause of the widespread corruption in China is the one-party rule is denied by the Chinese premier who holds the view that this anti-corruption issue has nothing significant to do with one-party rule or multi-party rule. In the target text, however, the Chinese premier's attitude towards the attributed material was scaled up by the interpreter when adding the noun phrase *'clear logic'*. Further, the emphatic *'in fact'* and the noun *'accomplishment'* were added by the interpreter, thereby "foregrounding (Fairclough 1995) China's positive achievements made in the enforcement of law as 'fact' that is irrefutable and praiseworthy. Such metadiscursive (re)framing leads to a more favourable presentation of the self, in this case the Chinese government" (Gu 2020: 183).

Attitudinal assessment

Attitudinal assessment whether 'affect', 'judgement', or 'appreciation' can be classified into positive or negative attitudes. Further, they can be classified into 'inscribed' (i.e. explicit regardless of the context, as in *'ugly'*) or 'invoked' (i.e. implicit and contextually based, as in *'big'*), as summarized below:

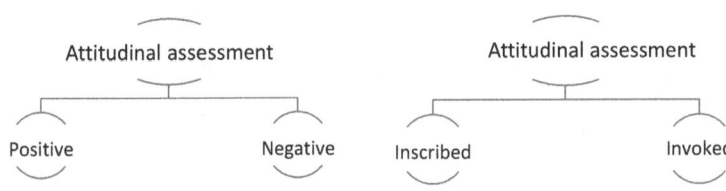

Invoked attitudes (also known as 'invocations') can be further subclassified into two main types: 'evocations' and 'provocations', as shown below:

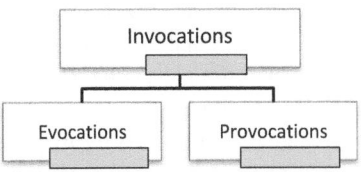

Evocations refer to informational content, which is content that invokes an attitudinal response by the text recipient (be it negative or positive) not because of the attitudinal qualities that they have, but because the text producer, with the intention to trigger an attitudinal response in the text recipient, decides to (1) select those evaluatively inactive elements, (2) place them beside evaluatively active elements, and then (3) implicitly invite the text recipient to make a connection among the evaluative and non-evaluative elements. So, the text producer triggers the attitudinal response in the text recipient only if they share the same assumption.

Identify the type of attitudinal assessment, whether it is an 'affect', 'judgement', or 'appreciation' in the following sentence: *'The film made me cry last night'.*

Identify the type of attitudinal assessment, whether it is 'inscribed' or 'invoked', in this sentence: *'The man with the red hair is handsome'.*

Provocation, on the other hand, is a mechanism employed by language users (be they writers or speakers) to trigger/provoke in their readers/listeners' minds a particular attitudinal response (negative or positive). According to Martin and White (2005), provocations can be realized by virtue of certain techniques, such as 'intensification through non-core lexis', 'metaphor', 'counter-expectancy', 'distancing formulations', and so on. Accordingly, provocations are not of themselves evaluative, but are rather contextually based, standing somewhere between 'inscribed', i.e. explicit attitudes, and 'evoked', i.e. implicit attitudes (Martin and White 2005: 67). To explain, let us consider the following example taken from a documentary film titled *The Fall: Final Days of the Caliphate* subtitled by *CNN Arabic* as: السقوط آخر أيام خلافة داعش المزعومة:

English	In defeat, the men of the so-called Islamic State bow their heads and cover their faces.
Arabic	بانهزام، أحنى مقاتلو ما تسمى بالدولة الإسلامية رؤوسهم وغطوا وجوههم.
Back translation	In defeat, the fighters of the so-called Islamic State bowed their heads and covered their faces.

Will the language user's attitude be changed if we remove the distancing formulation *'so called'*? Discuss.

In this example, there are certain evaluatively inactive materials, i.e. they are not evaluative in themselves, such as *'the men of the Islamic State'*, *'bow their heads'*, and *'cover their faces'*. However, by placing them with evaluatively active materials, such as the preposition phrase functioning as a comment adjunct *'in defeat'* and the distancing formulation *'so-called'*, the speaker invites his readers/listeners to make connections among those evaluative and non-evaluative materials with the potential to reinforce the negative response in his audience towards the men of ISIS and ISIS itself. These examples of inscribed attitude (*'in defeat'*), provoked attitude expressed by the distancing formulation *'so-called'*, and evoked attitude expressed by the evaluatively inactive materials *'the men of the Islamic State'*, *'bow their heads'*, and *'cover their faces'* were accurately reflected by the translator apart from changing *'men'* into مقاتلو *'fighters'*. It is worth noting that placing the lexical item مقاتلو *'fighters'* whose denotative meaning is narrower and less specific compared with *'men'* beside أحنى *'bowed'* scales up the speaker's attitude towards those men of ISIS. As such, this can be considered as an example of intervention by the translator. However, we are not sure whether the translator intervened on purpose or by accident.

Can we consider the translation of *'men'* into مقاتلو *'fighters'* as an example of 'particularization'?

Engagement

Engagement, as a semantic system, deals with the sources of the attitude. According to Bakhtin (1981), discourses can be classified into two main types: 'monoglossic', one voice, and 'heteroglossic', more than one voice, as shown below:

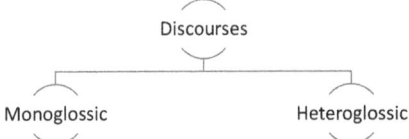

When a discourse is monoglossic, there is no reference to any external viewpoint other than the author's. However, when the discourse is heteroglossic, the source of voice refers to different voices, not only the author's. Martin (2003) holds that language users can "position one opinion in relation to another" in a variety of ways, such as "quoting or reporting, acknowledging a possibility, denying, countering, affirming and so on" (174).

As regards heteroglossic discourses, they are classified by Martin and White (2005) into two main types: 'expansion' (in the form of 'attribution' or 'entertainment') and 'contraction' (in the form of 'proclaiming' or 'disclaiming'), as shown below:

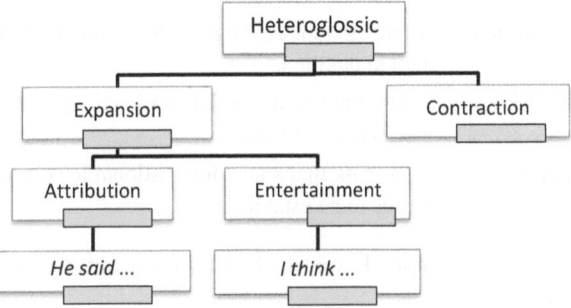

Note that 'entertainment' refers to the use of those words and structures (e.g. *'may'*, *'I think'*, *'possibly'*, etc.) that would indicate there are other possible positions other than the author's, thus making dialogic space for them.

To begin with 'contraction', it refers to the act of contracting the dialogic space instead of opening it up. Contraction is classified by Martin and White (2005) into two main types, namely 'proclaiming' and 'disclaiming', as shown below:

(1) 'Proclaiming' can be achieved by:
   (a) 'concurrence': using formulations that explicitly show the language user's agreement with a projected dialogic partner. Concurrence can be realized by certain words and expressions, including *'of course'*, *'naturally'*, *'certainly'*, and *'admittedly'* (122);
   (b) 'pronouncement': using a formulation that "involves authorial emphases or explicit authorial interventions" as in the use of *'I contend ... '*, *'the facts of the matter are ... '*, *'the truth of the matter is ... '*, etc. (127).

Identify the type of 'contraction' in the following sentence: *'Although she felt tired yesterday, she carried on teaching'.*

(2) 'Disclaiming' refers to the act of condensing the dialogic space instead of opening it up. This can be achieved by denying the current proposition (denial) or representing "the current proposition as replacing or supplanting, and thereby 'countering', a proposition which would have been expected in its place" (Martin and White 2005: 120).

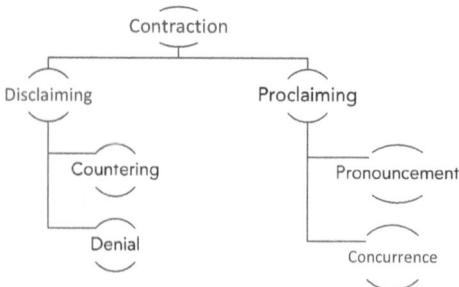

As regards 'expansion', the language user allows other voices to be heard in the form of 'attribution' or 'entertainment', i.e. it leaves good space for "dialogically alternative positions and voices" (Martin and White 2005: 102). Let us consider the following example quoted from Götz (2021: 157) to see how the interpreter managed to maintain the same dialogical space opened up by the effect of *'azt gondolom'* meaning *'I think'*.

ST (Hungarian)	… azt gondolom, hogy új nemzetközi jogi keretet kell kialakítani.
Back translation	… I think that a new international legal framework needs to be created.
TT (English)	… I think that a new international legal framework needs to be established.

In the following example, however, the translators acted differently, as shown here:

English	I think she has already travelled.
German	Sie ist schon gereist.
Back translation	She has already travelled.
French	Je pense qu'elle a déjà voyagé.
Back translation	I think she has already travelled.
Thai	เดาว่าหล่อนคงเดินทางไปแล้ว / dao wa lon khong doenthang pai laew.
Back translation	I guess [that] she has travelled already.
Arabic	بالطبع أنها سافرت.
Back translation	Of course she has travelled.

In this example, by means of the process of sensing expressed by the verb *'to think'*, we have a case of engagement (expansion: entertainment). This was reflected in French and Thai when opting for *'Je pense'* meaning *'I think'* and เดาว่า (dao wa) meaning *'I guess'*, respectively. However, in German, no space is opened up for alternative voices to be heard, thus changing the text type from a heteroglossic to a monoglossic one. In Arabic, however, by virtue of بالطبع *'of course'*, the shared belief, i.e. *'she has already travelled'*, is represented as very widely held in the current communicative context, thereby excluding any dialogistic alternatives from the ongoing colloquy. To put it differently, in Arabic through the use of بالطبع 'of course', we have an example of contraction, more accurately concurrence. Below is another example:

English	She claimed that he had attended yesterday's meeting.
French	Elle a dit qu'il avait assisté à la réunion d'hier.
German	Sie behauptete, er habe am gestrigen Treffen teilgenommen.
Spanish	Ella dijo que él había asistido a la reunión de ayer.
Thai	เธออ้างว่าเขาเข้าประชุมเมื่อวาน thoe ang wa khao khao prachum mueawan
Turkish	Dünkü toplantıya katıldığını söyledi.

By virtue of the framing verb 'to claim', we here have an example of engagement (expansion: attribution), where an external voice can be heard alongside the authorial voice. It is an example of 'distancing' where the writer explicitly distances him/herself from the attributed material. This was reflected in German and Thai, respectively, when the translators opted for 'behauptete' and อ้างว่า meaning 'claimed'. However, in the French, Spanish, and Turkish translations, the translators translated it into 'dit', 'dijo', and 'söyledi', respectively, meaning 'said', thereby changing the type of attribution from 'distancing' to 'acknowledging'. To reinforce this point, let us reconsider the following example adopted from Farghal (2008: 4) and discussed in Chapter 7:

ST (English)	In an interview with Newsweek yesterday, the Israeli Defense Minister said that the Palestinian suicide operations constitute the main cause for the Israeli troops entering cities in the West Bank.
TT (Arabic)	ادعى وزير الحرب الصهيوني في مقابلة مع مجلة النيوزويك أمس أن العمليات الاستشهادية الفلسطينية هي السبب الرئيس في اجتياح قوات الاحتلال الإسرائيلي للمدن الفلسطينية في الضفة الغربية المحتلة.
Back translation	In an interview with the Newsweek yesterday, the Zionist War Minister claimed that the Palestinian martyrdom operations are the main cause for the Zionist troops storming Palestinian cities in the occupied West Bank.

Here, as discussed in Chapter 7, the text is heteroglossic, i.e. there is more than one voice: the authorial voice and the Sayer of the process of saying expressed by the verb 'to say'. This neutral verb 'to say' was translated into ادعى 'to claim', thus changing the language user's attitude towards the attributed material. In the original text, it is an example of 'acknowledgement', where there is no explicit indication as to where the language user stands concerning the proposition. However, in the target text, by means of the framing verb ادعى *'to claim'*, we have a case of 'distancing' where the language user was presented as distancing him/herself from the attributed material.

Graduation

'Graduation', as a semantic system, is concerned with how the degree of appraisal, i.e. attitude or engagement, is adjusted; it deals with the main resources of grading that can be used by writers and speakers to scale up or scale down the strength of their attitude or engagement (Martin and White 2005: 135). Graduation resources are divided by Martin and White (2005) into two main types, 'force' and 'focus', as shown below:

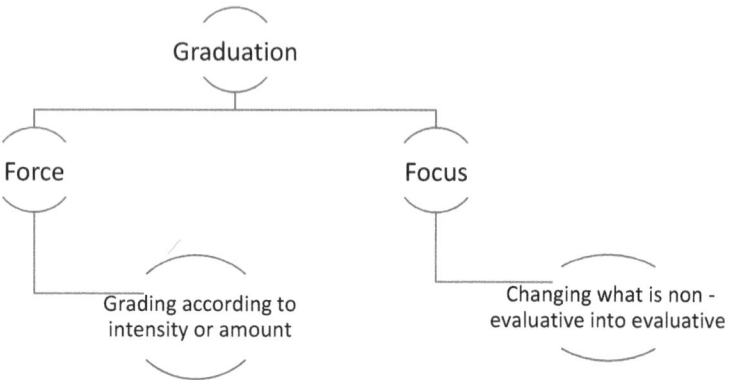

Identify the type of 'graduation', whether it is 'force' or 'focus' in the following sentence: *'He has helped us a great deal'.*

While the first type, 'force', is based on "grading according to intensity or amount", as in the use of *'extremely'*, *'fairly'*, *'a bit'*, *'somehow'*, *'fairly'*, *'very'*, *'utterly'*, etc., the second type, 'focus', is based on "grading according to prototypicality and the preciseness", as in the use of words and expressions like *'true'*, *'a kind of'*, and *'a sort of'* (Martin and White 2005: 137).

So, through the resources of graduation, the writer/speaker can add a personal meaning to the text that s/he is trying to produce, as shown in the following example:

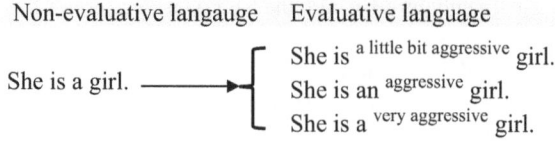

Here, without relying on the context, facial expressions, and so on, the simple sentence *'She is a girl'* is a non-evaluative sentence. However, by the effect of the evaluative words used, namely *'aggressive'*, *'a little bit'*, and *'very'*, in addition to adjusting the degree of the appraisal and changing a non-gradable word *'girl'* to a gradable one, a personal meaning is added that can help us figure out the language user's attitude towards the girl, whether negative or positive. This personal meaning along with the degree of appraisal should be given adequate consideration by translators. By way of illustration, let us consider the following example taken from a documentary film titled *The Fall: Final Days of the Caliphate* subtitled by *CNN Arabic* as السقوط: آخر أيام خلافة داعش المزعومة:

ST (English)	Syrian Democratic Forces have made good progress within the town, but they are encountering some resistance from the ISIS fighters. This despite the constant heavy coalition airstrikes on the town.
TT (Arabic)	قوات سوريا الديمقراطية حققت تقدماً جيداً في المدينة، لكنها تواجه مقاومة من مقاتلي داعش. هذا رغم القصف الجوي الكثيف للتحالف على البلدة.
Back translation	Syrian Democratic Forces have made good progress within the city, but they are encountering resistance from the ISIS fighters. This despite the heavy coalition airstrikes on the town.

Here, the evaluatively active words *'good'* and *'heavy'* were taken into account by the translator when opting for جيدًا *'good'* and كثيف *'heavy'*. Further, the lexical item *'town'*, which is a scaled-down version of the lexical item *'city'*, was given adequate consideration by the translator when opting for بلدة *'town'* rather than مدينة *'city'*. However, the evaluatively inert word *'constant'* was ignored. By virtue of the lexical item *'constant'*, the process of doing expressed implicitly through the compound complex word *'airstrikes'* is drawn out over a period of time. However, the translator decided not to translate it at all, thus weakening the relationship between the source text and the target text. Had s/he opted for the lexical item المتواصل *'constant'* in a rendering of the following kind هذا رغم القصف الجوي الكثيف والمتواصل للتحالف على البلدة, s/he would have created a similar mental image. Without the lexical item المتواصل *'constant'*, we are not sure if the process of doing is characterized by having breaks and interruptions or not. As regards the speaker's attitude towards these propositions, here the ideational content can guide the reader to the stance adopted by the speaker. However, the speaker decided to use indicators of counter-expectancy, such as *'but'* and *'despite'*, to further "alert the reader that attitudinal values" are there (Martin and White 2005: 67). So, the whole scene here is not dynamically neutral, but rather characterized by a 'force dynamic' value of forcing the Syrian Democratic Forces, who tend to carry on making more progress, not to make that progress (for more details on 'force dynamics', see Chapter 12).

Connecting the dots (3): Cohesion and translation

Any text, according to de Beaugrande and Dressler (1981), should include seven criteria:

(1) 'Cohesion', referring to the surface relationships among the components of the text.

(2) 'Coherence', referring to how the text hangs conceptually.
(3) 'Intentionality', referring to the language user's goals.
(4) 'Acceptability', referring to the relevancy and importance of the text to the reader.
(5) 'Informativity', referring to the amount of new information the text contains.
(6) 'Situationality', referring to the relevancy of the text to its context of situation.
(7) 'Intertextuality', referring to the relationship of the text with, and its dependency on, other texts.

The first two criteria (cohesion and coherence) can be defined as 'text internal', which make the text hang together cohesively and coherently, whereas other five criteria are 'text external' (cf. Titscher et al. 2000: 22; Almanna 2016: 126).

Cohesion is divided by Halliday and Hasan (1976) into two main types:

(1) 'Grammatical cohesion' that includes 'reference', 'substitution', 'ellipsis', and 'conjunction'.
(2) 'Lexical cohesion' that covers 'reiteration' and 'collocation'.

However, there are several cohesive devices that do not fall under any of these headings, such as thematic progression, parallel structures, and continuity of tense, aspect, and mood (cf. Hall 2008: 171), as explained below.

Reference

'Reference' refers to the use of pronouns, articles, or adverbs to refer backward or forward to an item in the text, thereby creating an anaphoric (referring backward to an item within the text) or cataphoric (referring forward to an item within the text) cohesive relation within the text, as in:

> Look at the girl. She is very tall. (the pronoun *'she'* refers back to the noun phrase *'the girl'*, thus creating an anaphoric reference)

> In addition to his visit to Kuwait, the prime minister visited Iraq. (the possessive adjective *'his'* refers forward to the noun phrase *'the prime minister'*, thus creating a cataphoric reference)

Substitution

'Substitution' refers to the act of replacing one lexical item or expression with another. In English, substitution is achieved by certain words, such as *'one'*, *'ones'*, *'same'*, *'do'*, *'does'*, *'did'*, *'so'*, and *'not'*, as in:

> This bottle of water isn't cold. Can you give me another one? (here the phrase *'this bottle of water'* is replaced with the pronoun *'one'*)

Ellipsis

'Ellipsis' refers to the omission of some elements from the text without affecting the overall meaning, as in:

> Last year, Tom <u>published</u> a book, but Suzan Ø an article. (here, the finite verb *'published'* is omitted, thus creating a cohesive relation within the text)

Conjunction

'Conjunction' makes the segments of a given passage hang together as a cohesive text. The relationship between the cojoined segments is marked when a conjunct is used, i.e. explicit conjunction; otherwise, it is unmarked when no conjunct is used, i.e. implicit conjunction, as shown in the following example:

> She invited all her friends to her birthday party, but nobody came. (here, these two finite clauses are in a countering relationship marked by virtue of the linking word *'but'*)

Reiteration

'Reiteration' refers to the process of making a passage hang together as a cohesive text by recruiting the different relations the lexical items have in a given language, such as 'synonymy' (as in *'child'* and *'kid'*), 'antonymy' (as in *'big'* and *'small'*), 'whole–part' (as in *'body'* and *'leg'*), 'part–whole' (as in *'window'* and *'room'*), 'part–part' (as in *'eye'* and *'nose'*), 'homophony' (as in *'buy'* and *'bye'*), 'polysemy' (as in the word *'eye'*), 'homonymy' (as in the word *'spring'*), and 'general words' (as in *'burger'* and *'hamburger'*). For more information, see Chapter 6 of this book.

Collocation

'Collocation' refers to the tendency of some words to collocate with others, thereby contributing to text connectivity. The word *'heavy'* collocates well with lexical items such as *'rain'*, *'meal'*, and *'smoker'*, and the word *'smart'* collocates well with lexical items such as *'boy'* and *'phone'*.

Repetition

'Repetition' refers to a repetition of the syntactic and semantic configuration so as to balance ideas of equal importance, as in this example quoted from Greene's (1980: 9–10) *The Bomb Party*:

> I think that I used to detest Doctor Fischer more than any other man I have known just as I loved his daughter more than any other woman.

Parallelism

'Parallelism', labelled 'iconic linkage' by House (1997: 45), refers to repeated occurrence of a particular syntactic and semantic configuration in juxtaposition, thereby contributing to text connectivity, as in:

> The boy was in the living room, reading a novel, while the girl was in the kitchen, preparing the lunch.

Thematic progression

'Thematic progression' refers to such features as the organization of the themes and rhemes and how they stay the same or change over the course of the text. In terms of markedness, themes (what the clauses are concerned with) are classified by Baker (1992) into two types: 'marked themes', i.e. unusual or atypical, and 'unmarked themes', i.e. usual or typical. When translating between languages, the issue of markedness should be given full consideration. Consider the following example:

English	It was the girl who helped the injured boy.
German	Das Mädchen half dem verletzten Jungen.
Back translation	The girl helped the injured boy.
Arabic	ساعدت الفتاةُ الولد المجروح.
Back translation	The girl helped the injured boy.

Here, the noun phrase *'the girl'* in English is a marked theme created by using a cleft structure. However, in German and Arabic, the theme becomes unmarked. This is an example of a shift in thematic progression.

Continuity of tense, aspect, mood, etc.

This refers to the use of the same combination of tense and aspect or mood in a passage, thus creating cohesive relations within the text, as in this example:

> One night, three thieves |stole| a lot of money from a rich man's house. They |put| the money in a bag and |went| to the forest. They |felt| very hungry. So, one of them |went| to a nearby village to buy food. The other two |remained| in the forest to take care of the bag of money.

Here, the events occurred in the past (tense) and the emphasis is placed on the completion of the actions (aspect). Combining tense and aspect in this passage in addition to other cohesive devices makes the passage hang together as a cohesive text.

Studies on cohesion shifts that occur while translating from language *A* to language *B* (cf. Blum-Kulka 1986/2004; Hoey 1991; Baker 1992; House 2004, 2006; Almanna 2016; among others) demonstrate that languages have different textual conventions and preferences in the use of certain patterns of cohesion, in particular with regard to lexical repetition, reference, substitution, and conjunction. Blum-Kulka (1986/2004) hypothesizes that translators tend to explicate what is implicitly expressed in the source text, thereby increasing the cohesive ties in the target language. But the question that arises here is related to the issue of directionality.

Using a corpus of translations of children's books from English into German and vice versa, House (2004) concludes that directionality should be given full consideration when the issue of explicitation is discussed. This is because procedures of explicitation which are common in translations from English into German are not traceable in the other translational direction (for more details, see the discussion on 'translation universals' in the first chapter of this book). The same holds true for Arabic–English translation. In translating a narrative text from English into Arabic, translators tend to add certain linking words, thus explicitating what is implicitly expressed in the source text. However, when translating from Arabic into English, translators tend to omit some of those linking words, in particular the additive connector و 'and' and ف 'so', etc. To explain, let us consider the into-Arabic translation of this short text extracted from Mary Ali's text titled *Women's Liberation through Islam* (published on 24 June 2013):

ST	Today people think that women are liberated in the West and that the women's liberation movement began in the 20th century. [Implicit connector] Actually, the women's liberation movement was not begun by women, but was revealed by God to a man in the seventh century by the name of Muhammad, may the mercy and blessings of God be upon him, the last Prophet of God. [Implicit connector] The Quran and the Sunnah of the Prophet are the sources from which every Muslim woman derives her rights and duties.
TT	يشيع اليومَ بين الناس اعتقاد بأن نساء الغرب ينعمن بالحرية وأن بداية حركة تحرير المرأة تعود إلى القرن العشرين. وَلَكِنْ، في الحقيقة، أن النساء لم يكن لهن يد في إطلاق شرارة هذه الحركة، بل أوحى بها الله سبحانه وتعالى على نبيه محمد (صلى الله عليه وسلم) خاتم الأنبياء والرّسل في القرن السابع الميلاديِّ، فَالقرآن الكريم والسّنة النّبوية هما المصدران اللذان يحددان للمرأة حقوقها وواجباتها.
Back translation	Today, it is widely believed that women in the West enjoy freedom and that the beginning of the women's liberation movement dates back to the twentieth century. But, in fact, the women did not have a hand in sparking this movement. Rather, God Almighty revealed it to His Prophet Mohammad (may God bless him and grant him peace), the Seal of the Prophets and Messengers in the seventh century AD. And the Holy Qur'an and the Sunnah are the two sources that determine women's rights and duties.

Here, the translator explicated the relationship between the first two sentences by opting for the linking word *'but'*, thus indicating that these two sentences are in a countering relation. Similarly, he added the linking word فـ *'so'* to connect the last two sentences. Added to this, he opted for increasing other cohesive ties, such as collocation when resorting to words and expressions that collocate well in Arabic, such as يشيع اعتقاد *'to be widely believed'*, ينعمن بالحرية *'to enjoy freedom'*, ليس لهن يد *'having no hand'*, إطلاق شرارة *'to spark'*, الأنبياء والرّسل *'prophets and messengers'*, and the like.

Connecting the dots (4): Translation assessment

In her original translation assessment model (1977/1981) and her revised models (1997, 2015, 2018a), House characterizes her approach as one in which translation is viewed as an act of 're-contextualization', emphasizing the crucial importance of the contextual embeddedness of any text. Without acknowledging the importance of context for a text, its meaning cannot be determined (House 2006). Another important concept underlying House's model is 'functional equivalence' and the question of whether such equivalence can be achieved in translation. Given such a view of translation, Hallidayan register analysis (see above) offered itself as an appropriate methodology for constructing a model for translation quality assessment. House modified and extended register analysis to include notions from discourse analysis, pragmatics, and corpus linguistics to provide a workable procedure for in-depth analysis of the source and the translation texts, facilitating a systematic comparison of the resultant textual 'profiles' and a final statement of the translation quality.

In House's view, 'field' refers to the subject matter and social action, covering the specificity of lexical items. Tenor refers to "the addresser's temporal, geographical and social provenance as well as his/her intellectual, emotional or affective stance (his/her) 'personal viewpoint')" (1997: 109; 2015: 64) and 'social attitude', referring to formal, consultative, or informal style. Mode refers to the channel of communication (spoken/written, etc.) and the degree of participation between addresser and addressee (monologue, dialogue, etc.).

The procedure suggested by House's model consists of the following steps:

(1) A detailed linguistic analysis of the source text is conducted using the register categories provided in the model. The outcome of this analysis is a textual profile of the source text.
(2) The source text's genre and the translation text's genre are compared.
(3) Then, a 'statement of function' of the source text is made. This function consists of ideational and interpersonal components. While the ideational component relates to what information is conveyed and how it is conveyed, the interpersonal function relates to what the relationship is like between the text's author and his/her audience.

(4) The same descriptive process is then carried out for the target text.

(5) The textual profiles of the source and target texts are compared, resulting in a statement of 'mismatches' or errors. These are categorized according to the situational dimensions of register and genre used in House's model. Such dimensional errors are referred to as 'covertly erroneous errors' (House 1997: 45) to distinguish them from 'overtly erroneous errors', which are 'denotative mismatches' (i.e. errors that give an incorrect semantic meaning compared to the source text) or 'target system errors' (i.e. errors which do not conform to the formal grammatical or lexical requirements of the target language).

(6) Then a 'statement of quality' is made of the translation.

(7) Finally, there is one of two types of translation: 'overt translation' or 'covert translation'.

Here is a diagram showing the parts of the model and how they are connected:

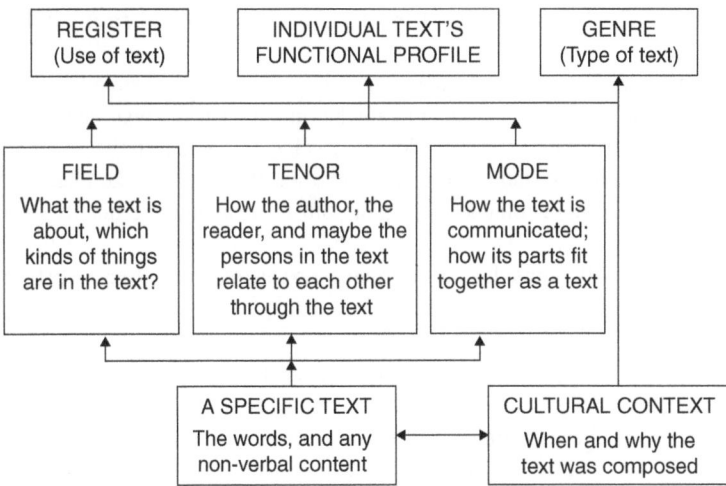

According to House (2018a:89), an overt translation, as explained in Chapter 8 of this book, is a type of translation in which functional equivalence cannot be achieved because of the singularity of the text as a source culture event (e.g. a speech at a certain time and place given by a prominent person). In an overt translation, the source text is, as far as possible, preserved such that the linguistic forms and structures often 'shine through' in the translation text. The translation is 'overt' because it is quite overtly a translation, not an original text.

A covert translation, on the other hand, is a type of translation in which the function of the source text can be maintained, such that the translation enjoys the status of an original source text in the target culture. The translation is covert because it is not marked pragmatically as a translation of a source text but may, conceivably, have been created

Think of any translation in which the translator inserted a 'cultural filter'?

in its own right as an independent text. In order to keep the function of the source text equivalent in the translation text, a so-called 'cultural filter' needs to be inserted between the source text and its translation. The cultural filter is an instrument by means of which a translator makes the translation compatible with target culture discourse norms and preferences.

In evaluating a translation, it is essential that the fundamental differences between these two types of translation be taken into account. Overt and covert translations clearly make very different demands on translation evaluation. The difficulty of evaluating an overt translation is reduced in that considerations of cultural filtering can be omitted. Overt translations are "more straightforward", the originals being taken over "unfiltered" and "simply" transposed from the source to the target culture in the medium of a new language. The major difficulty in translating overtly is, of course, finding linguistic- cultural 'equivalents', particularly along the dimension of tenor and its characterizations of the author's temporal, social, and geographical provenance. However, here we deal with overt manifestations of cultural phenomena which must be transferred only because they happen to be manifest linguistically in the original.

In translation quality assessment, it is important to be maximally aware of the difference between scientifically based linguistic analysis and social judgement (relating to values, ideology, identity, gender issues etc.) in evaluating any translation. In this volume we clearly prioritize linguistic analysis as a more reliable and valid path to assessing the quality of a translation.

To exemplify, consider the following text taken from House (2018b: 156).

ST (English)	Suppose *you* are a doctor in an emergency room and a patient tells *you* she was raped two hours earlier. She is afraid she may have been exposed to HIV, the virus that causes AIDS but has heard that there is a "morning-after pill" to prevent HIV infection. Can *you* in fact do anything to block the virus from replicating and establishing infection?
TT (German)	In der Notfallaufnahme eines Krankenhauses berichtet eine Patientin, sie sei vor zwei Stunden vergewaltigt worden und nun in Sorge, AIDS-Erregern ausgesetzt zu sein, sie habe gehört, es gebe eine „Pille danach", die eine HIV-Infektion verhüte. Kann der Arzt überhaupt etwas tun, was eventuell vorhandene Viren hindern würde, sich zu vermehren und sich dauerhaft im Körper einzunisten?

Back translation	In the emergency room of a hospital a patient reports that she had been raped two hours ago and was now worrying that she had been exposed to the AIDS-Virus. She said she had heard that there was an "After-Pill", which might prevent an HIV-Infection. Can the doctor in fact do anything which might prevent potentially existing viruses from replicating and establishing themselves permanently in the body?

In this example, we can see how in the English source text an effort is made to 'draw the reader into the text' by simulating interaction between the writer and reader. The reader is addressed directly (*'you'*) and asked questions. In the German translation, however, this is not the case: there is no interaction, just a sober description. The translation can be understood as governed by an attempt to adapt the text to the preferences of the German target audience, a clear case of the operation of a cultural filter. Note that the changes made in the translation mostly concern the tenor of the text. The scene in the hospital in the German translation is presented, as it were, 'from the outside', readers not being asked to actively engage with what is presented.

Exercises and discussion

Exercise 1: Mark the following statements (T) if they are true and (F) if they are false.

(1) Transitivity is defined by Halliday (1976) from a functional point of view as a set of transitive verbs that requires objects.	
(2) In the sentence *'My sister called me yesterday'*, there is one participant expressed by the noun phrase *'my sister'*.	
(3) Grammatical cohesion is classified by Halliday and Hasan (1976) into four types: 'reference', 'reiteration', 'ellipsis', and 'substitution'.	
(4) Written modes of discourse and spoken ones can be related by utilizing, for instance, dialectal features.	
(5) According to Halliday (1985), to transform our experiences in life into wording, we need first to transform them into meaning, which is, in turn, transformed into wording.	
(6) To create a feeling of solidarity and/or intimacy, writers usually emphasize the distance between them and their readers.	
(7) In *'He mentioned this to me yesterday'*, the text is monoglossic.	

(8) Appraisal theory proposed by Martin and White (2005) is made up of three main sematic systems: 'affect', 'judgement', and 'appreciation'.	
(9) According to Bell (1991), the mode of a given discourse can be signalled via four overlapping scales of level. These are (1) 'personalization' as opposed to 'impersonalization', (2) 'accessibility' as opposed to 'inaccessibility', (3) 'social distance' as opposed to 'standing', and (4) 'formality' as opposed to 'informality'.	
(10) The language in the sentence *'She is a kind of mother'* is not evaluative.	

Exercise 2: Select any literary text to conduct a simple register analysis before translating it into your own language.

Exercise 3: Before translating the following sentences into your own language, identify (1) the type of language ('evaluative' or 'non-evaluative') and (2) the type of attitudinal assessment ('affect', 'judgement', or 'appreciation').

(1) I feel tired.
(2) The film made me cry.
(3) The film was lovely.
(4) The lecture was boring.
(5) The paragraph was inconsistent.
(6) The essay is creative.
(7) The proposal is strong.
(8) The girl is strong.
(9) She is a girl.
(10) Your email pleased me.

Exercise 4: Select any journalistic text and:

(1) translate it into your language, by assuming that your translation will be published by a newspaper in your country;
(2) comment on your translation by using Martin and White's (2005) appraisal theory.

Discussion and research points
(1) In your opinion, what are the main criteria that can be used for judging one translation as appropriate or inappropriate for a particular situation?
(2) Is there any difference between 'provocations' and 'evocations' in the sense Martin and White (2005) use these terms? Discuss.
(3) Do you agree with Hatim and Munday (2004: 187) who view 'register theory' as "one of the most significant contributions to

our understanding of the interaction between translation and linguistics"?

(4) Go through any translated text from English into your own language and carry out a register analysis using House's (2015) model.

(5) Go through any translated book from your own language into English and identify some examples where the translator explicitly interpolates him/herself in the target text, thereby twisting the original message to varying degrees.

(6) Select any English text and translate it into your language. Then comment on your own translation by referring to such notions as 'reference', 'ellipsis', 'substitution', 'conjunction', 'collocation', and 'reiteration'.

References

Almanna, A. (2016). *The Routledge Course in Translation Annotation: Arabic-English-Arabic*. London/New York: Routledge.

Almanna, A. (2018). *The Nuts and Bolts of Arabic–English Translation: An Introduction to Applied Contrastive Linguistics*. Newcastle upon Tyne: Cambridge Scholars Publishing.

Al-Rubai'i, A. (1996). *Translation Criticism: A Model for Assessing the Translation of Narrative Fictional Texts*. Unpublished PhD thesis. Iraq: Al-Mustansiriya University.

Al-Rubai'i, A. (2005). *Translation Criticism*. Durham: Durham Modern Languages Series.

Baker, M. (1992). *In Other Words: A Coursebook on Translation*. London/New York: Routledge.

Bakhtin, M. M. (1981). *The Dialogic Imagination* (trans. C. Emerson and M. Holquist). Austin, TX: University of Texas Press.

Bayar, M. (2007). *To Mean or Not to Mean*. Damascus: Kadmous Cultural Foundation.

Beaugrande, R., de and Dressler, W. (1981). *Introduction to Text Linguistics*. London/New York: Longman.

Bell, R. T. (1991). *Translation and Translating: Theory and Practice*. London/New York: Longman.

Blum-Kulka, S. (1986/ 2004). "Shifts of Cohesion and Coherence in Translation". In Venuti, L. (ed.), *The Translation Studies Reader* (pp. 298–329). London/New York: Routledge.

Coffin, C. and O'Halloran, K. (2006). "The Role of Appraisal and Corpora in Detecting Covert Evaluation", *Functions of Language*, Vol. 13(1), pp. 77–110.

Curtiz, M. (1942). *Casablanca*. American film drama, released in 1942.

Eggins, S. (1994/ 2004). *An Introduction to Systematic Functional Linguistics*. London/New York: Continuum.

Fairclough, N. 1995. *Discourse and Social Change*. Cambridge: Polity Press.

Farghal, M. (2008). "Extrinsic Managing: An Epitaph to Translational Ideological Move", *STJ: Sayyab Translation Journal*, Vol. 1, pp. 1–26.

Götz, A. (2021). "Hedging in Interpreted Speech: Cognitive Hedges in English and Hungarian Interpreting". In Almanna, A. and Gu, C. (eds.), *Translation as a Set of Frames* (pp. 147–64). London/New York: Routledge.

Greene, G. (1980). *The Bomb Party*. Harmondsworth: Penguin Books.

Gregory, M. and Carroll, S. (1978). *Language and Situation: Language Varieties and Their Social Contexts*. London: Routledge/Kegan Paul.

Gu, C. (2020). "The Metadiscursive (Re)framing of Fact, Truth and Reality in Interpreted Political Discourse: A Corpus-based CDA on the Premier's Press Conferences in China". In Almanna, A. and Sierra, J. J. M. (eds.), *Reframing Realities through Translation* (pp. 169–94). Oxford: Peter Lang.

Gu, C. and Wang, B. (2021). "Interpreter-Mediated Discourse as a Vital Source of Meaning Potential in Intercultural Communication: The Case of the Interpreted Premier-Meets-the-Press Conferences in China", *Language and Intercultural Communication*, Vol. 21(3), pp. 379–94.

Hall, M. F. (2008). *Discourse Analysis of Fictional Dialogue in Arabic to English Translation*. Unpublished PhD thesis. London: University of London.

Halliday, M. A. K. (1964). "Comparison and Translation". In Halliday, M. A. K., McIntosh, M., and Strevens, P. (eds.), *The Linguistic Sciences and Language Teaching* (pp. 111–34). London: Longman.

Halliday, M. A. K. (1976). "Notes on Transitivity and Theme in English. Part 2", *Journal of Linguistics*, Vol. 3(1), pp. 199–244.

Halliday, M. A. K. (1978). *Language as a Social Semiotic*. London: Edward Arnold.

Halliday, M. A. K. (1985). *An Introduction to Functional Grammar*. London: Edward Arnold.

Halliday, M. A. K. (1994). *An Introduction to Functional Grammar*. London: Edward Arnold.

Halliday, M. A. K. and Hasan, R. (1976). *Cohesion in English*. London: Longman Group Ltd.

Halliday, M. A. K. and Matthiessen, C. (2004). *An Introduction to Functional Grammar*. London: Edward Arnold.

Hatim, B. and Munday, J. (2004). *Translation: An Advanced Resource Book*. London/New York: Routledge.

Hoey, M. (1991). *Patterns of Lexis in Text*. Oxford: Oxford University Press.

House, J. (1977/1981). *A Model for Translation Quality Assessment*. Tübingen: Narr.

House, J. (1997). *Translation Quality Assessment: A Model Revisited*. Tübingen: Narr.

House, J. (2004). "Linguistic Aspects of the Translation of Children's Books". In Kittel, H., Frank, A. P., Greiner, N., Hermans, T., Koller, W., Lambert, J., and Paul, F. (eds.), *Übersetzung – Translation – Traduction: An International Handbook* (pp. 683–97). Berlin: Mouton de Gruyter.

House, J. (2006). "Text and Context in Translation", *Journal of Pragmatics*, Vol. 38, pp. 338–58.

House, J. (2015). *Translation Quality Assessment: Past and Present.* London: Routledge.

House, J. (2018a). *Translation: The Basics*. London: Routledge.

House, J. (2018b). "Translation Studies and Pragmatics". In Ilie, C. and Norrick, N. (eds.), *Pragmatics and Its Interfaces* (pp. 143–63). Amsterdam: Benjamins.

Leech, G. and Short, M. (1981). *Style in Fiction: A Linguistic Introduction to English Fictional Prose*. London: Longman.

Mahfouz, N. (1959/1986). أولاد حارتنا. Beirut: Dār Al-Adab.

Martin, J. R. (1992a). "Macro-proposals: Meaning by Degree". In Mann, W. C. and Thompson, S. (eds.), *Discourse Description: Diverse Analyses of a Fund-Raising Text* (pp. 359–95). Amsterdam: Benjamins.

Martin, J. R. (1992b). *English Text: System and Structure*. Amsterdam: Benjamins.

Martin, J. R. (1995a). "Text and Clause: Fractal Resonance", *Text*, Vol. 15(1), pp. 5–42.

Martin, J. R. (1995b). "Interpersonal Meaning, Persuasion and Public Discourse: Packing Semiotic Punch", *Australian Journal of Linguistics*, Vol. 15(1), pp. 33–67.

Martin, J. R. (2003). "Introduction". *Text*, Vol. 23(2), pp. 171–81.

Martin, J. R., and White, P. R. (2005). *The Language of Evaluation: Appraisal in English*. London/New York: Palgrave Macmillan.

Matthiessen, M. I. M. (1985/2014). *Halliday's Introduction to Functional Grammar* (4th edn). London/New York: Routledge.

Munday, J. (2012). *Evaluation in Translation: Critical Points of Translator Decision Making*. London/New York: Routledge.

Stewart, P. (1997). *Children of Gebelawi* (trans.). London: Heinemann.

Thompson, G. (2004). *Introducing Functional Grammar* (2nd edn). London: Arnold.

Titscher, S., Meyer, M., Wodak, R., and Velter, E. (2000). *Methods of Text and Discourse Analysis*. London/New York: Sage Publications.

White, P. R. (1998). *Telling Media Tales: The News Story as Rhetoric*. Unpublished PhD thesis. Sydney: University of Sydney.

White, P. R. (2000). "Media Objectivity and the Rhetoric of News Story Structure". In Ventola, E. (ed.), *Discourse and Community: Doing Functional Linguistics* (Language in Performance 21, pp. 379–97). Tübingen: Gunter Narr Verlag.

White, P. R. R. (2003). "Beyond Modality and Hedging: A Dialogic View of the Language of Intersubjective Stance", *Text* – Special Edition on Appraisal, pp. 259–84.

Yule, G. (1985/ 1996). *The Study of Language.* Cambridge: Cambridge University Press.

Sociolinguistics

10

In this chapter, you are introduced to several sociolinguistic concepts, including 'social identity', 'social factors', 'social dimensions', 'code-switching', 'convergence', and 'divergence'. These concepts are also discussed in a direct link to translation.

After studying this chapter, readers should be able to find answers to such sociolinguistic questions as 'What is sociolinguistics?', 'What is social identity?', 'What are the main social factors and dimensions that should be taken into account while analysing and translating a text?', 'What is code-switching?', 'Why do people code-switch?', 'What are the main types of code-switching?', and 'How do translators deal with texts loaded with examples of code-switching?'.

Sociolinguistics is one of the branches of linguistics that utilizes the theories and approaches of sociology and linguistics to understand the relationship between 'society' and 'language'. Put at its simplest, sociolinguistics is an interdisciplinary subject where the primary focus is on studying the relationship between 'society' and 'language'. As shown in this chapter and the next one, sociolinguistics examines why people sometimes switch codes while communicating with each other and how their linguistic choices are influenced by aspects such as the social setting, social standing and rank, and the relations that they have with each other. Further, sociolinguistics explores the language variation that may occur at all levels (phonological, syntactic, semantic, etc.). Consider, for instance, the word *'advertisement'*. When you overhear a conversation between people talking about different types of advertisements, you might find that they pronounce it in a slightly different way. While some might pronounce it /əd'vɜː.tɪs.mənt/, others might pronounce it /æd.vɚ'taɪz.mənt/. Similarly, for the word 和, i.e. *'and'*, as in *'you and I'*, the standardized Mandarin version in mainland China is pronounced as /he/, whereas the same word tends to be pronounced as /han/ in Taiwan. Sociolinguists are interested in such language variation. They try to determine who are the people who use one pronunciation rather than another. But why should sociolinguists be interested in analysing this language variation? Because they are keen to find out why people use language as they do, how they pronounce words, why they opt for particular

> Why is sociolinguistics an interdisciplinary subject?

> How does your sense of belonging influence your behaviour? Discuss.

DOI: 10.4324/9781003228028-11

words or structures, and why and how they contribute to determining their social identity (for more details, see the next chapter).

Social Identity Theory

Why do you support your national football team when they play against other teams? Discuss.

It is worth noting that people have "multiple identities, some of which are more personal and idiosyncratic and some of which are group identifications" (Meyerhoff 2006/2011: 73). This theory, called Social Identity Theory, was developed from what is called in the literature mini-group studies, led by Henri Tajfel and his associates in the 1970s. In experiments conducted by this group, it was found that "people readily see contrasts between groups in terms of competition, and seek to find means of favouring" the in-group over the out-group.

How would you define Social Identity Theory (SIT)?

The aim of this theory is to identify the circumstances under which people think of themselves as members of one group rather than another, thus defining their place in society. Three psychological processes are given full consideration while studying people's social identity: 'social categorization', 'social comparison', and 'social identification'.

Social categorization

Think of people around you, identifying their place in society according to certain social categories.

Social categorization is a psychological process that refers to the tendency of people to think of themselves and others according to certain social categories. For example, one may think of oneself as a schoolteacher, a father, an activist, or a football fan.

Social comparison

Think of different groups in your society, including their social standing and group members.

Social comparison is the second psychological process by which people divide society into different groups; each group has a certain social standing and consists of certain members. Taxi drivers, for instance, may be seen by themselves and others as having a lower social standing compared with engineers. When people from a group with a lower social standing try to become members of a group with a higher social standing, they need to increase their cultural capital, among other things. Pierre Bourdieu (1986) holds that apart from economic capital, there are other types of capital, such as symbolic, cultural, and social capital. Here,

What are the main types of 'capital' according to Pierre Bourdieu?

Bourdieu adopts a broad perspective to reintroduce capital "in all its forms and not only in the one form which is recognized by economic theory" (1986: 242). It thus becomes possible to outline the practice of the social world as directed not only towards the acquisition of economic capital but of all forms of capital. Cultural capital, according to Bourdieu, takes one of three forms: (1) embodied, (2) objectified, and (3) institutionalized, as shown below:

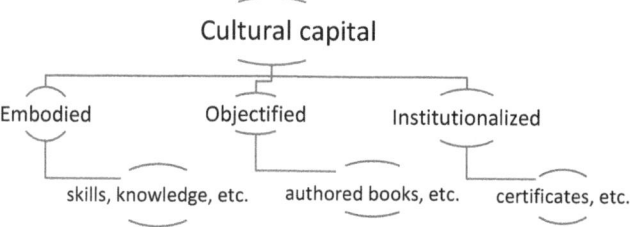

In its embodied form, cultural capital consists of dispositions embodied in the mind and body of the individual agent (Bourdieu 1986: 243), such as competences, skills, knowledge, and capacities that people develop deliberately through training and education or spontaneously through the unconscious processes of socialization. In its objectified form, cultural capital consists of human-created objects, such as pictures, books, instruments, or machines. In its institutionalized form, cultural capital includes certificates and degrees.

Why do people join schools and universities?

Social identification

Social identification is the third psychological process through which people, while observing other individuals and groups, take into account their sense of who they are and how they identify themselves in relation to others based on what they have in common or what they do not have in common. Identifying themselves in relation to others according to what they have in common motivates them to make every possible effort to achieve positive distinctiveness. Further, this sense of belonging motivates people to favour some people over others on the basis of whether they are from their own group or not, thus resulting in what is called 'in-group favouritism' or 'in-group bias' (Tajfel and Turner 1979).

How would you define 'in-group favouritism'?

To summarize, someone's social identity can be defined as their awareness of belonging to a particular group, involving (1) thinking of oneself and others according to certain social categories (social categorization), (2) comparing oneself with others in terms of having a higher social standing or a lower social standing (social comparison), and (3) identifying oneself in relation to other people based on shared characteristics (social identification).

Connecting the dots (1): Social identity and translation

Social identity, as hinted at above, refers to how we identify ourselves in relation to others based on what we have in common. The way we use the language "provides clues to others about who we are, where we come from, and perhaps what kind of social experiences we have had" (Holmes 1992/ 2013: 2). To elaborate, we can identify ourselves according to:

Can your social identity be identified in relation to others according to what you do not have in common?

- our relationships with others: mother and son, father and daughter, teacher and student, doctor and patient, lawyer and client, etc.;

- our religion: Muslim, Christian, Jewish, etc.;
- our occupation: teacher, mechanic, engineer, designer, artist, singer, actor, etc.;
- our nationality: Japanese, Chinese, English, etc.;
- our city: Basra, Hamburg, London, New York, etc.;
- gender: female or male;
- sexual orientation: straight, homosexual, bisexual, etc.

Identify your social identity according to your relationship with others by touching on religion, occupation, nationality, city, and gender.

However, identities are not always positive as sometimes some identities have negative overtones. In some countries in the Arab world, for instance, there is a huge number of people who are called بدون, which literally means 'without', referring to people who were born in a country and spent most of their life in it, but who do not have the nationality certificate of that country. Such identities are stigmatized, causing people who possess them to feel annoyed when they hear others labelling them with these identities, even though they do actually embrace such identities. Similarly, illegal immigrants who came from African colonies or the Middle East and North Africa to France, for instance, in the hope of finding a good job or being granted asylum are identified in relation to others on the basis of what they do not have in common – they are less likely speak French or to speak it not according to the established conventions and norms, and others look upon them as a threat to the supposedly refined manners and culture of the French. Again, such identities are stigmatized.

Think of other social identities which are stigmatized in your society.

Such social identities give people a sense of belonging to one group rather than another. Not only does this provide them with a framework for socializing, but it also influences their behaviour. In experiments carried out by Henri Tajfel and his associates in the early 1970s, it was found that people tend to support the members of their group. This explains why the same act performed by different people is sometimes praised and at some other times denounced. In this regard, van Dijk (1998: 33; emphasis his own) states that when we talk about good acts, "OUR people tend to appear primarily as the actors" of these acts. However, when bad acts are being talked of, they are assigned to THEIR people. This is because we identify ourselves in relation with others based on what we have in common.

Why do you prefer to socialize with one group of people rather than another?

Translation at its macro level is a complex activity as it involves more than one agent. According to Nord (2002: 35), translation is seen as an intercultural communicative interaction involving at least four social agents: (1) source culture sender, (2) commissioner of translation, (3) translator, and (4) target culture receiver. Each agent has his/her own identity (personal, social, or cultural), thus resulting in conflicting identities. As mediators, Nord (2002: 33) holds that translators "have a special responsibility" towards other agents, such as the author, commissioner, and target language readers as well as "themselves, precisely in those cases where there are differing views as to what a 'good' translation is or should be". This responsibility, termed 'loyalty' by Nord, can be considered as an "interpersonal category referring to a social relationship between people who expect not to be cheated in the process" (2002: 33). As such, it is the translator who has to prevent or reduce any 'communicative suffering' that "arises from not understanding something that you want to understand, from misunderstanding or inadequate understanding, and from not being able to get your own message across. It also arises from a lack of communication at all" (Chesterman 2001: 151). By way of example, let us consider the three translations of this passage extracted from *BBC News* (11 September 2021) and translated by three MA students:

Four of the six Palestinian inmates who escaped from a high-security jail earlier this week have been captured, Israeli police say.

TT1	قالت الشرطة الإسرائيلية إنها ألقت القبض في مطلع الأسبوع على أربعة من الأسرى الفلسطينيين الستة الذين تمكنوا من الهروب من سجن شديد الحراسة.
Back translation	The Israeli police said that at the beginning of the week, they arrested four of the six Palestinian prisoners who managed to escape from a high-security jail.
TT2	ادعت شرطة الاحتلال الإسرائيلي بأنه تم إلقاء القبض على أربعة من الأسرى الفلسطينيين الستة الذين تمكنوا من الفرار من سجن شديد الحراسة في مطلع هذا الأسبوع.
Back translation	The Israeli occupation police claimed that four of the six Palestinian prisoners who managed to escape from high-security jail earlier this week were arrested.
TT3	زعمت شرطة الكيان الصهيوني إنها ألقت القبض على أربعة من أصل ستة أسرى فلسطينيين هربوا من سجن شديد الحراسة في وقت سابق هذا الأسبوع.
Back translation	The police of Zionist entity said it had arrested four out of six Palestinian prisoners who escaped from a high-security jail earlier this week.

The second and third translators, being influenced by their own accumulated value systems, sense of belonging, commitment, orientation, and the like, opted for changing the author's attitude towards the attributed material (for more details, see the previous chapter). In TT2 and TT3, the verb *'to say'* (acknowledging) was translated into ادعت and زعمت, literally meaning *'to claim'* (distancing), and *'Israeli police'* (−ideologically motivated) was translated into شرطة الاحتلال الإسرائيلي *the Israeli occupation police'* and شرطة الكيان الصهيوني *'the police of Zionist entity'* (+ideologically motivated), respectively. In the original text, by means of the verb *'to say'* and the noun phrase *'Israeli police'*, there is no explicit indication as to where the author stands concerning the attributed material. In TT2 and TT3, however, the translators decided to interpolate themselves into the text by presenting the author as (1) distancing him/herself from the attributed material and (2) having a negative attitude towards *'Israel'* (see the previous chapter for more details). So, here, the translators decided not to prevent or reduce any 'communicative suffering'. Rather, they inflicted suffering on the target language readers.

Connecting the dots (2): Social dimensions and translation

In any situation, there are certain social factors which are relevant in accounting for the particular variety used in any interaction. While some of these factors are related to the language users (i.e. the participants), others are related to language uses (i.e. the social setting and function of the inter-action). In analysing any interaction, who is talking to whom (e.g. a father to a son, a wife to a husband, a customer to a shopkeeper, a worker to a boss, a student to a teacher, a patient to a doctor, a policeman to a crim-inal, a lawyer to a client) is an important factor. The setting or social con-text (e.g. at home in the morning, at the university in the afternoon, at a nightclub) is also a relevant factor. In some cases, the topic itself has an influence on people's linguistic choices. For instance, English teachers who are native speakers of another language find it easier to explain, discuss, or present their language-related ideas in English when participating in a conference. The main reason behind communicating with others may well be an important social factor that influences the language used. As such, there are four social factors that need to be taken into consideration when analysing any interaction:

(1) 'Participants' (who is talking to whom?).
(2) 'Setting' (where and when do they use the language?).
(3) 'Topic' (what is being talked about?).
(4) 'Purpose' of the interaction (why do they use the language?).

Closely related to the aforementioned social factors are social dimensions. Notions such as 'social distance', 'status', 'formality', and 'functional scale' are considered as indicators emphasizing the four social factors. In analysing an interaction between, for example, a mother and her daughter (participants) at home in the morning (setting) discussing a shopping list (topic and purpose), notions such as 'solidarity' (how intimate or distant they are), 'status' (who is superior to the other), 'formality' (how formal they are), and 'functional scale' (whether they are informative or expres-sive) should be taken into consideration. The main social dimensions can be summarized as follows:

(1) 'Solidarity' (intimate versus distant): our linguistic choices are influenced by the relationship that we have with other people and how well we know them.
(2) 'Status' (superior versus subordinate): our linguistic choices are influenced by our social standing and rank compared with that of our addressee. The choice of *'Sir'* or *'Miss'* by students, for instance, when addressing their teacher indicates their awareness that their teacher is of higher status and entitled to a term of respect.
(3) 'Formality' (formal versus informal): our linguistic choices are influenced by the social setting, i.e. where and when we are

communicating. In a formal situation, such as one with the university chancellor in his/her office, the language used will be influenced by the formality of the setting.

(4) 'Functional scale' (informative versus expressive): not only can language convey objective information of a referential kind (informative or referential), but it can express how someone is feeling (expressive or affective).

To maintain the register of the original text, the translator needs to give the social factors and dimensions full consideration. By way of explanation, let us consider the following extract, quoted along with its Arabic translation from the Air Wick: Oud العود product label:

English	Do not spray or place on painted or polished surfaces. Keep out of reach of children.
Arabic	لا يرش أو يوضع على الأسطح المطلية أو الملمعة. يحفظ بعيدًا عن متناول الأطفال.
Back translation	It should not be sprayed or placed on painted or polished surfaces. It should be kept out of reach of children.

By opting for the use of the imperative form in the original text *'do not spray'* and *'keep'*, the language user reduced the distance, thus creating a feeling of solidarity and/or intimacy. This should be reflected in the target text. However, the translator resorted to passivization, thereby emphasizing the distance as a social dimension on the one hand and, on the other hand, failing to reflect the degree of personalization (see Chapter 9 for more details).

Convergence versus divergence

When people communicate with each other, they sometimes become very close to each other, while at other times they move away from each other. When they become very close to each other, they are likely to converge their speech to be in line with the speech of their interlocutor. They do so by adjusting their way of speaking to be similar, to a certain degree, to that of their interlocutor, thus reducing the social distance between them. However, when speakers move away from each other, they may well adjust their way of speaking to differ, to a certain degree, from their interlocutors, thereby emphasizing the social distance between them (for more details, see, for example, Yule 1985/2014: 261; Holmes 1992/2013: 245–7; Spolsky 1998/2003: 41–3; Meyerhoff 2006/2011: 75–81).

Speakers can use two main strategies to adjust their way of speaking, namely 'convergence' and 'divergence'. Convergence involves speakers adjusting their way of talking to be very close to their interlocutors' way of speaking, thus increasing the similarities between them. By contrast, divergence involves speakers adjusting their way of talking to move away from their interlocutors' way of speaking, thereby increasing the differences

How would you define 'convergence' and 'divergence'?

between them. These are straightforward examples. But what happens when a speaker converges and his/her addressee diverges? Communication Accommodation Theory (CAT), which was developed out of research led by Howard Giles, is about when, how, and why people adjust their way of speaking (e.g. lexical choices, grammatical forms, pronunciation), and allows for the possibility of such cases. This theory shows "how complicated and important people's attitudes towards others are and how these attitudes can be played out in language use" (Meyerhoff 2006/2011: 77).

According to Le Page (1997: 28), people sometimes accommodate to their addressee's way of speaking to have a positive influence on them, thus creating a positive image, i.e. the image that they wish to project in a particular social context. Giles and Ogay (2006) maintained that people do not accommodate to what the addressee actually is, but rather to what they believe s/he is. When people misjudge the situation or accommodate to what they believe their interlocutor is (rather than to what their interlocutor actually is), they may well fail to achieve their communicative goal. The main reason behind this could be "because they do not have the necessary resources or skills to reach their goal accurately" (78).

There are many different ways in which speakers may accommodate to the speech of the person with whom they communicate, and the translator/interpreter needs to pay extra attention to this. People may converge or adapt:

- their speed of speech (e.g. slowing down when talking to foreigners or children);
- the length of their utterances (e.g. opting for simple sentences when talking to others);
- the frequency of their pauses;
- the structures used (e.g. simplifying their grammar when talking to others);
- the vocabulary used (simplifying their vocabularies when talking to others);
- their use of verbal fillers or pragmatic particles, such as *'sort of'*, *'you know'*, *'you see'*, etc., used by the addressee;
- their pronunciation (e.g. trying to use a similar pronunciation to that used by the addressee).

What is the difference between 'code-switching' and 'style shifting'?

In addition, code-switching is also a common practice in certain countries, such as India where Hindi, for instance, is used along with the former colonial language, English. Another example is the Philippines where people sometimes code-switch from Tagalog to English or the other way round.

In the actual act of translating, the translator needs to give these two strategies, i.e. convergence and divergence, full consideration. By way of example, let us consider the following example extracted from Husni and Newman (2008: 44–5):

ST (Arabic)	يقول الشيخ سعيد: "إذن تريدين أن يرجع إليك زوجك؟".
	أجابت عزيزة بتردّد: "أريد أن يرجع إليّ".
	فابتسم الشيخ سعيد بينما أردفت قائلة باكتئاب: "أهله يريدون تزوجيه مرة ثانية".
	قال الشيخ سعيد وهو يرمي في وعاء الجمر نتفًا من البخور: "سيعود إليك زوجك، ولن يتزوج مرة ثانية".
Back translation	Sheikh Said says: "So, you want your husband to return to you?"
	Aziza replied, hesitantly: "I want him to return to me".
	Sheikh Said smiled as she went to say, mournfully: "His family wants him to get married again".
	Sheikh Said while throwing bits of incense into the dish filled with live coal: "Your husband will return to you, and he will not marry again".
TT (English)	Sheikh Said said: "So, you want your husband to return to you?"
	"I want him to return to me," Aziza replied, hesitantly.
	Sheikh Said smiled as he added, mournfully: "His family wants him to get married again". He threw bits of incense into the dish filled with live coal, and said: "Your husband will return to you, and he will not take another wife".

Here, as the back translation shows, Sheikh Said opts for certain lexical items and structures with the potential to reduce the distance between him and Aziza. This was reflected in the target text by the translators when selecting simple words and structures. However, they superimposed a certain directionality/narrativity when mistranslating فابتسم الشيخ سعيد بينما أردفت قائلة باكتئاب"أهله يريدون تزوجيه مرة ثانية" into *Sheikh Said smiled as he added, mournfully: "His family wants him to get married again"* ', thereby changing the Sayer from Aziza to Sheikh Said. Further, in the original text, there is no time lapse between the process of saying expressed by the verb قال *'to say'* and the process of doing expressed by the verb يرمي *'to throw'*. In the target text, however, the process of saying occurred shortly after the process of doing, which is reduced, by the effect of the grammatical form and content specification, to be seen as a point on the timeline (for more details on this, see Chapter 12 of this book).

Connecting the dots (3): Code-switching and translation

Code-switching can be defined as the practice of moving back and forth between two codes, i.e. between two languages or between two dialects or registers. Bilingual speakers (speaking two languages) and multilingual speakers (speaking more than two languages) can switch from one language to another while communicating with each other. This is clear. But what about monolingual speakers (speaking one language only)? Can they also code-switch? Although monolingual speakers are not able to use more than one language, they can code-switch intralingually, i.e. within the same language; they move from one dialect to another or from one level to another, and so on.

Switching from one level to another in the same language may lead to what is called 'style shifting', rather than 'code-switching'. Discuss.

Code-switching occurs far more often in conversation than in writing. However, this does not exclude the possibility of having it in writing or in multi-modal texts. It is common among immigrant families. Imagine, for example, an Egyptian family who moved from Egypt to the UK and the children grew up speaking the Egyptian dialect as their mother tongue and English as a second language outside the family domain, such as with their schoolmates. In such a situation, when the children talk to their parents, for example, they may well code-switch from Arabic (low level) to English and vice versa. By way of example, the following interview with an Egyptian–Scottish duo called the *Ayoub Sisters* can be considered:

Speaker:	... احنا الاثنين ابتدينا بيانو بنفس الوقت وبعدين گربنا other instruments أنا الكمنگا (احنا الاثنين الكمنگا) ... وبعدين رحنا مدرسة (music school) specific to music ...
Gloss:	... we both started piano at the same time, then we tried other instruments: I [tried] a violin [actually] we both [tried] violin. After that we joined a school specific to music [i.e.] a music school ...

How would you define the 'matrix language'?

Personally, I (the first author of this book) remember when I moved to the UK, and I met many Arabs there. When we communicated with each other, the dominant language, technically called the matrix language, was Arabic. However, when we came across words such as *'home office'* and *'underground'*, we switched to English, which is called the additional language in such a situation.

People code-switch for a variety of different reasons, including:

● when there is a change in the situation, such as the arrival of a new person who does not have access to the code used by the participants before his/her arrival. Here, the newly arrived person might be included or excluded from the conversation, depending on the interlocutors' attitudes towards him/her;
● when there is a change in the topic;
● when there is a perceived gap in the code used;
● when there is a difficulty in expressing one's ideas. Sometimes people are not able to express their ideas easily; therefore, they code-switch to another language to express their ideas more easily and clearly;
● when there is a change in the function of the code, for example, from informative to expressive or the other way round. People sometimes code-switch from one language to another to better express their feelings, opinions, or sense of identity;

- to indicate social-group membership, in particular when they live in another country speaking a different language from their mother tongue;
- to show their solidarity, in particular when they switch to a code understood by the person who has joined them;
- to show distance when they switch to a code which is not shared by the new person who has joined them;
- to make their messages clear or emphasize it. People sometimes code-switch from one language to another or repeat the same idea in both languages to clarify or emphasize it;
- to emphasize their social class;
- to indicate that their relationship has become strong or the other way round;
- to comment on something. When people hear or say something in one language, sometimes they switch to another language to comment on it;
- to make jokes. People sometimes embed some words into the matrix language to make jokes;
- to quote a person.

<aside>Think of other reasons for 'code-switching'.</aside>

There are three main types of code-switching: (1) 'inter-sentential code-switching', (2) 'intra-sentential code-switching', and (3) 'tag code-switching' or 'extra-sentential code-switching', as shown below:

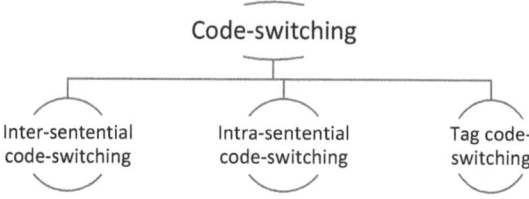

	Code-switching	
Inter-sentential code-switching	Intra-sentential code-switching	Tag code-switching

Inter-sentential code-switching

Inter-sentential code-switching is a kind of code-switching in which the language user code-switches from one language to another at the level of clause or sentence, as in the following two examples:

English to German	It seems that you are thirsty. Was wollen Sie trinken? [What do you want to drink?]
English to Spanish	Some people start their sentences in English y las terminan en español [and finish in Spanish]

The matrix language in the above two examples is English. The embedded language in the first example is German where the language user embedded the interrogative sentence '*Was wollen Sie trinken?*' (*What do you want to drink?*) into the matrix language, thus resulting in inter-sentential code-switching. The embedded language in the second example is Spanish,

<aside>How would you define the 'embedded language'?</aside>

where the language user embedded *'y las terminan en español'* (and finish in Spanish) into the matrix language.

Intra-sentential code-switching

Intra-sentential code-switching, by contrast, occurs when the language user switches within the same clause or sentence, as in:

English to Arabic	I'm really مشغول [I'm really busy].

In the above sentence, the matrix language is English, and the embedded language is Arabic. The language user embedded the word مشغول *'busy'* into the matrix language, thus resulting in code-switching. As this word is embedded within the same sentence, it is a case of intra-sentential code-switching.

Tag code-switching

The last type of code-switching is tag code-switching (also called 'extra-sentential code-switching'). It is a type of code-switching where a tag question from another language is embedded into the matrix language, as in the following examples:

English to French	She is beautiful, n'est-ce pas? [She is beautiful, isn't she?]
German to English	Das Wetter ist schön, isn't it? [The weather is lovely, isn't it?]

In the first example, the tag question (in French) is inserted into the matrix language (English). In the second example, the tag question (in English) is inserted into the matrix language (German).

A question that may arise is, 'How do translators deal with texts loaded with examples of code-switching?' Following Cincotta (1996), we can suggest five strategies that can be used by translators depending on the text type, genre, purpose of translation, readership, interfacing languages, and so on. They are:

(1) making the target text monolingual;
(2) keeping the embedded language without translation;
(3) transliterating the embedded language;
(4) using a colloquial variety, thus causing a style shift;
(5) using another dialect or language, if possible.

By way of explanation, let us consider the following example quoted from Ahmed (2018: 19–20), who discusses many examples of code-switching taken from a Hebrew novel written in 2005 by Eli Amir (2005) and translated into four languages, namely English, German, Italian, and Arabic:

ST (Hebrew)	"מה אתה מחפס ברדיו של הערבים? כוס אמם! ואני הסברתי והפצרתי, עד שנענה באי-רצון.
Back translation	"What are you listening to on the radio of the Arabs? [Insulting expression in Arabic]." And I explained and pleaded, until he reluctantly complied.
TT1 (English)	"What the hell do you want the Arabic station for? Screw them!" I explained and pleaded and finally he relented.
TT2 (German)	"Was suchst du im Radio der Araber?" Und er fügte einen unflätigen Fluch hinzu. Ich erklärte und bettelte, bis er unwillig nachgab.
TT3 (Italian)	Ma cosa cerchi nelle transmissioni delgi Arabi? Che vadano all'inferno! – Io insistetti finché lui, di malavoglia, mi accontentò.
TT4 (Arabic)	(ما الذي تبحث عنه في راديو العرب) فأخذت أشرح له وأناشده إلى أن استجاب عن غير رضا.

In the above example, we have a case of code-switching from Hebrew (matrix language) to Arabic (embedded language), but it is transliterated into Hebrew. In all these translations, the translators opted for keeping the target text monolingual. By contrast, in the following example quoted from Ahmed (2018: 9), the translators decided to keep the embedded language, thereby reflecting the code-switching used in the original text.

ST (Hebrew)	שוב צלצל הטלפון. "אהלן, כבוד ראש העיר, ת_פ_ד_י'ל," אמר המושל והאזין, משחק בעט המונח על שולחנו
Back translation	The phone rang again. "Hello, Mr Mayor, tafaddal" said the governor and listened, playing with the pen on his desk.
TT1 (English)	The phone rang again. "Ahlan, Mr Mayor go ahead." As he listened, the governor fiddled with a pen on his desk.
TT2 (German)	Wieder klingelte das Telefon. "Ahlan, verehrter Herr Bürgermeister, tafadal, bitte", sagte der Gouverneur und lauschte, während er mit dem Stift spielte.
TT3 (Italian)	Il telefono squillò ancora. – Ahlan, signor sindaco, tafaddal –. Il governatore rimase in ascolto giocherellando nervosamente con una pe.

Here, we have two examples of code-switching from Hebrew to Arabic: *'Ahlan'* meaning *'hello'* and *'tafaddal'* meaning *'Yes, sir/madam'*. Guided partially by the 'initial acceptability norm' (Toury 1995) and 'expectancy norm' (Chesterman 1997/2000), the first translator decided to keep *'Ahlan'* and to translate *'tafaddal'* into its equivalent, i.e. *'go ahead'*. In German and Italian, however, the translators, guided by the 'initial adequacy norm' (Toury 1995) and 'relation norm' (Chesterman 1997/ 2000), decided to keep both examples of code-switching (for more details on 'norms', see the next chapter).

Exercises and discussion

Exercise 1: Mark the following statements (T) if they are true and (F) if they are false.

(1) Code-switching refers to switching from written to spoken codes only.	
(2) When we have typical participants in a typical setting discussing typical issues, then we will have what is called a 'social dimension'.	
(3) When speakers try to reduce the social distance, they are likely to diverge their speech to be in line with that of the other speaker.	
(4) To converge is to change, for instance, your pronunciation, thus pronouncing words clearly.	
(5) People sometimes code-switch to indicate that their relationship has become strong or the other way round.	
(6) In a sentence of the following kind, إن شاء الله, *I'll call her later*, we have an example of what is called 'intra-sentential code-switching'.	
(7) Social identity refers to how people identify themselves in relation to others based on what they do not have in common.	
(8) Social identities are always positive as it is difficult to have negative identities.	
(9) In social psychology, Social Identity Theory (SIT) is a social-psychological theory stating that people can be identified as having many identities, not just one.	
(10) Social Identity Theory (SIT) developed from what is called in the literature 'mini-group studies', led by Henri Tajfel and his colleagues in the early 1970s.	
(11) Cultural capital, according to Bourdieu, takes one of three forms: (1) embodied, (2) objectified, and (3) institutionalized.	
(12) People's sense of belonging motivates them to be in favour of some people over others on the basis of whether they are from their group or not, thus resulting in what is called 'in-group favouritism'.	
(13) Code-switching is common among emigrant families.	

(14) In a sentence of the following kind, *That's kind of you. Vielen Dank*, the embedded language is English and the dominant language is German.	
(15) When people accommodate to what they believe their addressee is (rather than to what their interlocutor actually is), they may well fail to achieve their goal.	
(16) Code-switching is also a common practice in certain countries, such as India or the Philippines.	

Exercise 2: Identify the type of code-switching in the following examples:

Example	Type
(1) *Das Wetter ist schön* [the weather is nice]*, isn't it?*	_____
(2) *Excuse me,* وين مكتب العميد [Where is the dean's office?]	_____
(3) *You did your homework. n'est-ce pas* [didn't you]*?*	_____
(4) *Have you finished tes devoirs* [your homework]*?*	_____
(5) Mon dieu [oh my God]! It has been broken.	_____
(6) *Please,* كتابت را به من قرض بده [give me your book]*	_____
(7) No problem! 我现在就去做, 做完了告诉 你。(Wo xianzai jiu qu zuo, zuo wan le gaosu ni) [I am going to do it now. I will let you know when I finish.]	_____
(8) من [I am] *not only* خسته هستم [tired] *but also* هم هستم گُشنه [hungry]*	_____

Exercise 3: Read the following conversation between a teacher and one of his students, who is multilingual. Then, analyse the text by touching on:

(a) the 'social factors' relevant in accounting for the particular variety used by the participants;

(b) the 'social dimensions' that are related, in one way or another, to social factors;

(c) examples of 'code-switching', if any, along with their types;

(d) examples of 'convergence' or 'divergence', if any.

Student: May I come in, أستاذ?
Teacher: Why do you always come late?
Student: Je suis désolé Monsieur, it is the bus which makes me late.
Teacher: What time do you leave home?
Student: Je te jure Monsieur, I always leave home at سبعة ونص.
Teacher: In English, please. How far is your home from here?
Student: Trois kilometres, sorry three kilometres, from here.
Teacher: My dear. It is a bad habit. Change your routine. Always get up early in the morning.

Exercise 4: The short story titled "Two Nights at Neempani" written by Arnaba Saha can be accessed using this link: www.americanliterature.com. Your task is:

(a) to translate the text into your own language;
(b) to comment on your translation by adopting a sociolinguistic approach.

Discussion and research points
(1) Why do people code-switch while communicating with each other?
(2) Why do people sometimes spend time, money, and energy to achieve something for free, such as translating a book?
(3) It is argued in this chapter that translation is a complex activity. Do you agree? Discuss.
(4) Go through any translated book from English into your own language to identify any examples of 'communicative suffering' arising from the translator's failure to understand what is meant by the original writer.
(5) Select any English text that has some examples of code-switching and translate it into your language. Then comment on your own translation by referring to the main strategies you adopted to handle examples of code-switching.

References

Ahmed, M. A. H (2018). "Codes across Languages: On the Translation of Literary Code-Switching", *Multilingua: Journal of Cross-Cultural and Interlanguage Communication*, Vol. 37 (5), pp. 483–514. https://doi.org/10.1515/multi-2017-0060.

Amir, E. (2005). *Yasmin* (Sifriyah la-'am 535). Tel Aviv: Hotsa'at 'Am 'oved.

Bourdieu, P. (1986). "The Forms of Capital". In Richardson, J. G. (ed.), *Handbook of Theory and Research for the Sociology of Education* (pp. 241–58). New York: Greenwood Press.

Chesterman, A. (1997/2000). *Memes of Translation: The Spread of Ideas in Translation Theory*. Amsterdam/Philadelphia, PA: John Benjamins.

Chesterman, A. (2001). "Proposal for a Hieronymic Oath", *The Translator*, Vol. 7(2), pp. 139–54.

Cincotta, M. S. (1996). "Naturalising Linguistic Aliens: The Translation of Code-Switching. Conference on Interpreting and Translation". http://files.eric.ed.gov/fulltext/ED404868.pdf.

Giles, H. and Ogay, T. (2006). "Communication Accommodation Theory". In B. Whaley and W. Samter (eds.), *Explaining Communication: Contemporary Theories and Exemplars* (pp. 293–310). Mahwah, NJ: Erlbaum.

Holmes, J. (1992/ 2013). *An Introduction to Sociolinguistics* (4th edn). London/New York: Routledge.

Husni, R. and Newman, D. (2008). *Modern Arabic Short Stories: A Bilingual Reader*. London: Saqi Books.

Le Page, R. B. (1997). "The Evolution of a Sociolinguistic Theory of Language". In Coulmas, F. (ed.), *The Handbook of Sociolinguistics* (pp. 15–32). Oxford: Blackwell.

Meyerhoff, M. (2006/ 2011). *Introducing Sociolinguistics*. London/ New York: Routledge.

Nord, C. (2002). "Manipulation and Loyalty in Functional Translation", *Current Writing: Text and Reception in Southern Africa*, Vol. 14, pp. 32–44.

Saha, A. (n.d.). "Two Nights at Neempani". Retrieved on 21 June 2022 from https://americanliterature.com/author/arnaba-saha/short-story/two-nights-at-neempani.

Spolsky, B. (1998). *Sociolinguistics*. Oxford: Oxford University Press.

Tajfel, H. (1979). "Individuals and Groups in Social Psychology", *British Journal of Social and Clinical Psychology*, Vol. 18 (2), pp. 183–90.

Tajfel, H. and Turner, J. C. (1979). "An Integrative Theory of Intergroup Conflict". In Austin, W. G. and Worchel, S. (eds.), *The Social Psychology of Intergroup Relations* (pp. 33–47). Monterey, CA: Brooks/Cole.

Toury, G. (1995). *Descriptive Translation Studies and Beyond*. Amsterdam: John Benjamins.

van Dijk, T. (1998). "Opinions and Ideologies in the Press". In Bell, A. and Garrett, P. (eds.), *Approaches to Media Discourse* (pp. 21–63). Oxford: Blackwell.

Yule, G. (1985/ 1996). *The Study of Language*. Cambridge: Cambridge University Press.

Language variation

11

The previous chapter considered some sociolinguistic concepts and notions, such as 'social identity', 'social factors', 'social dimensions', 'code-switching', 'convergence', and 'divergence'. This chapter completes the introduction to these sociolinguistic concepts and notions by touching on language variation, including 'regional variation', 'social variation', 'stylistic variation', 'diglossia', 'polyglossia', 'pidgins', and 'creoles'. Dialects, accents, and styles as examples of language variation are discussed in a direct link to translation.

After studying this chapter, readers should be able to analyse texts and discourses in terms of the type of variation they exhibit, and they should be able to define the notions of diglossia and polyglossia, as well as pidgins and creoles. Readers should also be knowledgeable about the difficulties of translating styles, dialects, and accents into different languages.

How would you define 'language variation'?

As stated in the previous chapter, sociolinguistics explores, among other issues, the different forms of language that may occur at all levels (phonological, syntactic, semantic, etc.). When we ask Arabs from different countries, for instance, how they are, we might hear words such as زين, بخير, كويّس, باهي, and امنيح, all meaning *'fine'*. Although these are very simple utterances, they do reveal information about the language user, such as his/her country and wish to be friendly and informal. Similarly, to say *'very'* as in *'very good'* in Chinese, you might hear native speakers from different dialectal regions say 很 (*hen*), 非常 (*fei chang*), 特别 (*te bie*), 挺 (*ting*), 蛮 (*man*), 忒 (*tei*), 贼 (*zei*), and 几 (*gei*). This is similar in English where speakers, for example from Scotland or Northern England, might say *'aye'* for *'yes'* and some speakers from certain geographical and socio-ethnic backgrounds tend to say *'innit'* and *'eh'* for *'right'* or *'isn't it'*. In France, for example, a lexical item such as *'vingt'* meaning *'twenty'* is pronounced differently in the northeast compared to the south, northwest, and southeast. Similarly, to refer to chocolate bread, people from the north use *'pain au chocolat'*, while people from the south use *'chocolatine'*. Again, although these are fairly simple utterances, they reveal information about their users.

DOI: 10.4324/9781003228028-12

Types of language variation

These different forms of language, technically known as 'language variation', are used in sociolinguistics to refer to "the study of those features of a language that differ systematically as we compare different groups of speakers or the same speaker in different situations" (Parker and Riley 1994/2010: 148). There are three main types of language variation: 'regional variation', 'social variation', and 'stylistic variation'.

Regional variation

The geographical areas that language users come from are given full consideration when features of pronunciation, vocabulary, and grammar are studied. With this in mind, we could have regional dialects, such as 'American dialect' versus 'British dialect'. It is worth noting that there are sub-regional dialects within each regional dialect, thus having 'Northern', 'Midlands', and 'Southern' as sub-regional dialects within American English. The line that demarcates these regional varieties or dialects is called an 'isogloss'. An isogloss "represents the boundary of any linguistic feature or set of features which separate one speech variety from another" (Romaine 1994/2000: 136).

Social variation

Here, the social group of the language users, which is usually evaluated on the basis of a range of scales, such as education, occupation, social class, and income level, is given serious consideration. Building on this, features of pronunciation, vocabulary, and grammar according to the social group of the speakers are studied to identify social varieties, which are also called 'social dialects'. Examples of social dialects include a 'standard dialect' versus a 'non-standard dialect'. The use of *'ain't'*, *'bɒʔəl'*, and *'eh eh man'*, for instance, which are referred to as socially marked forms, might cause the addressee "to form a negative social judgment of the speaker" as being an uneducated person or a person who might come from a lower social class (Parker and Riley 1994/2010: 161). Living in the UK, you might hear sentences of the following kind uttered by native speakers:

'Her flat messed up'	in place of	'Her flat is messed up'
'I have not seen her yesterday'	in place of	'I did not see her yesterday'
'She watching TV right now'	in place of	'She is watching TV right now'
'Where it is?'	in place of	'Where is it?'
'Did you receive the le?ə?'	in place of	'Did you receive the letter?'

These sentences are examples of socially marked variation. These non-standard varieties can be classified, following Parker and Riley 1994/2010: 163–73), into three main types:

What is wrong with these sentences? Discuss.

(1) Non-standard syntactic variation, as in:
I have not seen her yesterday.
Where it is?
She watching TV right now.
(2) Non-standard morphological variation, as in:
She watching TV right now.
Her flat messed up.

Can you guess the dialect?

(3) Non-standard phonological variation, as in:
Did you receive the le?ə?

Hearing or reading such sentences uttered by native speakers might cause the addressee to form a negative social judgement of the language user as being, for instance, uneducated. This is why some literary writers inject their texts with ungrammatical or non-standard sentences. The main reason behind this is to inject the text with vividness and credibility, thus letting their audience form a particular social judgement by identifying the character's social identity, including aspects such as his/her education, age, and gender. Consider in this connection the following example extracted from a short story titled طبلية من السماء by Yusuf Idris translated into English by Husni and Newman (2008: 276–7) as *A Tray from Heaven*:

ST	... كان يقول موجهاً كلامه إلى السماء:
	ـ أنت عايز مني ايه. تقدر تقول لي أنت عايز مني ايه؟
Back translation	He was saying addressing the sky:
	- You want what from me? Can you tell me what you want from me?
TT	He said, addressing the sky: "What do you want from me? Can you tell me what is it that you want from me?"

Here, the use of عايز *'want'* and ايه *'what'* in place of the standard words, such as تريد and ماذا, gives us some extra information about the language user, such as his country (Egypt).

Stylistic variation

How would you define 'stylistic variation'?

Stylistic variation refers to the study of those varieties of language that range from extremely formal to quite informal. As stated in the previous chapter, in a formal social context (setting), native speakers of English may well be more likely to pay extra attention to their way of using the language than they would in an informal social context. For example, they may opt for pronouncing words ending in '*–ing*' with a velar nasal instead of an alveolar nasal (e.g. '*walking*', not '*walkin*'). They may choose more formal words, such as '*father*' instead of '*dad*', '*child*' instead of '*kid*', or '*mother*' instead of *'mom'*. They may well tend to avoid the use of certain words which are considered non-standard, such as *'ain't'*.

Different stylistic varieties can be identified by studying different types of stylistic variation, such as (1) stylistic lexical variation (e.g. *'children'* versus *'kids'*), (2) stylistic phonological variation (e.g. *'walking'* versus *'walkin'*), (3) 'stylistic morphological variation (e.g. *'I will'* versus *'I'll'*), and (4) stylistic syntactic variation (e.g. *'Do you want another cup of tea?'* versus *'You want another cup of tea?'*).

What are the main types of 'stylistic variation?

Diglossia and polyglossia

'Diglossia' is a Greek term used in sociolinguistics to describe a situation where two distinct codes or varieties are used for clearly distinct purposes in certain situations (for more details, see Holmes 1992/ 2013: 27; Spolsky 1998/2003: 63). Diglossia is close to bilingualism, rather than monolingualism or multilingualism. In some languages, such as Arabic, two distinct varieties are used by native speakers; one is regarded as a high variety and the other is considered a low variety. Each variety is used for a quite distinct function, and the two varieties complement each other. It is worth noting that native speakers do not use the high variety in everyday conversations; they use the low variety instead. When there are two codes or varieties, then we have a diglossic community; however, when there are more than two distinct codes or varieties, we have a polyglossic community. The term 'polyglossia' is related to multilingualism rather than to monolingualism or bilingualism. An example of polyglossia is the distinct varieties used in Singapore. Two distinct varieties, namely Mandarin and formal Singapore English, are used in Singapore in formal situations, and they are considered to be high varieties. Further, three distinct varieties, namely Hokkien, Cantonese, and Singapore English, are regarded as informal or low varieties and they are used in informal situations.

Why is the term 'diglossia' modelled on the word 'bilingualism'? Discuss.

Why is the term 'polyglossia' modelled on the word 'multilingualism'? Discuss.

Pidgin and creole

Pidgin

A pidgin can be defined as a code which comes into existence when people who do not have a common language come into contact with each other. A pidgin is not a particular group's native language; rather, it evolves "as a means of communication between people who do not have a common language" (Holmes 1992/ 2013: 85). Imagine that you find yourself in another country working with another person and you both do not have a common language. In such a situation, both of you may work without uttering a single word. However, if you have to work on a daily basis and for a longer period of time, then you need to communicate. One of the solutions is to resort to what is called a 'lingua franca', i.e. a language used by people when they need to communicate with each other, but their languages are not mutually intelligible. But what happens if you do not have any common language and there is an urgent need for interacting? The only solution that you may have is to develop a means of communicating from your languages and some other existing languages, such as English or French. The resulting language is what is called a 'pidgin'. In this respect, Parker and Riley (1994/2010: 327) state that a pidgin is a "mixture of two existing languages brought into contact by trade or colonization". It is worth mentioning that people start using a pidgin developed by them for certain purposes, such as work-related activities. However, over time, people may start using such a pidgin in different domains, such as the family domain. Such an expanded pidgin will then be passed from one generation to another as a non-native lingua franca among people who speak different languages.

How would you define the term 'lingua franca'?

Can a 'pidgin' be used as a lingua franca? Discuss.

Creole

What are the main differences between a 'pidgin' and a 'creole'?

When a pidgin develops over time in a certain way into a more complex linguistic system in terms of sound system, vocabulary, structures, and so on, and it is then adopted by later generations as their own native language, it becomes a 'creole'. From this one may well conclude that a creole differs from a pidgin in terms of having native speakers, having increased lists of vocabulary, sound systems, and structures, and being used in a wide range of domains.

Tok Pisin, the English-based creole of Papua New Guinea, can be considered as an example of a creole language. In Papua New Guinea, Tok Pisin, one of the official languages, is used as a lingua franca among the people living there. Most of the words in this creole are taken from English, but they are used in different domains and pronounced quite differently, as shown below:

Tok Pisin	English	Meaning
brata	*brother*	the same meaning, *brother*
inap	*enough*	the same meaning, *enough*
bepo	*before*	the same meaning, *before*
sak	*shark*	the same meaning, *shark*
ples	*place*	meaning hometown

The words in the above table are derived from English. However, there some words which are derived from other languages, as shown below:

Tok Pisin	German	Meaning
rausim	*raus*	meaning *out*
gumi	*gummi*	meaning *rubber*
maski	*macht nichts*	meaning *it does not matter*

Tok Pisin	Malay	Meaning
susu	susu	meaning *milk*

Tok Pisin	Portuguese	Meaning
save	*saber*	meaning *to know*
pikinini	*pequenino*	meaning *child*, *little*, and the like

Connecting the dots (1) Translating dialects and accents

The term 'dialect' has been used by linguists, and occasionally by lay people, to refer to "a subordinate variety of a language" (Romaine 1994/ 2000: 2). If two people speak different varieties of the same language, say Arabic, and they can understand each other, then we talk about two different dialects. However, if they do not understand each other, then, in theory, they speak two different languages. To determine whether people speak the same language or different languages, some linguists rely on what is called 'mutual intelligibility', i.e. the criterion of understanding each other or not (for more details, see van Herk 2012: 13). These two simple sentences written in the language used by people who live in a tiny village called Kumzar in the northern tip of Oman were given to 30 native speakers of Arabic to see whether they are understood by other Arabs, including Omanis, or not.

Some people assume that a 'dialect' is a subordinate variety of a language. So, can we say that a language is a superordinate variety of a dialect? Discuss.

تاتم بسوالتتكم بي امتحاناتتو.
Literal meaning: I want to ask a question about your exams.
نواز سيارت نو تخيرمخو.
Literal meaning: I will buy a new car tomorrow.

All of the speakers failed to understand the entire meanings of these sentences, apart from the words امتحاناتتو and سيارت, which are somewhat similar to their equivalents in Arabic, i.e. امتحان meaning *'exam'* and سيارة meaning *'car'*. Building on the mutual intelligibility criterion, it suggests that this variety is a different language because it is not understood by Arabs. However, most people in Oman still consider it to be a dialect. It seems that the border that divides a language from a dialect is not always clear. To illustrate this further, let us consider Mandarin and Cantonese. Although these are two different dialects of Chinese, the speakers of these two dialects do not have mutual intelligibility as they are not able to understand each other. By way of explanation, consider the following two Mandarin and Cantonese sentences meaning *'I don't have time now'* in English:

Mandarin:	我 (wo) 现在 (xian zai)没有 (mei you) 时间 (shi jian)
Literal meaning	*I now don't have time.*
Cantonese:	我 (ngo) 而家 (yi gaa) 冇 (mou) 时间 (si gaan)
Literal meaning	*I now don't have time.*

Although both Mandarin and Cantonese are written in Chinese characters and share general structures, there is next to zero mutual intelligibility between them. This is evidenced in the different use of vocabulary and pronunciation, among other things. For example, consider in the two varieties, i.e. Mandarin and Cantonese, the words for *'now'* are 现在 (xian zai) and 而家 (yi gaa), respectively and the words for *'don't have'* are 没有 (mei you) and 冇 (mou), respectively. Even for the words shared in both varieties in the written form, the pronunciations are very different. For instance, the personal pronoun *'I'* 我 is /wo/ in Mandarin but /ngo/ in Cantonese. Similarly, the word *'time'* 时间 is pronounced as /shi jian/ in Mandarin and /si gaan/ in Cantonese. A combination of these factors explains the lack of mutual intelligibility between the two varieties of the Chinese language.

By contrast, Urdu and Hindi are considered to be two different languages, although the speakers of these two languages have mutual intelligibility as they are able to understand each other.

It seems we cannot rely on mutual intelligibility as the sole criterion to determine whether people speak different languages or different dialects of the same language. Instead, other sociopolitical issues should be taken into consideration as well. The often social, political, and even ideological dimensions in determining what is a language and what is a dialect are aptly illustrated in the oft-quoted saying among linguists that 'a language is a dialect with an army and navy'.

Dialect differs from 'accent' in the sense that while the former refers to the differences among varieties of the same language in terms of three main levels, namely pronunciation, structure, and vocabulary, the latter refers to the differences in terms of pronunciation only, as shown below:

	British	**American**
Vocabulary	I'm looking for a small flat.	I'm looking for a small apartment.
Structure	I don't have friends in this city.	I haven't friends in this city.
Pronunciation	/əd'vɜː.tɪs.mənt/	/æd.vɜˈtaɪz.mənt/

Consider the word *'cut'*. In England, the word *'cut'* is used by people from different geographical areas to talk about their haircut in a structure of the following kind *'I had my hair cut'*. However, it can be pronounced differently. In cities such as Durham, Sunderland, or Newcastle, the vowel in the middle of the word is a high back vowel where the tongue is articulated

---

What are the criteria that can be used to distinguish a language from a dialect?

What is the difference between a 'dialect' and an 'accent'?

Is RP (Received Pronunciation), which you may hear when you watch *BBC News*, an accent or dialect? Discuss.

in the back of the oral cavity (horizontally) and in the high part of the mouth (vertically), thus being pronounced /ʊ/, rhyming with words like *'good'* or *'push'*. In some other cities, however, it is a low central vowel where the tongue is articulated in the centre of the oral cavity (horizontally) and in the low part of the mouth (vertically), thus being pronounced /ʌ/, rhyming with words like *'blood'* or *'flood'* in Southern Standard British English. As the difference here is in terms of pronunciation only, we talk about an accent, rather than a dialect or sub-dialect. Another interesting example is the word *'three'*, which is pronounced in most parts of the English-speaking countries as /θriː/. However, this word is pronounced by Londoners with a cockney accent /friː/, thus resulting in what is linguistic-ally called a 'homophone', i.e. two words (*'free'* and *'three'*), which have different spelling and meaning, are pronounced in exactly the same way. It is worth mentioning that Londoners with a cockney accent conflate the interdental /θ/ with a labiodental sound /f/ not only in this word.

Now the question that might be raised here is: How can a text made up of different variations of language be translated? To show the difficulty of answering such a question, let us consider this example extracted from a short story titled صورة ياسمين 'Yasmine Picture' by Hanan al-Shaykh translated by and cited in Husni and Newman (2008: 152–3):

ST	يتمشى في البيت، يدخل كلّ الغرف. يكتفي بالنظر، يفتح الخزائن، الأدراج، وزوجته تقول له وهي تبتسم: ولو شو صاير لك. رد كاذبًا: "بفتش على كتاب ...".
Back translation	He (was) walking around the house, going into every room. He was content with just looking; he (was) opening cupboards and drawers. His wife said to him while smiling: "So, what happened to you?" He answered with a lie: "I am looking for a book ...".
TT	He walked around the house, going into every room. He was content with just looking; he opened cupboards and drawers. His wife smiled and told him: "So, what are you up to?" He answered with a lie: "I am looking for a book ...".

In the above example, as Arabic speakers may notice, there is an example of intralingual code-switching from standard Arabic into non-standard Arabic: ولو شو صاير لك 'So, what happened to you' and بفتش على كتاب 'I'm looking for a book'. Here, the author, presumably intending to inject her text with vividness and credibility, opts for code-switching, thereby impli-citly revealing some information about the speaker. The translators, as can be seen, opted for *'So, what are you up to?'* and *'I am looking for a book ...'*, respectively, thereby failing to maintain this dialectal feature. Their failure has nothing to do with their translation competence, but rather has something to do with the notion of the 'untranslatability' of such dialectal features. Untranslatability, as defined by Cui (2012: 826), refers to "a prop-erty of a text, or of any utterance in one language, for which no equivalent

Are the words *'thin'* and *'fin'* examples of homophones in the cockney accent?

Can we consider the words that are used in a cer-tain area local words? And can these local words be considered as examples of dialects? Discuss.

What about opting for a non-standard variety, as in *'Tha mi a 'coimhead airson leabhar'* (Scottish English) or *'Táim ag lorg leabhar'* (Irish English). Discuss.

text or utterance can be found in another language". Examining what the translators did in the above example, in particular in بفتش على كتاب, which was translated somewhat formally into *'I am looking for a book'*, one can readily see that the dynamics created by the mode of discourse in the original text is largely lost in the target text (see also the chapter on untranslatability in House 2018). Translators can use a variety of different local strategies when facing any difficulty; however, in translating dialects and accents, the story is different. This clearly shows how translators suffer when dealing with a text made up of different varieties of language. To reinforce this point, let us consider this example quoted from Al-Rubai'i (2005: 37) and translated in two different ways:

ST	"Listen at you, now", Luster said. "Ain't you something, thirty-three years old, going on that way …".
TT1	قال لستر [بالعامية التي يتحدثها السود]: اسمع أنينك الآن. أليس عجيبًا أنك في الثالثة والثلاثين من عمرك وتستمر على هذا النحو؟
Back translation	Luster said [in a vernacular spoken by black people]: "Listen to yourself now. Isn't it strange that you thirty-three years in your age, and you continue in this way."
TT2	اطّلع عنفسك هسا. مش غريب أنك ثلاث وثلاثين ولسا بعدك عهلحال؟
Back translation	Look at yourself now. Isn't it strange that you are thirty-three and you are still like this?

In the first translation, the translator added between square brackets بالعامية التي يتحدثها السود, i.e. *'in a vernacular spoken by black people'* to reflect the speaker's way of using language. Further, she misunderstood the Black American English expression *'Listen at you, now'*, which means *'look at yourself now'*, thus mistranslating it into اسمع أنينك الآن *'Listen to yourself now'*. In the second translation, the translator opted for Levantine Arabic. However, a question that may arise here is: 'Is this variety of language equivalent to what is used in the original text?' The answer is 'No'. This leads us again to the issue of 'untranslatability'.

Connecting the dots (2): Translating styles and style shifts

Style (derived from the Latin word *'stylus'* meaning stake or pointed instrument for writing), obviously, is the object of study for stylistics. Within any language, the same idea can be communicated in various linguistic forms, thus resulting in different styles. Leech and Short (1981: 10–11) define style as "the linguistic habits of a particular writer …, genre, period, school". Style is seen by other stylisticians as "the dress of thought" (Hough 1969: 3). However, it is defined by formalists as "a deviation from language norms". Nida and Taber (1969) in their definition of style touch on the patterning of choices, as well as the generic constraints that play crucial roles in determining an author's style. Style, according to Yule (1985/2014: 259), is defined as "a social feature of language". When you, as a speaker, pay extra attention to your way of using language in terms of structure, lexical choices, pronunciation, etc., then your style is 'formal' or 'careful'. However, when you do the opposite, i.e. you pay less attention to how you are speaking, then your style is 'informal' or 'casual'. Building on this, when you change your style while communicating from a 'formal style' to an 'informal style', there will be a 'style shift'. In place of having only two styles, 'formal' and 'informal', Martin Joos, in his book *The Five Clocks: A Linguistic Excursion into the Five Styles of English Usage* (1962), talks of five styles in spoken English. They are 'frozen', 'formal', 'consultative', 'casual', and 'intimate' (see here House 1977/1981, where Joos' classification is used in her model of translation assessment).

> How would you classify 'style' according to Martin Joos?

Frozen style

This is also known as 'static register'. This style, referring to printed unchanging language, is characterized by the use of archaic expressions, such as the use of some quotations from the Quran or the Bible.

> How many styles are there which are one-way participation?

Formal style

This style is characterized by a one-way participation, as is the case in the use of technical words. As it involves a one-way participation, this means there is no interruption and feedback.

Consultative style

Unlike the 'formal style', this style is characterized by a two-way participation where background information is provided, and prior knowledge is not assumed. Further, verbal fillers, such as *'I see'*, are common. As we have here a two-way participation, interruptions are allowed in this style. A good example of this style is that used, for instance, between a teacher and student, a doctor and patient, etc., where interruptions are allowed to seek clarification or further information.

Casual style

This style is used among friends and acquaintances where background information need not be provided, and prior knowledge is not always assumed. As it is not a one-way participation, interruptions, ellipsis, and slang are common among friends and acquaintances in an informal setting.

> What are the differences between a 'casual style' and an 'intimate style'?

Intimate style

This style is characterized by a two-way participation. Like the 'casual style', it is used among family members, close friends, and acquaintances. In this style, intonation and non-verbal messages are given a front seat, while wording or grammar is given a back seat.

Think of some situations where style shifting may occur.

When you change your style from an 'intimate style' to a 'consultative style' while communicating with one of your family members, for instance, there will be a style shift. Similarly, changing your style as a doctor while communicating with your patient, from a 'consultative style' to a 'casual style', for instance, will result in a style shift.

The questions that arise here are: 'Shall we cater for style while translating?' and 'How can a style shift be translated?' Priority should be given to the meaning as the translator's role is to translate the meaning first, and only then style (Nida and Taber 1969/1974: 12). However, this does not mean that the author's way of using the language, or any style shift, should be completely ignored. Rather, the translator needs to make use of the potential sources available to reflect the author's style and/or any style shift. To explain, let us consider the following example extracted from Maḥmūd Saīd's story البديلة 'The Stand-in' (cited in Almanna and Al-Rubai'i 2009: 67):

Arabic	أصبح العالم قرية صغيرة يشرب فيها الكل الكوكاكولا ويأكلون "الهم" بركر ويلبسون نفس الزي ويحلقون رؤوسهم بنفس الطريقة وو.. ونحن ما زلنا متخلفين.. يا ويلي علينا..
Back translation	The world has become a small village in which everyone drinks Coca-Cola, eats 'ham' burgers, wears the same clothes, and has the same haircut, and (and) … we are still lagging behind. Oh my God.

Here, certain rhetorical devices are employed by the author:

(1) 'Alliteration' in the repetition of the sound-cluster الكل at the beginning of the words الكل and الكوكاكولا.
(2) 'Assonance' in the repetition of the letters ك, و, and ل.
(3) 'Pun' on the words هم 'grief' and همبركر 'hamburger'.

In addition to these rhetorical devices, there is a style shift from formal to casual, as shown below:

أصبح العالم قرية صغيرة يشرب فيها الكل الكوكاكولا ويأكلون "الهم" بركر ويلبسون نفس الزي ويحلقون رؤوسهم بنفس الطريقة وو.. ونحن ما زلنا متخلفين.. [formal] يا ويلي علينا [casual]

Returning to the question raised earlier, can we reflect some of the style shifts, if not all of them, in the target text? Due to (1) the differences between the interfacing languages and (2) the fact that each language has its own preferences, we might fail. It would be advisable for the target text to retain as much as possible of such an effect. To convey the character's tone of indignation, one may opt for the addition of an adjectival expletive, such as 'damn' or 'bloody'. To reflect the style shift, however, one may use expressions such as 'O gosh', 'Holy moly', and 'Holy crap'.

The world has become a small village where everybody drinks Coca-Cola and eats the bloody hamburger, wears the same clothes and has the same haircut, and we are still lagging behind. O gosh.

In the following example quoted from Strikauskaitė (2016: 73), style is given a back seat due to the differences between the interfacing languages.

English	Grievers, we call 'em.
Lithuanian	Mes juos vadiname grizais.
Back translation	We call them grievers.

With the potential to lay more emphasis on the lexical item *'grievers'*, the author decides to foreground it. This becomes a stylistic feature that needs to be given full consideration after reflecting the meaning, i.e. *'We call them grievers'*. Guided by the 'initial acceptability norm' (Toury 1995) and 'expectancy norm' (Chesterman 1997/2000; for more details, see the next section), the translator decided not to translate this stylistic inversion as translating it would strike the Lithuanian reader as very unusual (Strikauskaitė 2016). Due to the flexibility that Arabic has in word order, such a stylistic feature can be easily reflected without striking the target language readers as unusual.

Arabic		تَعساء، نسميهم.
Back translation	Grievers, we call them.	

In German with its similar word order flexibility, inversion is also possible: *'Trauernde nennen wir sie'*.

To finish off this section, let us translate the following example extracted from Greene (1980: 9–10; also discussed after being translated to other languages in Chapter 2 of this book) into Thai:

English	I think that I used to detest Doctor Fischer more than any other man I have known just as I loved his daughter more than any other woman.
Thai	ผมคิดว่าผมเคยเกลียดหมอฟิสเชอร์มากกว่าที่เคยเกลียดใครคนไหนที่ผมได้รู้จักมา ในแบบเดียวกับที่ผมรักลูกสาวของเขามากกว่าผู้หญิงคนไหน phom kit wa phom koei kliat mo Fischer mak-kwa thi kliat khai-khon-nai thi phom dai ru-chak ma nai baep diaw kap thi phom rak luk-sao khong kao mak-kwa phu-ying khon-nai.
Back translation	I think I used to hate Doctor Fischer more than I hate any other person I have known in the same way as I loved his daughter more than any other woman.

In the original text, parallelism is used, as shown below:

I	used to detest	Doctor Fischer	more than	any other	man
I	loved	his daughter	more than	any other	woman

Added to this, two antonyms, i.e. *'detest'* versus *'love'* and *'man'* versus *'woman'*, are employed by the author. These antonyms acquire stylistic features that need to be reflected in the target text, providing that such a reflection would not distort the linguistic and stylistic norms of the target language.

Having paid attention to the style used by the author, the translator managed to reflect the parallel structures in his translation into Thai. Further, an experienced Thai translator may use assonance to create a literary effect in addition to the phonological features that emerge from the repetition of the terms *'kliat'* meaning *'hate'* and *'mak-kwa'* meaning *'more than'*. Assonance is created by the choice of the /ai/ sound, as in *'khai-khon-nai'* meaning *'any other person'*, *'dai'* which is a lexis-based aspect for the past perfect, *'nai'* meaning *'in'*, and *'khon-nai'* meaning *'any other'*. This rendition compensates for the loss of alliteration in *'detest'* and *'doctor'*, which sound entirely different in Thai: *'kliat'* and *'mo'*, respectively.

Connecting the dots (3): Audience type and translation

Try to reflect on a situation in which you changed your way of speaking because of your audience.

Language users in general and speakers in particular modify their way of using language when they know for sure who they are talking to. Talking to a professor of English while discussing a linguistic issue is different from talking to a level-one student to discuss the same topic. Added to this, talking to a person when you are sure that there is nobody lurking around is different from talking to a person when you know that there are some people around you listening in to your speech. In this regard, Allan Bell (1984) distinguishes between four types of audience, namely (1) addressee, (2) auditor, (3) over-hearer, and (4) eavesdropper. The addressee has more impact on the speaker's way of using the language compared with other types of audience. This is because the addressee is the person who the speaker is talking to directly, while the auditor, over-hearer, and eavesdropper are not addressed directly by the speaker. Bell (Ibid.) proposes three criteria through which these types of audience can be distinguished:

(1) 'Known' (this is the wider circle covering all people that are part of the speech context, such as speaker, addressee, auditor, and over-hearer).
(2) 'Ratified' (this is the second largest circle covering the speaker, addressee, and auditor, indicating that the speaker is aware of the auditor's presence without addressing him/her).
(3) 'Addressed' (this is the smallest circle covering only the speaker along with the addressee).

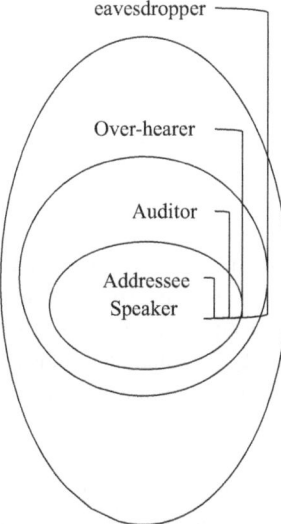

These different types of audience according to their relationship with the speaker can be modelled here (adapted from Bell 1984: 160):

	known	ratified	addressed
Addressee	✓	✓	✓
Auditor	✓	✓	X
Over-hearer	✓	X	X
Eavesdropper	X	X	X

To make this point clear, let us imagine a situation in which a head of department is talking to a teacher in an official meeting in front of the other teachers when he suddenly realizes that someone is lurking around. Here, the head of department (the speaker) is talking to one of the teachers (addressee) in front of the other teachers (auditors who are 'known', 'ratified', but not 'addressed') and realizes that someone is lurking around (over-hearer who is 'known', but neither 'ratified' nor 'addressed'). In such a situation, the head of department, being influenced by (1) the presence of the other teachers and (2) the realization of someone lurking around, may well influence his way of using language, thus resulting in what is called 'intra-speaker style shifting'.

Building on this, we can imagine an interpreting situation in which the interpreter, being influenced by the audience type or the presence of other people who are experts in the field, modifies his/her way of using language, thus resulting in what is called in this book 'intra-interpreter style shifting'.

As far as translation is concerned, audience type can be discussed from a different perspective. To achieve effective communication, Hall (2008: 23) states that "the translator needs to take account of the cognitive

How would you define 'intra-speaker style shifting'?

How would you define 'intra-interpreter style shifting'?

and cultural environment of the targeted language community and its likely expectations of the transmitted text and make his/her translation as informative and accessible as possible". However, it is worth noting that translators, as special readers, do not have direct access to the cognitive environment of their target readers, but they rely on certain beliefs and assumptions as well as their own intuitions (Gutt 1991: 112). Before translating the text at hand, the translator needs to take into account the target language readers' expectations, as well as their level of education, familiarity with the topic discussed, event narrated, entities referred to, structures and lexical items used, and so on. To this end, s/he needs to take into consideration several fundamental decisions regarding such notions as acceptability, readability, idiomaticity, authenticity, accessibility, and well-formedness that feed into naturalness. Almanna (2016: 41) expresses this situation as follows:

> Through careful reading and analysis, translators can make some guesses as to the degree of formality as opposed to informality, generality as opposed to specificity, accessibility as opposed to inaccessibility, explicitness as opposed to implicitness, and so on.

Acceptability, as Baker (1992: 219) states, has almost nothing to do with "how closely it corresponds to some state in the world". Rather, it depends on how the target language readers access the target text and decide on its reality, "whether believable, homogenous or relevant" (Ibid.). Acceptability, according to Toury (1995), is one of the social regulation mechanisms, i.e. norms, that make certain choices more likely than others. Toury (1995: 56–9; also discussed in Almanna 2014: 119–20; Farghal and Almanna 2015: 34) distinguishes three types of norms, namely:

Norms, in general, are conventional, social, behavioural routines, according to which members of a certain culture behave when they find themselves under particular circumstances.

(1) 'Preliminary norms' referring to the 'translation policy' and 'directness of translation'.
   (a) 'Translation policy' referring to the factors that determine the selection of the original text for translation.
   (b) 'Directness of translation' dealing with the question of whether the target text is directly translated from the source language or through another language.
(2) 'Initial norms' referring to the general choices made by translators when they make decisions to either pay attention to the norms of the source language, thus guaranteeing adequacy, or to take into account the norms of the target language, thereby achieving the acceptability of the original text in the target language.
(3) 'Operational norms' covering both 'matricial norms' and 'textual-linguistic norms'.

(a) 'Matricial norms' referring to the completeness of the target text, thereby questioning issues such as omission, addition, and relocation.

(b) 'Textual-linguistic norms' referring to linguistic materials, such as lexical items, phrases, and stylistic features.

Chesterman (1997/2000: 68–9) classifies translation norms into four types:

(1) 'Expectancy norm' referring to the translator's decisions to make the target text grammatical, acceptable, appropriate, and so on in a certain text type.

(2) 'Accountability norm' referring to how translators consider tricky points and complex, sophisticated, and sometimes confusing language by double-checking their translation and/or asking professionals for their opinion.

(3) 'Relation norm' referring to the relationship between the components of the original text and those of the target text.

(4) 'Communication norm' referring to the communicative maxims in terms of quantity, quality, relevance, and manner (see Chapter 8 of this book for more details).

In order to see how these norms put pressure on the translator, thus determining, among other factors, the final shape of the target text, let us consider the following example quoted from a short story titled حكاية القنديل 'The Tale of the Lamp' by 'Izz al-Dīn al-Madanī, translated by and cited in Husni and Newman (2008: 26–7):

ST	فقال الرجل: (نعم يا موالي السلطان إنه والله قنديل من النحاس).
Back translation	So the man said: Yes, O my lord, the Sultan; it is by God a lamp made of copper.
TT	Yes, my lord – a lamp made out of copper.

Here, the translators, guided by the initial acceptability norm (Toury 1995) and the expectancy and communication norms (Chesterman 1997/2000), decided not to translate the lexical items سلطان 'Sultan' and والله 'and by God' (an operational norm/matricial norm). Such decisions affect the communication norm in terms of quantity. In this regard, Farghal and Almanna (2015: 35) hold that this "kind of tug of war between conflicting norms sometimes results in one winning over the other … or, alternatively, a balance being struck or a compromise being reached between them". To reinforce this point, the following example extracted from Haddon (2003: 1; also discussed in Pillière 2018: 234) and translated by Demange (2004: 13) into French can be considered:

ST	There was a garden fork sticking out of the dog. The points of the fork must have gone all the way through the dog and into the ground because the fork had not fallen over. I decided that the dog was probably killed with the fork because I could not see any other wounds in the dog and I do not think you would stick a garden fork into a dog after it had died.
TT	Il avait une fourche plantée dans le ventre. Les dents avaient dû le traverser de part en part et s'enfoncer dans le sol, parce qu'elle n'était pas tombée. Je me suis dit que le chien avait sans doute été tué avec la fourche, parce que je ne voyais pas d'autres blessures. Et je ne pense pas que quelqu'un irait planter une fourche dans un chien qui serait mort.
Back translation	There was a garden fork sticking out of its stomach. The points Ø must have gone through it and into the ground because it had not fallen over. I decided that the dog was probably killed with the fork because I could not see any other wounds Ø and I do not think you would stick a garden fork into a dog after it had died.

As the back translation shows, the translator, guided by the initial acceptability norm (Toury 1995) and the expectancy and communication norms (Chesterman 1997/2000), decided to:

(1) omit the lexical items *'fork'* in *'the points of the fork'* and *'dog'* in *'I could not see any other wounds in the dog'* when opting for *'les dents avaient dû le traverser meaning'* meaning *'the points must have gone through it'* and *'je ne voyais pas d'autres blessures'* meaning *'I didn't see any wounds/injuries'* respectively;
(2) replace the lexical items *'fork'* and *'dog'* with pronouns when translating *'the fork had not fallen over'* into *'elle n'était pas tombée'* literally meaning *'she did not fall'* and *'the fork must have gone all the way through the dog'* into *'les dents avaient dû le traverser'* literally meaning *'the points must have gone through it'*.

Omitting these two lexical items and substituting them on other occasions with pronouns do not affect the initial adequacy norm (Toury 1995) and relation norm (Chesterman 1997/2000), as is the case with the previous example. Rather, the translation hangs together as a cohesive and coherent text.

These examples and other examples consulted show the amount of pressure put on translators in their attempt to reach an adequate decision.

Exercises and discussion

Exercise 1: Mark the following statements (T) if they are true and (F) if they are false.

(1) When you communicate with your teacher in front of your classmates, your classmates, in such a situation, are 'known', 'ratified', and 'addressed' according to the criteria proposed by Allan Bell (1984).	
(2) 'Intra- interpreter style shifting' occurs when the interpreter, influenced by the audience type or presence of other people who are experts in the field, modifies his/her way of using language.	
(3) 'Translation policy', according to Toury (1995), refers to the factors that determine the global strategy that should be adopted by the translator.	
(4) To determine whether people speak different languages or different dialects of the same language, one can rely on the mutual intelligibility criterion.	
(5) The line that demarcates regional varieties, i.e. dialects, within a given language is called an 'isogloss'.	
(6) The use of *'to seek'* in place of *'to look for'* can be considered as an example of regional variation.	
(7) Consultative style according to Martin Joos (1962) is characterized by a one- way participation and thus by a heavy use of fillers.	
(8) 'Polyglossia' is very close to bilingualism, rather than monolingualism or multilingualism.	
(9) Dialectal features can be easily translated by experienced translators.	
(10) A 'pidgin' is different from a 'creole' in the sense that the former has native speakers.	

Exercise 2: In the following sentences, different figures of speech are used. Identify them before translating the sentences into your own language:

Example	Type
(1) "All animals are equal, but some animals are more equal than others" – George Orwell, *Animal Farm*.	
(2) My brother won the lottery, so he's a bit excited.	
(3) The famous chef said people should live to eat, not eat to live.	

Example	Type
(4) Recently, he has lost his wife, his house, and his car.	
(5) I have told you a million times not to touch my laptop!	
(6) Opportunity seldom knocks twice, dude. You'll always regret it if you don't go for it".	
(7) Her husband is an onion; to understand him, she has to peel back the layers.	
(8) The strawberry cake made by your mom was awfully good.	
(9) The burning fire warmed the whole house.	
(10) Speech is silver, but silence is golden.	

Exercise 3: Try to search for Earnest Hemingway's short story titled 'Very Short Story' (1942) and:

(1) translate it into your language, assuming that your translation will be published by a literary magazine in your country;
(2) comment on your own translation by adopting a stylistic approach.

Discussion and research points

(1) What is the difference between 'intralingual code-switching' and 'intra-sentential code-switching'? Discuss with illustrative examples.
(2) Find out the main differences between 'dialect' and 'idiolect'.
(3) How would you define a 'reader-oriented translation'?
(4) Think of the main local strategies that a translator can resort to while dealing with translating certain dialectal features.
(5) Select any English text and translate it into your own language. Then comment on your translation by referring to Toury's (1995) norms.

References

Almanna, A. (2014). *Translation Theories Exemplified from Cicero to Pierre Bourdieu*. Munich: Lincom Europa Academic Publishers.

Almanna, A. (2016). *The Routledge Course in Translation Annotation: Arabic-English-Arabic*. London/New York: Routledge.

Almanna, A. and Al-Rubai'i, A. (2009). *Modern Iraqi Short Stories: A Bilingual Reader*. London: Sayyab Books Ltd.

Al-Rubai'i, A. (2005). *Translation Criticism*. Durham Modern Languages Series. Durham: Durham University.

Baker, M. (1992). *In Other Words: A Coursebook on Translation*. London/New York: Routledge.

Bell, A. (1984). "Language Style as Audience Design", *Language in Society*, Vol. 13, pp. 145–204.

Chesterman, A. (1997/ 2000). *Memes of Translation: The Spread of Ideas in Translation Theory*. Amsterdam/ Philadelphia, PA: John Benjamins.

Cui, J. (2012). "Untranslatability and the Method of Compensation", *Theory and Practice in Language Studies*, Vol. 2(4), pp. 826–30.

Demange, O. (2004). *Le bizarre incident du chien pendant la nuit*. (trans.). Paris: Pocket jeunesse.

Farghal, M. and Almanna, A. (2015). *Contextualizing Translation Theories: Aspects of Arabic–English Interlingual Communication*. Newcastle upon Tyne: Cambridge Scholars Publishing.

Greene, G. (1980). *The Bomb Party*. Harmondsworth: Penguin Books.

Gutt, E- A. (1991). *Translation and Relevance: Cognition and Context*. Oxford: Blackwell.

Haddon, M. (2003). *The Curious Incident of the Dog in the Night-Time*. London: Jonathan Cape.

Hall, M. F. (2008). *Discourse Analysis of Fictional Dialogue in Arabic to English Translation*. Unpublished PhD thesis. London: University of London.

Hemingway, E. (1942). "Very Short Story". Retrieved on 11 February 2023 from http://ouallinator.com/blog/wp-content/uploads/2017/08/A-Very-Short-Story.pdf.

Holmes, J. (1992/ 2013). *An Introduction to Sociolinguistics* (4th edn). London/New York: Routledge.

Hough, G. (1969). *Style and Stylistics*. London: Routledge/Kegan Paul.

House, J. (1977/ 1981). *A Model for Translation Quality Assessment*. Tübingen: Narr.

House, J. (2018). *Translation. The Basics*. London/New York: Routledge.

Husni, R. and Newman, D. (2008). *Modern Arabic Short Stories: A Bilingual Reader*. London: Saqi Books.

Joos, M. (1962). *The Five Clocks: A Linguistic Excursion into the Five Styles of English Usage*. New York: Harcourt Brace.

Leech, G. and Short, M. (1981). *Style in Fiction: A Linguistic Introduction to English Fictional Prose*. London: Longman.

Nida, E. and Taber, C. R. (1969). *The Theory and Practice of Translation*. Leiden: Brill.

Parker, F. and Riley, K. (1994/2010). *Linguistics for Non-Linguists*. Boston, MA: Pearson.

Pillière, L. (2018). "Style and Voice: Lost in Translation?" *Études de stylistique anglaise*, Vol. 40(12), pp. 225–52.

Romaine, S. (1994/ 2000). *Language in Society. An Introduction to Sociolinguistics*. Oxford: Oxford University Press.

Spolsky, B. (1998). *Sociolinguistics*. Oxford: Oxford University Press.

Strikauskaitè, R. (2016). "Translation of Stylistic Devices in Contemporary Young Adult Fiction", *Jaunųjų mokslininkų darbai*, Vol. 2(46), pp. 71–7.

Toury, G. (1995). *Descriptive Translation Studies and Beyond.* Amsterdam: John Benjamins.

Van Herk, G. (2012). *What is Sociolinguistics?* Hoboken, NJ: Wiley-Blackwell.

Yule, G. (1985/1996). *The Study of Language.* Cambridge: Cambridge University Press.

Cognitive linguistics

12

In this chapter, you will learn about the main theories and approaches of cognitive linguistics. In particular, you will become aware of the difference between cognitive grammar and cognitive semantics and about fundamental commitments in cognitive linguistics and imaging systems and its components. You will further learn about translation and its relations to the configurational, attentional, perspectival, and force dynamic systems.

After studying this chapter, you will be in a position to apply the above theoretical concepts to the process of translation, thus managing to make your own translation more in line with the underlying cognitive systems of the original text.

Cognitive linguistics was first developed in the late 1970s out of dissatisfaction with strictly formal approaches to language and with the aim of providing a holistic account of language by focusing on such cognitive abilities as distribution of attention, image schemas, viewing frames, scope of intention, extent of causation, memory, and perception (Evans and Green 2006: 3). Since the mid-1970s, several scholars have contributed to the development of cognitive linguistics, such as Charles Fillmore and Paul Kay (Construction Grammar), William Croft (Radical Construction Grammar), Adele Goldberg (Cognitive Construction Grammar), Benjamin Bergen and Nancy Chang (Embodied Construction Grammar), Eleanor Rosch (Prototype Theory), Gilles Fauconnier (Mental Spaces Theory), Gilles Fauconnier and Mark Turner (Conceptual Blending Theory), Charles Fillmore (Frame Semantics), Ronald Langacker (Theory of Domain), Mark Johnson (Image Schema Theory), George Lakoff and Mark Johnson (Conceptual Metaphor Theory), and Leonard Talmy (Imaging Systems Theory) (for more details, see Evans and Green 2006; Abdulkareem 2021).

Cognitive linguistics can be divided into two main areas: 'cognitive grammar' and 'cognitive semantics'; the former depends on the latter as it "assumes a cognitive semantics" (Evans and Green 2006: 48), as explained below:

> Ronald Langacker, George Lakoff, and Leonard Talmy are the founders of cognitive linguistics. Do you agree?

DOI: 10.4324/9781003228028-13

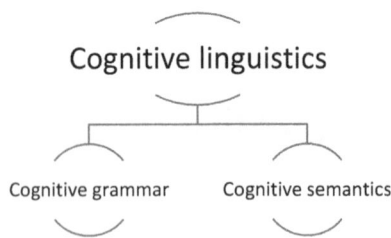

Cognitive grammar

Unlike the traditional approaches to grammar, cognitive grammar "attempts to model the cognitive mechanisms and principles that motivate and license the formation and use of linguistic units of varying degrees of complexity" (Evans 2007: 20). In cognitive linguistics, cognitive grammar is viewed as an image-based approach to grammar, and thus grammatical universals need to be "flexible enough to accommodate the variability actually encountered" (Langacker 1987: 47). Surface structures, as Langacker argues, do not "conceal a 'truer', deeper level of grammatical organization; rather, it itself embodies the conventional means a language employs for the structuring and symbolization of semantic content" (1987: 46–7). Consider the following two sentences:

> She goes to school with her dad in the morning.
> She went to school with her dad in the morning.

In the second sentence, an open path with windowing, i.e. emphasis, over the final portion is recruited.

In these two simple sentences, we have a process of doing expressed by the verb *'to go'* that invokes in our mind a *moving*-frame as well as an open path where the starting point and endpoint are not the same. But is the same mental image conjured up in our mind by virtue of these two sentences? The answer is 'No'. In the first sentence, the process of doing expressed by the verb *'to go'* is characterized by multiplexity, i.e. the quantity of the action is made up of more than one action, while in the second sentence it is characterized by uniplexity, i.e. the quantity is made up of one action that occurred in the morning. In the first sentence, we talk about a series of actions. Not only is the action of going to school drawn out over a long period of time in the first sentence, but it is characterized by having breaks or intervals.

Cognitive semantics

In cognitive semantics, the focus of attention is shifted towards the relationships among a certain sociocultural experience, the conceptual system, and the semantic structure encoded by language. Approached from this perspective, linguistic units utilized by language users to conceptualize a certain sociocultural experience are used by cognitive linguists to study the cognitive phenomena evoked in their minds. To make this point clear, let us consider the following simple sentence:

The girl is digging a hole in the sand.

In this sentence, we have two noun phrases: *'the girl'* and *'a hole in the sand'*. While the first noun phrase, i.e. *'the girl'*, fills a semantic role of Actor and a verb-specific semantic role of Digger, the second noun phrase, i.e. *'a hole in the sand'*, fills a semantic role of Affected Participant and a verb-specific semantic role of something Dug.

Now, hearing or reading such a sentence conjures up in our mind an image where a girl is digging a hole in the sand with something, such as a spade, garden fork, mattock, crowbar, or auger. This spade, for instance, used by the girl fills a semantic role of Instrument. However, it is worth mentioning that the language user decides not to mention it while communicating, thus backgrounding it in attention. In the above sentence, we have two semantic roles, while there are three visual roles, as shown in the following table which summarizes the relationships among syntactic, semantic, and visual roles:

Discuss the difference between 'The girl is digging a hole in the sand' and 'The girl is digging a hole in the sand with a spade'.

Identify the semantic and visual roles assigned to each noun phrase used in this simple sentence: 'The man is painting the wall right now'.

Syntactic roles	The girl ^{Subject} is digging the sand ^{Predicate}.
Semantic roles	The girl ^{Actor} is digging ^{process of doing} the sand ^{Affected Participant}.
Visual roles	The girl ^{Actor} is digging ^{process of doing} the sand ^{Affected Participant} (with something ^{Instrument}).

Commitments of cognitive linguistics

George Lakoff (1990), one of the pioneering figures in cognitive linguistics, argues that cognitive linguistics is based on two fundamental commitments: 'the generalization commitment' and 'the cognitive commitment', as shown below:

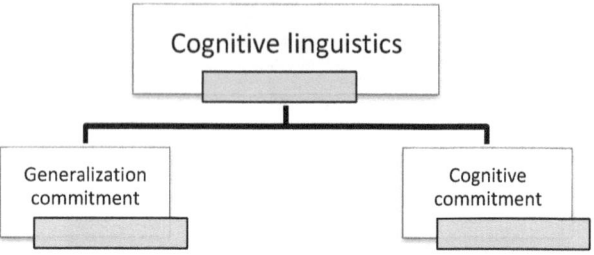

The generalization commitment is a commitment adopted to characterize regular and irregular structuring principles that account for all aspects of human language (Evans and Green 2006: 28). In English, for instance, there are a number of suffixes, such as '–er', '–or', '–ress', '–ant', and '–ist', that can be added to verbs or nouns in order to denote the agent or doer of the actions. The verb 'to teach', for example, can be changed to a noun referring to the doer of the act of teaching by virtue of the suffix '–er'. The same holds true for the word 'artist', which is made up of two morphemes: the root, 'art', and the suffix '–ist'. These suffixes function as agentive morphemes, as modelled below (for more details, see Chapters 3 and 4 of this book):

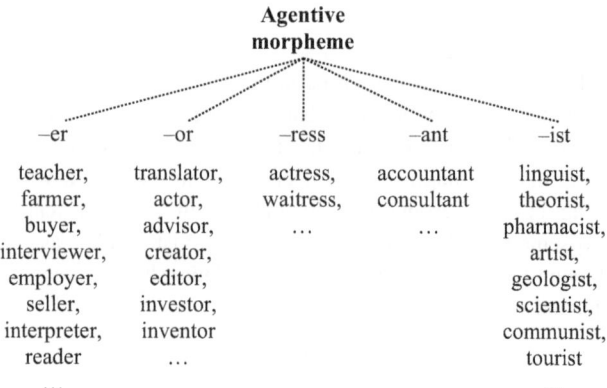

This grammatical category contains certain members, and those members are representative of this category having almost the same function. As such, these members share common structuring principles, thus forming a family. In this respect, Evans and Green (2006: 43) hold that those common structuring principles result in "a set of members related by family resemblance rather than a single criterial feature, or a limited set of criterial features possessed by every member of the category".

Find out in your language a grammatical category that contains certain members that have almost the same function.

In Italian, for example, the diminutive suffixes, such as '*–ino*', '*–etto*', and '*–ello*' can be added to nouns, adjectives, or verbs to convey different but related meanings, thereby forming a category with a family resemblance, as shown in the following examples quoted from Evans and Green (2006: 30–1):

paese (village)	→	paesano (small village)
cena (supper)	→	cenetta (light supper)
bene (well)	→	benino (quite well)
lavorare (to work)	→	lavoricciare (to work half-heartedly)

In Arabic, morphological causatives are created by the process of affixation, as shown in the following examples quoted from Almanna (2016: 41):

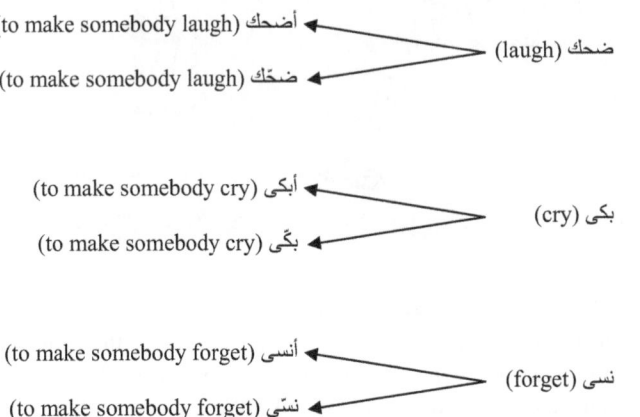

As we can see, these verbs and similar ones (for more details, see Almanna 2016: 40–1) can be changed from intransitive verbs to transitive ones, and then act as morphological causatives through the same process, thus forming a family.

Cognitive commitment, on the other hand, is a "commitment to providing a characterization of general principles for language that accords with what is known about the mind and brain from other disciplines" (Evans and Green 2006: 27–8). As such, our knowledge of language should not be separated from other types of knowledge and experience that we have acquired and developed over time. Approached from such a perspective, decoding the meaning of any linguistic unit relies on (1) the conceptual content that a linguistic unit has, and (2) a certain construal that

What does the word '*buy*' mean? Can you tell us its meaning without imagining a particular situation? Discuss.

a language user may adopt "to conceive and portray the same situation in alternate ways" (Langacker 2008: 43). To make this point clear, consider the following three sentences:

The man raised his hand and pressed the bell.
The man raised his hand to press the bell.
The bell was pressed by the man.

Note that in this book, terms such as 'tensed clause' and its opposite 'non-tensed clause' are used as synonyms for such terms as 'finite clause' and 'non-finite clause', respectively.

In the first sentence, which is a compound one, two tensed clauses, expressing two processes of doing, are used. The emphasis is here placed on the completion of the two actions, i.e. raising his hand and pressing the bell.

How would you translate the above three sentences into your language without changing the mental images that might be conjured up in your readers' minds?

Cognitively speaking, as it is asserted that he raised his hand and pressed the bell, the extent of causation is greater than the scope of intention. We can see in our mind's eye that there is no distance between his finger and the bell should we take the picture at the moment of pressing the bell.

In the second sentence, however, there are two clauses where two processes of doing are utilized. However, only one clause is tensed, that is, *'The man raised his hand'* where the emphasis is placed on the completion of the act of raising his hand.

In the second clause, which is a non-tensed clause, the scope of intention is greater than the extent of causation as it is not asserted that he pressed the bell – he might change his mind at any moment and for any reason.

In the third sentence, the language user decided not to mention that the man had raised his hand with the potential to press the bell, thus backgrounding it in attention, but it can be predicted as it is still in the scope of prediction. To put it differently, while in the first two examples, the language user decided to profile the entire scope of prediction, in the third sentence, s/he decided not to profile the first part, thereby providing us with less details.

Main theories and approaches

Cognitive linguistics is not one single theory or approach; rather, it covers several theories and approaches that share certain fundamental theoretical principles and hypotheses, such as (1) meaning is conceptualization, (2) meaning is encyclopedic, (3) meaning is based on usage and experiences, (4) language has a symbolic function, and (5) language structures invoke conceptual structures characterized by universality (for more details, see Evans and Green 2006). These theories and approaches are classified into two main groups, as already hinted at above. They are (1) cognitive approaches to grammar, such as 'Construction Grammar' by Charles Fillmore and Paul Kay, 'Radical Construction Grammar' by William Croft, 'Cognitive Construction Grammar' by Adele Goldberg, and 'Embodied Construction Grammar' by Benjamin Bergen and Nancy Chang; and (2) cognitive semantics, such as 'Frame Semantics' by Charles Fillmore,

'Mental Spaces Theory' by Gilles Fauconnier, 'Theory of Domain' by Ron Langacker, 'Prototype Theory' by Eleanor Rosch, 'Conceptual Blending Theory' by Gilles Fauconnier and Mark Turner, 'Image Schema Theory' by Mark Johnson, 'Conceptual Metaphor Theory' by George Lakoff and Mark Johnson, and 'Imaging Systems Theory' by Leonard Talmy (for more details, see Evans and Green 2006; Abdulkareem 2021).

In this chapter, we look at Leonard Talmy's 'Imaging Systems Theory' in which he describes imaging systems (also known as 'schematic systems'). By employing certain grammatical forms and content specifications, a given scene may turn out to be of paramount importance for the actual work of translators. 'Frame Semantics' by Charles Fillmore is another important theory, and is explained in Chapter 6 of this book.

Imaging systems

A scene, according to Leonard Talmy (2000), which is expressed by language is structured by a kind of collaboration among the imaging systems (also known as 'schematic systems') which each and every person has. Each imaging system "contributes different structural aspects of the scene, resulting in the overall delineation of the scene's skeletal framework" (Evans and Green 2006: 194). These imaging systems explained by Talmy in several academic papers were later republished in his book titled *Toward a Cognitive Semantics* (2000) in two volumes.

Imaging systems are divided, following Talmy (2000), into four systems:

(1) 'Configurational system' referring to all forms of conceptualization of quantity or relations between quantities, in dimensions like TIME and SPACE.

According to Evans and Green (2006: 199), while the first three imaging systems focus on visual perception, force dynamics "derives from kinaesthesia, i.e. our bodily experience of muscular effort or motion and somesthesia, i.e. our bodily experience of sensations such as pressure and pain".

(2) 'Attentional system' referring to the distribution of attention over the aspects of the scene along with its participants.
(3) 'Perspectival system' referring to how people fix their mind's eye to look upon a scene and its participants.
(4) 'Force dynamic system' dealing with the forces that each element in the scene may exert on another element.

These imaging systems, as hinted at above, work hand in hand to structure a given scene, which is, in turn, expressed by virtue of certain grammatical forms (grammar) and content specifications (semantics). It is worth mentioning that each imaging system has certain features and categories that can be used to study the mental image(s) conjured up in the minds of the target language readers when we talk about translating from language *A* to language *B*, as shown in what follows.

Connecting the dots (1): Configurational system and translation

The configurational system refers to all forms of conceptualization of quantity or relations between quantities, in dimensions like TIME and SPACE. According to Talmy (2000), this imaging system is made up of eight schematic categories, namely 'plexity', 'state of dividedness', 'state of boundedness', 'disposition of quantity', 'degree of extension', 'pattern of distribution', 'axiality', and 'scene partitioning'. Almanna (2022), in an attempt to link them to the actual work of translators, has modified them slightly, thus suggesting seven categories, as explained in this chapter.

(1) Plexity

'Plexity' refers to the quantity of the action expressed by the verb or matter expressed by the noun phrase, whether it is made up of one element (uniplex) or more than one element (multiplex).

(2) State of boundedness

'State of boundedness' refers to the matter or action, whether it has boundaries (bounded) or not (unbounded).

(3) State of dividedness

'State of dividedness' refers to the internal segmentations that the quantity of the matter or action has. So, if the quantity has some kinds of breaks or interruptions through the process of composition, then it is internally 'discrete'. Otherwise, it is internally 'continuous' if it has no breaks or interruptions.

(4) Degree of extension

'Degree of extension' refers to the quantity of the matter or action, in terms of whether it is reduced to a single point or drawn out over a period or space. When it is drawn out over a period or space, it could be bounded (for boundaries, see 'state of boundedness') or unbounded.

(5) Scene partitioning

'Scene partitioning' refers to how the whole scene along with its main parts and participants is conceptualized. 'Part' here refers to the process itself typically expressed by the verb and the noun phrases used. 'Participant', however, refers to the personation type in terms of whether there is one participant (monadic) or two participants (dyadic).

What is the difference between these two sentences in terms of 'plexity', 'state of dividedness', 'state of boundedness', and 'degree of extension'?
'He travelled to the UK last week' and 'He has travelled to the UK many times recently'.

Identify the personation type, parts, and noun phrases used in this simple sentence:
'I received a text message from her yesterday'.

(6) Point of emphasis

'Point of emphasis' refers to the aspect of the action which the sentence focuses on. This emphasis can be on completion, duration, continuity, habituality, regularity, frequency, and the like.

(7) Pace of events and time lapse

'Pace of events' and 'time lapse' refer to the quality of actions immediately following one another, with a time gap to separate them or not.

Let us discuss the process of behaving expressed by the verb *'to watch'* in these two sentences:

> I was watching TV when my friend came to visit me last night.
> I used to watch TV when I was young.

Profile of the process in the first sentence:

- **Plexity:** the process of behaving is characterized by uniplexity as the quantity of the process is made up of one element.

- **State of boundedness:** as we are not able to determine the starting point and endpoint, it is unbounded.

- **State of dividedness:** according to the grammatical form and content specification used, it is without breaks or interruptions.

- **Degree of extension:** it is drawn out over a short period of time.

- **Scene partitioning:** it is made up of three parts (the process itself expressed by the verb and two noun phrases, namely *'I'* and *'TV'*), and one participant (monadic).

- **Pace of events and time lapse:** there is no time lapse between the process of behaving and the process of doing as the latter occurred in the middle of the former.

- **Point of emphasis:** the emphasis is shifted from the beginning and end of the action towards the middle phase, thus presenting the action as an ongoing activity that occurred in the past.

Profile of the process in the second sentence:

- **Plexity:** the process of behaving is characterized by multiplexity as the quantity of the process is made up of more than one element.

- **State of boundedness:** it is unbounded as no boundaries can be determined.

- **State of dividedness:** it is not internally continuous, but it has many breaks and interruptions.

- **Degree of extension:** it is drawn out over a long period of time – we are talking about years here.

- **Scene partitioning:** the whole scene is made up of three parts (the process itself and two noun phrases, namely '*I*' and '*TV*') and one participant (monadic).

- **Pace of events and time lapse:** not applicable

- **Point of emphasis:** the emphasis is placed on the habituality of the action in the past.

Now, to produce a similar mental image in the mind of the target language readers, these details should be given serious consideration by the translator. Translating them into German, for instance, an experienced translator might opt for:

How would you translate these two sentences into your language accurately?

ST (English)	TT (German)
I was watching TV when my friend came to visit me last night.	Ich sah fern, als mein Freund mich letzte Nacht besuchte.
I used to watch TV when I was young.	Ich habe in meiner Jugend immer ferngesehen.

Translating these sentences into Arabic, we might use the same grammatical form and content specification in the first part of the above sentences, i.e. كنتُ أشاهدُ التّلفازَ, literally meaning '*I was watching TV*', as shown below:

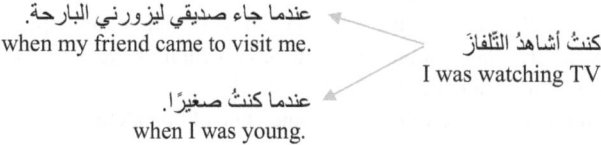

عندما جاء صديقي ليزورني البارحة.
when my friend came to visit me.

كنتُ أشاهدُ التّلفازَ
I was watching TV

عندما كنتُ صغيرًا.
when I was young.

Does that mean we failed to translate accurately, thereby producing a different mental image in the mind of the target language reader? The answer is 'No', simply because we managed to reflect all categories of the configurational system despite the use of the same grammatical form and content specification.

To reinforce this point, let us translate this sentence into different languages:

Translate this sentence into your language to produce a similar mental image in the mind of the target language reader.

I have told him several times not to wear this shirt.

Arabic	أخبرته ألا يرتدي هذا القميص.
Back translation	I (have) told him not to wear this shirt.
German	Ich habe ihm mehrmals gesagt, dass er dieses Hemd nicht tragen soll.
Back translation	I have told him several times that he should not wear this shirt.
French	Je lui ai dit plusieurs fois de ne pas porter cette chemise.
Back translation	I told him many times not to wear that shirt.
Chinese	我已经告诉他几次不要穿这件衬衫。
Back translation	I already told him several times not to wear this shirt.

All the above translations reflect a similar mental image in the minds of the target language readers, except for the translation into Arabic where the translator decided not to translate *'several times'*. In the original text, by virtue of the grammatical form (present perfect) and content specification (several times), the verbal process expressed by the verb *'to tell'* is characterized by multiplexity, i.e. the quantity of the action is made up of more than one element with breaks or intervals (state of dividedness) and without boundaries (state of boundedness) because we are not able to determine its starting point and endpoint. The emphasis is placed on the duration of the process that started in the past (unspecified) and is seen as relevant to the present (specified: the moment of speaking), so it is partially bounded (degree of extension and state of boundedness). The scene is made up of four parts (the process itself, two noun phrases *'I'* and *'him'*, and verbiage/content) and a dyadic personation type (Sayer and Addressee).

In Arabic, however, the verbal process expressed by the verb أخبر *'to tell'* is characterized by uniplexity, i.e. the quantity of the action is made up of one element without breaks or intervals (state of dividedness). The emphasis by the effect of the grammatical form and content specification used by the translator is placed on the completion of the action (point of emphasis), thus reducing the process, which is now seen as a single point on the timeline (degree of extension and state of boundedness).

Connecting the dots (2): Attentional system and translation

In this imaging system, the distribution of attention over the aspects of the scene is given adequate consideration by concentrating on issues such as scope of attention, profile selection, foregrounding versus backgrounding in attention, windowing of attention, and strength of attention, whether it is placed on the extent of causation or the scope of intention (Almanna and Al-Shehari 2019: 122). By way of illustration, let us go back to one of the examples discussed earlier in this chapter with the potential to translate it to several languages:

The man raised his hand and pressed the bell.

Arabic	رفع الرّجلُ يدَهُ وضغطَ جرسَ البابِ.
Back translation	The man raised his hand and pressed the doorbell.
German	Der Mann hob seine Hand und drückte auf die Klingel.
Back translation	The man raised his hand and pressed on the bell.
French	L'homme a levé la main et a appuyé sur la sonnette.
Back translation	The man raised his hand and pressed the doorbell.
Chinese	这个男的抬起他的手，按了下门铃。
Back translation	This man raised his hand, (and) pressed the doorbell.
Spanish	Levantó la mano y apretó la campana.
Back translation	He raised the hand and pressed the bell.

What about opting for translating the additive connector into a full stop, thus having two simple sentences, particularly in literary translation? Discuss.

In the original sentence, a compound sentence is used with two processes of doing expressed by two finite verbs: *'to raise'* and *'to press'*. The emphasis in the two processes is placed on the completion of the actions, thus being reduced to being seen as points on the timeline. Each process, to elaborate, is made up of one element (uniplex) and without breaks or interruptions (state of dividedness) or boundaries (state of boundedness). In both of them, it is asserted that the man raised his hand and pressed the bell, so they are past oriented, i.e. part of reality. By means of the additive connector *'and'*, there is no time lapse between the two processes, and the pace of events is sped up. In the translations suggested above, as one may notice, all these cognitive categories were given serious consideration, thereby producing a similar mental image in the target language readers' minds.

To reinforce this point, let us consider the following example taken from *BBC News* (2 December 2015) and translated into Arabic and German:

English	One of the workers died at the scene, while the other was rushed to a nearby hospital where he succumbed to his injuries. Their two colleagues were unharmed.
Arabic	وقتل أحد المستخدمين فورا فيما نقل الآخر إلى مستشفى محلي حيث فارق الحياة. ولم يصب الموظفان الآخران في الحادث.

Translate this text into your language to produce a similar mental image in the mind of the target language reader.

Back translation	And one of the workers was killed immediately, while the other one was taken to a local hospital, where he died. The other two employees were not injured in the accident.
German	Einer der Arbeiter starb noch vor Ort, während der andere in ein nahe gelegenes Krankenhaus gebracht wurde, wo er seinen Verletzungen erlag. Ihre beiden Kollegen blieben unverletzt.
Back translation	One of the workers died at the scene, while the other was taken to a nearby hospital where he succumbed to his injuries. Their two colleagues remained unharmed.

In the English example above, a process of happening expressed by the verb *'to die'* is used. While this process was translated into Arabic as a process of doing expressed by قتل *'to kill'*, it was translated into German as a process of happening expressed by the verb *'sterben'*, i.e. *'to die'*. It is worth noting that each verb used here has a certain profile in a given semantic frame. The verb *'to die'* is profiled in a frame where it contrasts with the verb *'to kill'*. While the verb *'to die'* is characterized by having a monadic personation type, i.e. it requires only one participant, the verb *'to kill'* is characterized by having a dyadic personation type, i.e. it requires at least two participants: 'Agent' and 'Patient'. The verb *'to die'* invokes in our minds an *accident*-frame which has nothing to do with issues such as the intention to cause death to somebody. By contrast, by resorting to the verb *'to kill'*, a *killing*-frame is activated that has something to do with issues such as the intention to cause somebody to die (causativity) – flow of energy from the Agent to the Patient (transitivity). In the Arabic version, by virtue of the lexical item فورا, i.e. *'immediately'*, the pace of events is sped up, thus indicating that there is no time lapse between the act of shooting, backgrounded in attention, but it can be predicted as it is in our scope of attention. This was not reflected in the German translation where the translator opted for *'gebracht wurde'* meaning *'was taken/ brought'*.

Connecting the dots (3): Perspectival system and translation

This imaging system is concerned with "how people fix their mind's eye to look out upon a scene and its participants" (Almanna and Al-Shehari 2019: 132). To translate accurately, thus producing a similar mental image, four schematic categories need to be given adequate consideration by translators. They are 'location', 'distance', 'mode', and 'direction', as explained below with a direct link to translation.

Location

'Location' refers to how the text readers, as observers, are invited by the author, and later supposedly by the translator, to locate their perspective point somewhere inside or outside the depicted place in the scene (Talmy 2000: 69; Almanna and Al-Shehari 2019: 132). There are two main perspective points: 'interior' (from inside) and 'exterior' (from outside).

Distance

'Distance', as a schematic category, refers to the distance between the reader as an observer and the scene with its various elements. By virtue of certain grammatical forms and content specifications, the author, and later supposedly the translator, invite the reader to adopt a particular perspective to view the scene. This perspective can be 'proximal', resulting in a restricted frame, or 'distal', resulting in a less restricted frame (Evans and Green 2006; Evans 2007; Almanna and Al-Shehari 2019: 134). Closely related to distance as a schematic category is 'zooming', with its two cognitive operations, namely 'zooming in' and 'zooming out' (Almanna and Al-Shehari 2019: 134).

Mode

'Mode' in the sense used by Talmy (2000: 70) refers to the motion of the perspective point. If it is in motion, then it is in a sequential mode, and the perspective adopted by the reader is proximal with a restricted frame. Otherwise, it is a synoptic mode, and the perspective adopted by the reader is distal with a less restricted frame.

Direction

'Direction', as the name suggests, refers to the direction from which the scene at hand is viewed. Two directions are suggested by Talmy (2000; also discussed in Evans and Green 2006; Evans 2007; Almanna and Al-Shehari 2019: 136), namely 'prospective' (forward) and 'retrospective' (backward).

By way of illustration, let us consider the translation of the following example quoted from "Mix War, Art, and Dancing" by Ernest Hemingway (www.americanliterature.com):

> Identify the location and distance as schematic categories in a sentence of the following kind: *'The man entered the shop and bought a bottle of water'.*

> Identify the 'mode' and 'direction' as schematic categories in a sentence of the following kind: *'After her husband died, she travelled to the UK to live there'.*

English	After the last car had gone, the woman walked along the wet sidewalk through the sleet and looked up at the dark windows of the sixth floor.
Arabic	بعد أن اختفت السيارة الأخيرة، مشت المرأة على الرصيف المغطى بالجليد ونظرت عاليًا إلى النوافذ المظلمةِ في الطابق السادس.
Back translation	After the last car disappeared, the woman walked down the pavement covered with ice and looked up at the dark windows on the sixth floor.

In the original text, by means of the grammatical forms and content specifications used by the author, readers as observers are invited to locate their perspective point outside the building, thus being able to see the woman walking down the wet pavement looking up at the dark windows of the sixth floor. To have a less restricted frame, readers are invited to adopt a somewhat distal perspective. Further, readers as viewers are induced to place their perspective point on the finite clause *'the last car had gone'* from which a line of viewing in a prospective direction goes forward to the process of doing expressed by the verb *'to walk'* and then to the process of behaving expressed by the phrasal verb *'to look up at'*. All these schematic categories were given adequate consideration by the translator.

To reinforce this point, let us translate the following sentence into several languages:

Having cleaned her flat, she sat with her kids watching cartoons.

Arabic	بعد أن نظفت الشقة، جلست مع أطفالها تشاهد أفلام الكرتون.
Back translation	After she had cleaned the flat, she sat with her children watching cartoons.
German	Nachdem sie ihre Wohnung sauber gemacht hatte, saß sie bei ihren Kindern und schaute Cartoons an.
Back translation	After she had cleaned her flat, she sat with her children and watched cartoons.
French	Après avoir nettoyé son appartement, elle s'est assise avec ses enfants en regardant des dessins animés.
Back translation	After cleaning her apartment, she sat with her children watching cartoons.
Spanish	Después de limpiar su piso, se sentó con sus hijos a ver dibujos animados.
Back translation	After cleaning her flat she sat with her children to watch cartoons.
Chinese	打扫完公寓之后，她和她的孩子们坐在一起看卡通。
Back translation	After cleaning the flat, she and her children sat together to watch cartoons.

As can be observed, the translators managed to produce similar mental images in the minds of their targeted readers by considering such schematic categories as 'location', 'distance', 'mode', and 'direction', in addition to other cognitive categories.

Connecting the dots (4): Force dynamic system and translation

This imaging system is concerned with the forces that the elements of a given scene may have and then exercise over one another. These forces can take different forms, such as forcing an entity to act in a certain way, resisting such a force, overcoming such a resistance, blocking such a force or resistance, or removing such a blockage (for more details, see Talmy 2000; Almanna and Al-Shehari 2019: 128). In discussing the force dynamic patterns, we assume two entities: 'agonist' and 'antagonist' (Talmy 2000: 413; also discussed in Evans 2007: 83; Almanna and Al-Shehari 2019: 128). The agonist, to begin with, refers to "the entity that receives focal attention". The antagonist, however, refers to "the entity that opposes the agonist, either overcoming the force of the agonist or failing to overcome it" (Evans 2007: 83). Let us translate the following example quoted from Almanna (2018: 264) into several languages:

No sooner had the lecture begun than the professor left the class due to the bad behaviour of one of the students.

Is there any time lapse between the beginning of the lecture and the act of leaving the class?

TT1 (Arabic)	ما إن بدأت المحاضرة حتى غادر الأستاذ الصّف بسبب سوء تصرّف أحد الطلبة.
Back translation	No sooner had the lecture begun than the professor left the class due to the misbehaviour of one of the students.
TT2 (German)	Kaum hatte der Unterricht begonnen, da verließ der Professor auch schon den Unterricht aufgrund des schlechten Benehmens eines Studenten.
Back translation	The lesson had hardly started when the professor already left the class due to the misbehaviour of one student.
TT3 (French)	Dès que le cours a commencé, le professeur a quitté la classe en raison de la mauvaise conduite d'un des élèves.
Back translation	As soon as class started, the teacher left the class due to the misbehaviour of one of the students.
TT4 (Chinese)	讲座刚刚开始，那个教授便因为一个学生的不正当行为离开了教室。
Back translation	The lecture just began, the professor due to a student's misbehaviour left the classroom.
TT5 (Thai)	เลคเชอร์ไม่ทันจะเริ่ม อาจารย์ก็เดินหนีจากชั้นเรียน เพราะนักเรียนคนหนึ่งแสดงกิริยาแย่
Back translation	The lecture had not properly begun, the professor walked away from the class because one student showed bad behaviour.
TT6 (Turkish)	Ders başladıktan hemen sonra, öğrencilerden birinin yaramazlığı nedeniyle öğretmen sınıftan ayrıldı.

Translate this text into your language to produce a similar mental image in the minds of your readers.

Back translation	Immediately after the lesson began, the teacher left the classroom because of the misbehaviour of one of the students.
TT7 (Persian)	به محض شروع درس، استاد بهدلیل رفتار بد یکی از دانشجویان کلاس را ترک کرد.
Back translation	As soon as the lecture started, the professor left the class due to the bad behaviour of one of the students.

In the original text, the scene is not dynamically neutral; rather, it is characterized by having a force dynamic value of forcing the professor – who tends, in normal circumstances, to stay in the class – to leave the class. To elaborate, the finite cause *'the professor left the class'* is an expected result of the non-finite clause *'the bad behaviour of one of the students'*. This force dynamic framework enables us to capture the causing (the bad behaviour of one of the students) of the result (the professor left the class), as modelled here:

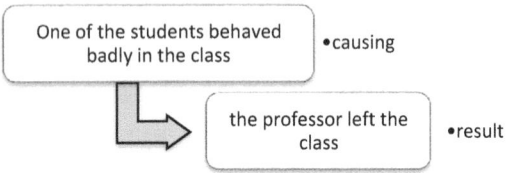

This force dynamic pattern was given serious consideration by all the translators, thereby producing similar mental images in their targeted readers.

In the following example, the whole scene is not force-dynamically neutral; rather, it is characterized by having a force dynamic value of forcing the experiencer/enjoyer, expressed by the pronoun *'he'*, not to enjoy his work due to the fact that he does not earn much money. However, in this example, by means of the counter indicator *'but'*, the experiencer/enjoyer overcomes this force, thus continuing enjoying his work.

He doesn't earn much, but he does enjoy his work.

Translate this sentence into your language to produce a similar mental image in the minds of your readers.

TT1 (Italian)	Guadagna poco, ma in compenso il lavoro gli piace.
Back translation	Earn little, but, on the other hand, he likes work.
TT2 (German)	Er verdient nicht viel, aber er genießt seine Arbeit.
Back translation	He does not earn much, but he enjoys his work.
TT3 (Arabic)	على الرغم من أنه لا يكسب كثيرًا من عمله، فهو مستمتع به.
Back translation	Although he does not earn much from his work, he enjoys it.

TT4 (Chinese)	他挣的不多，但却享受他的工作。
Back translation	He doesn't earn much but enjoys his work.
TT5 (Thai)	ถึงเขาได้เงินน้อย แต่ก็มีความสุขกับงาน
Back translation	Although he earns less, [but he] is happy with his job.
TT6 (Turkish)	Çok kazanmasa da işine severek yapıyor.
Back translation	Although s/he does not earn much, s/he loves his/her job.
TT7 (Persian)	درآمد زیادی ندارد اما از کارش لذت می‌برد.
Back translation	(He) does not have much earnings, but enjoys his work.

This force dynamic pattern was reflected by the translators. In TT1 (Italy), the translator, guided by the initial acceptability norm (Toury 1995) and expectancy norm (Chesterman 1997/2000), decided to change the conjunction but without changing the force dynamic pattern. In TT2 (German), the translator opted for a translation which is close to the original text, apart from the emphasis put on the verb *'enjoy'* in English by virtue of the verb *'does'* that could have been reflected had the translator opted for an adverb like *'wirklich'* to emphasize the enjoyment expressed by *'does'* in English. In TT3 (Arabic), the translator changed the structure without changing the force dynamic pattern. It cannot be argued that the Arabic translator, for the sake for acceptability, readability, authenticity, idiomaticity, and other issues that would feed into naturalness, decided to change the structure as having one very close to the original text, such as لا يكسب كثيرًا، لكنه يستمتع بعمله *'he does not earn much, but he enjoys his work'*, will not strike the target language readers as unusual.

To finish off this section, let us consider the following example quoted from Gu and Wang (2021: 387):

ST (Chinese)	我说要向雾霾等污染宣战, 这是因为这是社会关注的焦点问题。
Back translation	I said (I) will declare war against pollution like smog. This is because this is a focal issue that the society focuses on.
TT (English)	I said the government will declare war against smog pollution as a whole, because this has become a serious issue on the top of minds of our people.

As the back translation shows, the Sayer/Declarer in the original text is 我, i.e. *'I'*. So, by virtue of the grammatical form and content specification employed by the language user in the original text, the Sayer is presented as being characterized by being-able-to-do, thus presupposing authority. In the target text, however, the Declarer is the government. As such, the speaker's authority is lost through translation. In the original text, the scene is not dynamically neutral; rather, it is characterized by having a force dynamic value of forcing the Sayer/Declarer – who tends, in normal circumstances, not to declare war against smog pollution – to declare it. The clause *'I will declare war against smog pollution'* is an expected result of *'a focal issue that society focuses on'*. This force dynamic framework enables us to capture the causing (a focal issue that society focuses on) of the result (I will declare war against smog pollution). However, one may argue that *'a focal issue that society focuses on'* is different from *'a serious issue on the top of minds of our people'* as the experiencer is different in these two versions. While the experiencer in the original text is 'society', in the target text, it is assigned to 'people'.

Exercises and discussion

Exercise 1: Mark the following statements (T) if they are true and (F) if they are false.

(1)	In a sentence of the following kind, *'He is reading right now'*, there is one sematic role and two visual roles.	
(2)	By employing certain grammatical forms and content specifications, language users can structure a given scene.	
(3)	Cognitive linguistics is a single theory that first developed in the late 1970s out of dissatisfaction with strictly formal approaches to language and with the aim of providing a holistic account of language.	
(4)	Cognitive linguistics, according to Lakoff (1990), is based on two fundamental commitments: the 'generalization commitment' and the 'cognitive commitment'.	
(5)	In the second clause, which is non-finite, of the following sentence, *'She went to the mall to buy a new laptop'*, the scope of intention is greater than the extent of causation.	
(6)	According to Talmy (2000), there are four imaging systems: the 'configurational system', 'attentional system', 'perspectival system', and 'force dynamic system'.	
(7)	In a sentence of the following kind, *'She led him by the hand to his room'*, the whole scene is not dynamically neutral, but is characterized by having a force dynamic value.	

(8)	In a sentence of the following kind, *'I used to smoke when I was young'*, the action of smoking is characterized by having breaks and interruption.
(9)	In a sentence of the following kind, *'She is stirring the coffee'*, there are three semantic roles and three visual roles.
(10)	The action in *'She kept smiling'* is characterized by 'multiplexity', i.e. it consists of more than one smile.

Exercise 2: In the following sentences, a process of doing expressed by the verb *'to visit'* is used. Your task is to analyse them cognitively by referring to such notions and categories as 'plexity', 'state of dividedness', 'state of boundedness', 'degree of extension', 'scene partitioning', and 'point of emphasis' before translating them into your own language.

(1)   He has been visiting his close friend for many years.
(2)   He has been visiting his close friend since morning.
(3)   He visited his close friend yesterday morning.
(4)   He had not visited his close friend till yesterday morning.
(5)   He used to visit his friend when he was young.

Exercise 3: The following short text is extracted from *BBC News* (1 November 2017).

Carles Puigdemont triggered a crisis in Spain by holding an independence referendum in early October in the semi-autonomous region despite Madrid's opposition and the Constitutional Court declaring the vote illegal.

Before translating it into your own language, read it carefully to identify whether the scene is construed as having a force dynamic value or not.

Exercise 4: Translate the following text quoted from Almanna (2018: 40–1) into your own language, and then comment on your translation by referring to the imaging systems discussed in this chapter.

There was a man. The man was illiterate. He did not know how to read and write. He often saw people wearing spectacles for reading books or papers. So, he decided to buy a pair of spectacles for himself.

One day he went to the town. There, he entered a spectacles shop and asked the shopkeeper for a pair of spectacles for reading. The shopkeeper gave him various pairs of spectacles and a book. The man tried all the spectacles one by one, but he could not read anything. He told the shopkeeper that all those spectacles were useless for him as he wasn't able to read. The shopkeeper didn't understand him. Then he looked at the book. It was upside down!

Discussion and research points

(1) Select any English text where the scenes are not dynamically neutral and translate it into your language. Then comment on your own translation by referring to the force dynamic system.

(2) Go through any translated text from your own language into English and comment on the translation by referring to the attentional system.

(3) Select any English text and translate it into your language. Then comment on your own translation by referring to the configurational system.

References

Abdulkareem, M. A. (2021). *Viewing Arrangement in Dan Brown's Works: A Cognitive Semantic Study*. Unpublished PhD thesis. Babylon: University of Babylon.

Almanna, A. (2016). *Semantics for Translation Students: Arabic-English-Arabic*. Oxford: Peter Lang.

Almanna, A. (2018). *The Nuts and Bolts of Arabic–English Translation: An Introduction to Applied Contrastive Linguistics*. Newcastle upon Tyne: Cambridge Scholars Publishing.

Almanna, A. (2022). "A Configurational System-based Approach to Translating Tenses from Arabic to English", *BJTLL: British Journal of Translation, Linguistics and Literature*, Vol. 2, pp. 1–14.

Almanna, A. and Al- Shehari, A. (2019). *The Arabic–English Translator as Photographer: A Linguistic Account*. London/ New York: Routledge.

Chesterman, A. (1997/2000). *Memes of Translation: The Spread of Ideas in Translation Theory*. Amsterdam/Philadelphia, PA: John Benjamins.

Evans, V. (2007). *A Glossary of Cognitive Linguistics*. Edinburgh: Edinburgh University Press.

Evans, V. and Green, M. (2006). *Cognitive Linguistics: An Introduction*. Edinburgh: Edinburgh University Press.

Gu, C. and Wang, B. (2021). "Interpreter-Mediated Discourse as a Vital Source of Meaning Potential in Intercultural Communication: The Case of the Interpreted Premier- Meets- the- Press Conferences in China", *Language and Intercultural Communication*, Vol. 21(3), pp. 379–94.

Lakoff, G. (1990). "The Invariance Hypothesis: Is Abstract Reason Based on Image-Schemas?" *Cognitive Linguistics*, Vol. 1(1), pp. 39–74.

Langacker, R. (1987). *Foundations of Cognitive Grammar, Volume I*. Stanford, CA: Stanford University Press.

Langacker, R. (2008). *Cognitive Grammar: A Basic Introduction*. Oxford: Oxford University Press.

Talmy, L. (2000). *Toward a Cognitive Semantics: Vol. 1: Concept Structuring Systems*. Cambridge, MA: MIT Press.

Toury, G. (1995). *Descriptive Translation Studies and Beyond*. Amsterdam: John Benjamins.

Index